THE
SALISBURY TO EXETER LINE

With the regulator closed and with just a whisper of steam issuing from the safety valves, N class 2-6-0 No. 31810 rattles out of Honiton Tunnel and heads down the bank with an eastbound special vans train on 1 June 1963. *Rodney Lissenden*

With steam sanding gear fully applied to assist adhesion, rebuilt 'West Country' class 4-6-2 No. 34104 *Bere Alston* leaves Salisbury and heads towards Waterloo with an 'up' Exeter relief on 12 September 1964.

S. C. Nash

As part of our ongoing market research, we are always pleased to receive comments about our books, suggestions for new titles, or requests for catalogues. Please write to: The Editorial Director, Oxford Publishing Co., Sparkford, Near Yeovil, Somerset, BA22 7JJ

THE
SALISBURY TO EXETER LINE

Recollections of the Southern route to the West

DEREK PHILLIPS & GEORGE PRYER

OPC

Oxford Publishing Co.

S15 4-6-0 No. 30843 (72A) barks her way up the bank out of Templecombe with the 3.5 pm Salisbury–Exeter Central on 14 August 1963. With just four coaches and a van on the tail, this is a boy's load for a superb steaming engine such as this, which was one of Exmouth Junction's finest.

S. C. Nash

A catalogue record for this book is available from the British Library.

ISBN 0 86093 525 6

Oxford Publishing Co. is an imprint of Haynes Publishing, Sparkford, Nr Yeovil, Somerset BA22 7JJ

Printed in Hong Kong

Typeset in Times Roman Medium

Note: The signal box diagrams and track plans do not always show lines as viewed from the same direction.

Acknowledgements

Preparation of a book such as this would be impossible without the kind assistance of many people through their photographs or recollections of the line; thank you: Hugh Ballantyne, Bob Barnard, Ralph Bartlett, Colin Caddy, R. M. Casserley for the use of the H. C. Casserley photographs, John Cornelius, Hugh Davies, John Day, Barry Eagles, Terry Gough, Barry Hayward for the use of the Kenneth Leech Collection, Brian Jackson, Ron Lacey, David Lawrence, Rodney Lissenden, Locomotive Club of Great Britain, Jim Maidment, J. S. Perry, R. C. Riley, Gerald T. Robinson, John Scrace, The Signalling Record Society, R. E. Toop, Adrian Vaughan. Photographs from the Mowatt and other Brunel University collection prints are available from Mr W. Burton, 3 Fairway, Clifton, York, Y03 6QA.

Contents

Bibliography

Our Home Railways Vol. 1 W. J. Gordon. Frederick Warne 1910.

General & Western Appendices 1934 Southern Railway 1934.

Salisbury to Yeovil Railway (reprint of *The History of a Railway* by Louis Ruegg). David & Charles 1960.

The London & South Western Railway O. S. Nock – Ian Allan 1965

Locomotives at the Grouping 1 Southern Railway H. C. Casserley & S. W. Johnston. Ian Allan 1965.

Southern Steam O. S. Nock. David & Charles 1966.

The Drummond Greyhounds of the L&SWR D. L. Bradley. David & Charles 1977.

Main Lines to the West Simon Rocksborough-Smith. Ian Allan 1981.

BR Steam Motive Power Depots S.R. Paul Bolger. Ian Allan 1983.

The Southern West of Salisbury Terry Gough. Oxford Publishing Company 1984.

Somerset Railways Robin Madge. Dovecote Press 1984.

Steam around Yeovil – The Final Years John Day. Badger Publications 1985.

The Somerset & Dorset Railway Robin Athill. David & Charles 1985.

Working Yeovil Steam Derek Phillips. Fox & Co. 1989.

Working Somerset & Dorset Steam Derek Phillips. Fox & Co. 1990.

British Railways Locomotives 1948 Chris Banks. Oxford Publishing Company 1990.

Waterloo-Exeter Heyday Gerald Siviour & Mike Esau. Ian Allan 1990.

L&SWR Engine Sheds Western District Chris Hawkins & George Reeve. Irwell Press 1990.

Working Yeovil to Taunton Steam Derek Phillips. Fox & Co. 1991.

Working the Chard Branch Derek Phillips & Ron Eaton-Lacey. Fox & Co. 1991.

The North Devon Line John Nicholas. Oxford Publishing Company 1992.

L&SWR West Country Lines Then & Now Mac Hawkins. David & Charles 1993.

The Story of the Westbury to Weymouth Line Derek Phillips. Oxford Publishing Company 1994.

The Somerset & Dorset Aftermath of the Beeching Axe Tim Deacon. Oxford Publishing Company 1995.

Signal Box Diagrams of the Great Western & Southern Railways Vol. 5 Exeter Central-Templecombe & Branches. George Pryer 1995.

The line from Salisbury to Exeter, with its branches

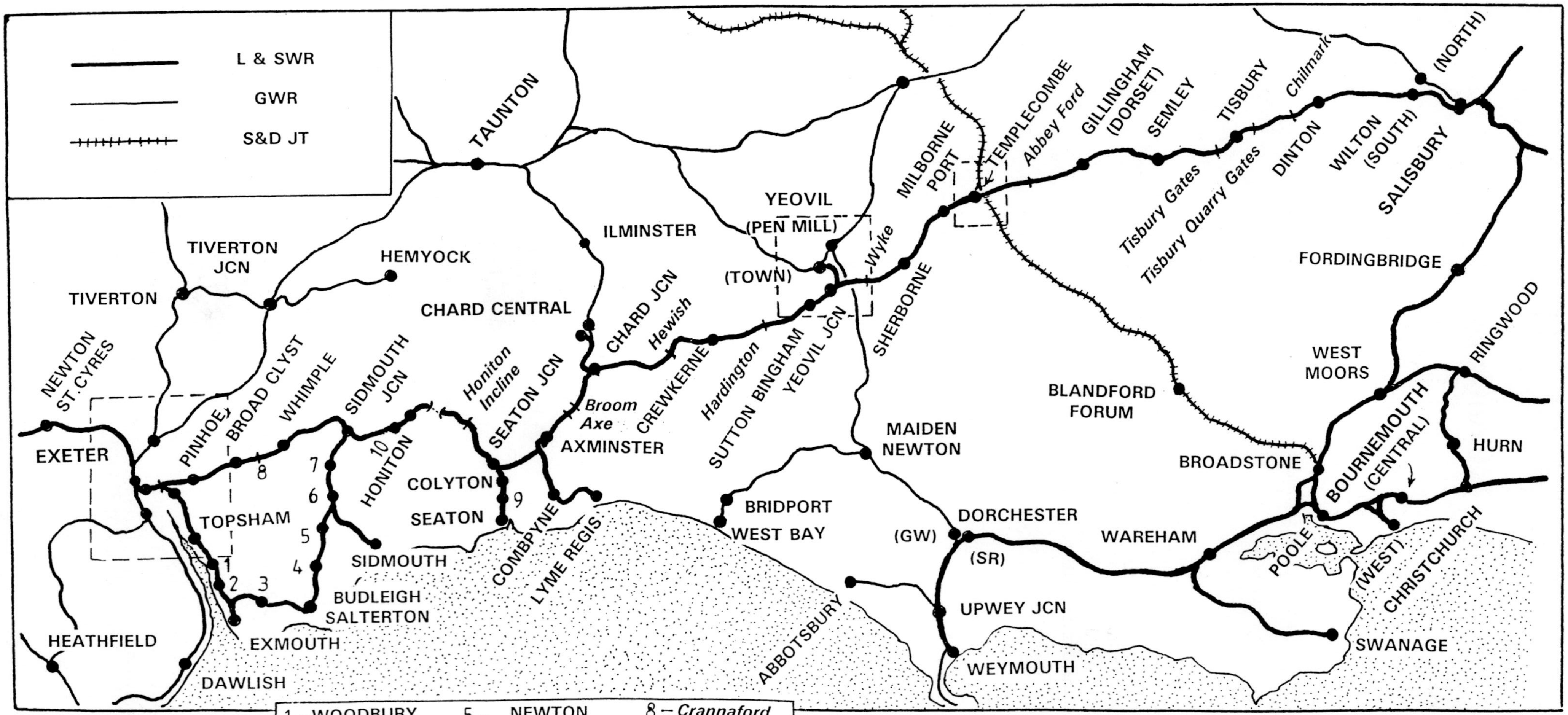

Legend:
- L & SWR
- GWR
- S&D JT

1 – WOODBURY ROAD
2 – LYMPSTONE
3 – LITTLEHAM
4 – BUDLEIGH
5 – NEWTON POPPLEFORD
6 – OTTERY ST. MARY
7 – TIPTON ST. JOHN'S
8 – Crannaford Crossing
9 – COLYFORD
10 – ROUNDBALL HALT

Introduction

For George Pryer and myself the line from Salisbury to Exeter Central brings back many memories of our working days when it was, first and foremost, a superb main line. When the first sod of the Salisbury & Yeovil Railway was cut at Gillingham on 3 April 1856, the Company had a grand total of £4 2s 4d in the bank! However, the line proved to be so successful that it was doubled throughout by July 1870 and it is interesting to recall that the Salisbury & Yeovil had calculated optimistic returns for the first five years at £20 per mile at the opening, and £25 per mile for the next ten years. The actual returns for 1877 totalled a grand figure of £55 19s 8d per mile! Such was the prosperity of the line. The top echelon of British steam locomotive power and design was always used on the route. The classical and beautiful designs of the early Gooch, Beattie and Adams locomotives, the superb T9 4-4-0s of Dugald Drummond – so richly deserved of the name 'Greyhounds'. These were followed by Robert Urie's three classes of 4-6-0, one of which formed the basis of the 'King Arthur' class later developed by Richard Maunsell, the unmistakable Pacifics of Oliver Bulleid – who turned locomotive design and evolution into a dimension which has never been equalled – then the Jarvis rebuilds of the Bulleid Pacifics which were the final and supreme accolade of all time. I count myself very fortunate indeed to have been a footplateman working on some of the very best steam power ever designed.

The beautiful umber and salmon coaches of the London & South Western Railway eventually gave way to the green coaches of the Southern Railway and its successor – the Southern Region of British Railways. No other region ran its coaches in the distinctive and attractive coat of green, the 'Atlantic Coast Express' and the short-lived all-Pullman 'Devon Belle' will long be remembered as being the premier trains of the day, as well as the succession of fast trains starting 'on the hour' from Waterloo. Bulleid Pacifics streaking along the main line, 'King Arthurs', U class 2-6-0s on the stopping locals, S15s plodding away on freight, stone and milk trains, the large locomotive sheds at Salisbury and Exmouth Junction, plus my own engine depot at Yeovil Town; M7 and O2 branch tanks meeting the mainline services at the junction stations – including the beloved Adams Radial tanks at Axminster, the hustle and bustle at Salisbury, the splitting and rejoining of trains at Exeter Central – are now just memories and we shall never see their like again.

With the line being taken over by the Western Region, the wilderness years came into being, and the line was brought almost to the point of closure through mismanagement and ineptitude. Today, the stations that are left are served by the Class 159 'Super Sprinters' of South West Trains, a Stagecoach company and the remaining branch line from Exeter to Exmouth is still alive and thriving. Through the many steam photographs in this book the line is alive again – the trains are running, the stations are open, with the sound of block bells and slamming levers ringing out from the signal box windows, with the sound of panting engines echoing over the countryside. As this book is concerned with the main line, the branch lines are mentioned in passing, as the various lines, Yeovil Town, Chard, Lyme Regis, etc., will form the basis of a further volume which is now in preparation.

Derek Phillips
Yeovil
Somerset

Rebuilt Bulleid Pacific No. 34109 *Sir Trafford Leigh-Mallory* runs into Salisbury with the 9.15 am Exmouth–Waterloo on 12 September 1964. S15 4-6-0 No. 30823 stands alongside the former GWR signal box to the right during a shunting manoeuvre.

S. C. Nash

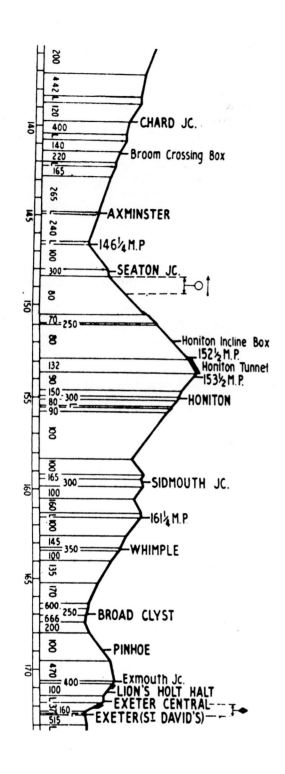

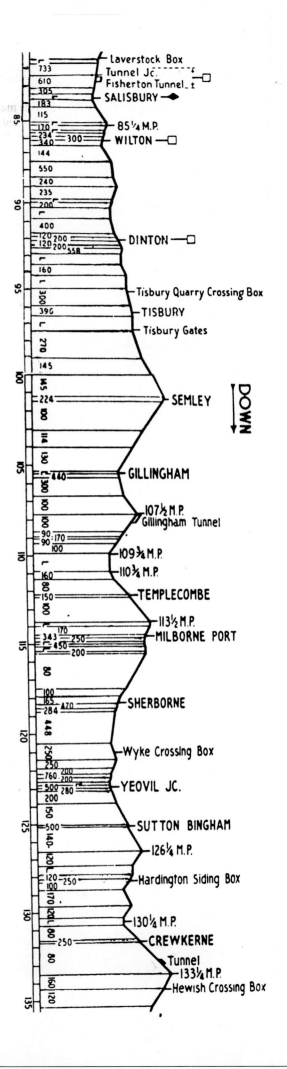

General History

The London & South Western Railway had never made a secret of its intention of reaching the far West, and had secured a foothold in that area as early as 1847 when it acquired the Bodmin & Wadebridge Railway. In fact, although much had happened before that year, the details really belong to another period of railway history and it will be sufficient for our purposes to look at the situation as it stood at the time.

In June 1847 the standard gauge Southampton & Dorchester Railway was opened throughout, this line being leased and worked by the L&SWR. The promoter of the line was one Charles Castleman, a Wimborne solicitor, and it is clear that from the outset he envisaged it as something more than a local line through the heathlands of East Dorset as his Dorchester terminus was laid out to facilitate ready conversion to a *through* station. During the same year the L&SWR also opened a branch from Bishopstoke (later to be known as Eastleigh) to Salisbury, and whilst this could be seen as a possible alternative launching point for a drive into Devon, Castleman and his supporters considered their line to be better placed. There was some justification in this belief. The mileage from Dorchester to Exeter was considerably less than that from Salisbury, but against it were the facts that the Southampton & Dorchester had been built on the cheap with many sharp curves while the country west of Dorchester was very hilly and therefore difficult for the construction of a well-aligned railway. These considerations played no small part in the eventual choice of the Salisbury route.

Also against the extension from Dorchester were the various plans of the broad gauge companies – the GWR and Bristol & Exeter – who saw western Dorset and everything beyond as *their* territory. The GWR's early attempts to secure this area against 'narrow gauge' infiltration do not concern us directly, suffice it to say that their Wilts, Somerset & Weymouth line from Thingley Junction (Chippenham) to Weymouth via Frome and Yeovil had been making painfully slow progress since 1846, and that connected with it was a scheme for a Yeovil–Exeter line running via Bridport and Axminster. As a through route between London and the West it was useless, the distance being even greater than that incurred travelling via Bristol, but its publication should have spurred the L&SW Board into urgent action, for had it been built any westward advance would have been almost impossible. In fact little happened, partly because the GWR's project was not taken too seriously in view of the financial troubles besetting the WS&W line, but also because the Board was sharply divided on the whole issue of the Exeter line. The shareholders of the L&SWR could at that time be divided into three camps. One, led by Castleman and his Engineer, Moorsom, almost *demanded* that any westward extension should be through Dorchester. Another, championed by Locke – Engineer of the original London & Southampton Railway but now MP for Honiton – actively campaigned for the Salisbury line. These two factions became known as the 'Coastal' and 'Central' parties respectively, but there was also a sizeable group who pronounced themselves as opposed to any westward extension. This resulted in a total lack of progress with either option, despite a legal battle with the broad gauge companies which had cost an estimated £400,000 and the financial difficulties following the 'Railway Mania' ensured that nothing happened until 1851 when independent companies were formed to exploit both schemes.

No standard gauge line, no matter how independent,

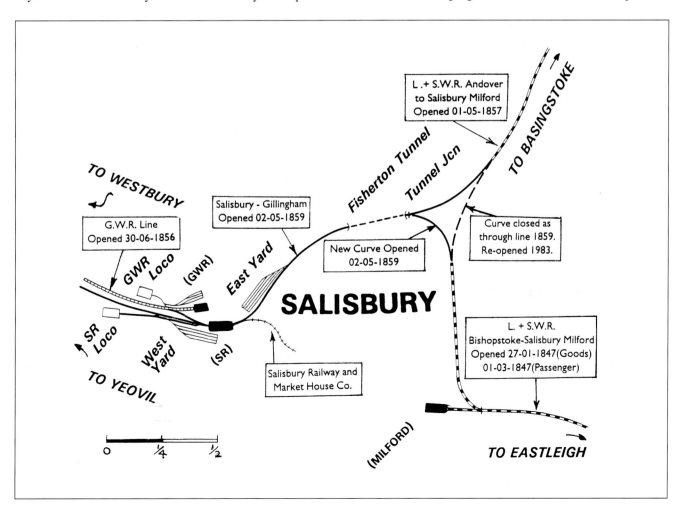

could hope to succeed without the support and investment of the L&SWR, but that Company remained an uncertain ally. At first the 'Coastal' route gained a majority, but it failed on Standing Orders and a Company known as the Salisbury & Yeovil Railway quickly issued a prospectus in which it claimed L&SWR backing. However, a shareholders meeting on 26 October 1852 voted against any arrangement with the Yeovil company, and the GWR decided to add further confusion to the already very confused situation by publishing plans for a broad gauge route known as the Devon & Dorset Railway – joining the Wilts, Somerset & Weymouth line at Maiden Newton and running through Bridport and Axminster to Exeter. This was even more circuitous than their 1846 plan, and can hardly have been a serious proposition. No doubt its sole function was to delay any advance by the standard gauge by provoking another lengthy Parliamentary battle, but it had the opposite effect. The L&SWR Board, now fearful that the district could fall once and for all into Great Western hands, rallied the shareholders and won their support for a double-track 'Coastal' line. The newly-elected Chairman, Francis Scott, made a pledge before the Commons Select Committee that this line would be commenced as soon as possible, whereupon the Devon & Dorset Bill was defeated. But the shareholders proved fickle, and at their next meeting it was voted not to proceed with the coastal line despite their Chairman's solemn undertaking. This left Scott in an impossible position – he promptly resigned, and was replaced by W. J. Chaplin.

Chaplin was a less aggressive character than Scott, and he soon convened another meeting at which he managed to obtain a decisive vote from the shareholders – this time to support the Salisbury & Yeovil. This line then received the Royal Assent without undue difficulty on 7 August 1854, but still nothing happened! By now the population of West Dorset and East Devon were despairing of ever seeing a railway, and any prosperity those districts had enjoyed was steadily draining away. Meanwhile, Yeovil had been reached by a broad gauge branch of the Bristol & Exeter which ran from Durston (near Taunton), to a terminus on the western edge of the town at Hendford. This line opened on 1 October 1853, and offered a reasonable route between Yeovil, Exeter and the West but a very indirect one to anywhere else. The Wilts, Somerset & Weymouth eventually reached Yeovil from the North on 1 September 1856 and opened up further travel opportunities for the district, but the route to London it provided was far from convenient. The extension of this line to Weymouth finally opened on 20 January 1857, and as it cut across the path of any westward extension of the Southampton & Dorchester line it more or less killed off the 'Coastal' line to Exeter – although there were to be feint rumblings in later years.

By this time the military authorities were becoming concerned over the lack of a direct standard gauge route between Plymouth and other Naval bases in the West and Dover, and were prepared to add their weight to any railway scheme that offered to provide one. Pressure from that quarter manifest itself in 1855 when the L&SWR went to Parliament for a Bill authorising extra time for the completion of its Basingstoke–Andover line, intending to provide a more direct route between London and Salisbury. The authority was granted, but the occasion was also used to order the Company to honour it's commitment to an Exeter extension. Of course, this could have meant either a coastal or a central choice, the Government appearing not to have a preference, but early the following year it was announced that a firm agreement had been reached with the Salisbury & Yeovil company. Construction went ahead rapidly, the works

being formed to accommodate a double track but only a single line was laid. However, it now emerged that there were those in Parliament who thought that the original commitment was to the coastal route, and following some awkward questions in the House – work on the Salisbury & Yeovil virtually ceased. In fact, the coastal scheme was not finally buried until the following year, when work on the Yeovil line commenced with renewed vigour. The L&SWR obtained the Act for its Exeter–Yeovil line on 21 July 1856, this line being planned to join the Salisbury & Yeovil at Bradford Abbas. It is almost certain that the L&SWR would have reached Exeter in the end, its interests in the far West dictating that it must, but it would have preferred to let either the Salisbury & Yeovil or some other independent company do the initial work. Had it not been for the strong attitude adopted by the Government of the day, many more years could have elapsed before rail communication came to this part of the West Country. The Salisbury & Yeovil was opened in stages as the work progressed, although the Company placed itself on a firm financial footing by only using main stations as temporary terminal points. Many lines at the time opened to traffic up to the limit of construction work, resulting in isolated and inconvenient railheads, but this temptation was resisted. Salisbury to Gillingham came into service on 2 May 1859, Gillingham to Sherborne on 7 May 1860, and Sherborne to the Bristol & Exeter's Hendford station in Yeovil a few weeks later, on 1 June. In connection with the opening of the first section to Gillingham the original line from Bishopstoke to Salisbury and the direct line via Andover were diverted away from the old Milford terminus and extended through a tunnel to a better-located station in Salisbury. Meanwhile construction of the Exeter Extension was going well, for whilst the country could not be called 'easy' and engineering works were by no means light – including several tunnels – it presented no problems and Yeovil to Exeter opened to traffic on 19 July 1860. The junction between the two lines at Yeovil was triangular, *through* trains depositing Yeovil passengers at the new junction station for onward transmission to Hendford by a shuttle service. Hendford itself was scarcely convenient, being some way from the town centre and very congested with the traffic of both the standard and broad gauge companies. Improvements were urgently needed and, on 1 June 1861, a new Town station – joint with the GWR – was opened on a good central site, Hendford being relegated to a goods depot.

Initially the Salisbury & Yeovil and the Exeter Extension railways were single track with engineering features wide enough for doubling, passing loops being provided at the stations. Between Salisbury and Yeovil these were: Wilton, Dinton, Tisbury, Semley for Shaftesbury, Gillingham, Templecombe, Milborne Port, and Sherborne, and there was never any development in the area which made it necessary to add to these. Exeter Extension stations were: Yeovil Junction, Sutton Bingham, Crewkerne, Chard Road, Axminster, Colyton for Seaton, Honiton, Feniton, Whimple, Broad Clyst and Exeter (Queen Street). Several of these were to be renamed, and there were one or two additions. Traffic built up quickly, the Salisbury & Yeovil becoming one of the most profitable lines in Britain, and it soon became necessary to undertake some doubling. The first section, from Sherborne to Bradford Abbas Junction, came into use early in 1861, but thereafter work proceeded in fits and starts, double line not being available throughout until July 1870. The Exeter Extension was outright L&SWR property, the Salisbury & Yeovil being leased and worked by that Company for the exceptionally low figure of $42\frac{1}{2}\%$ of gross receipts. The smaller company was not acquired until

Argus, a handsome Joseph Beattie outside-cylindered 2-4-0 of 1863 with 6ft 6in coupled wheels, stands in the yard at Exeter Queen Street. The plate on the cabside reads 'L&SWR Beattie's Patent'.

Derek Phillips Collection

January 1878, when its shareholders were finally persuaded to sell out at a huge profit. The financial success of the Salisbury & Yeovil was unusual, particularly for a line through such a rural area, but there were several contributing factors. Those stations which served towns were well placed, and there was a steady flow of through traffic over the line. Perhaps more importantly, the Company was never tempted to build costly branch lines or make extensions, many railways of the period overstretching their modest resources in this way. If the Salisbury–Exeter line had one weakness, it was that it missed all of the coastal towns of Dorset and Devon plus several other centres of population such as Shaftesbury and Chard. Branch lines were therefore proposed in plenty, some of which materialised while others, like one from Gillingham to Mere and Zeals, were destined never to be built, although in some cases they later became horse-bus routes run in connection with the trains. The first branch to appear in the area was that between Exeter and Exmouth, which left the main line on the eastern outskirts of the city at a point later to become well-known as Exmouth Junction – the branch opened on 1 May 1861, trains sharing Queen Street station.

The next few years were to see a variety of schemes to link the long established if small ports of Bridport and Lyme Regis to the Exeter line. The former had achieved a broad gauge branch from Maiden Newton in 1857, but the townspeople had always hoped for a *through* line which now seemed unlikely, a second branch to Axminster or Crewkerne being the next best thing. This never materialised, but Lyme Regis did eventually get a railway in the following century. So, despite all the planning and public meetings taking place in the Dorset/Devon border country, the second station to become a junction was actually in Somerset. In 1862 the Somerset Central line from Highbridge, which had reached Glastonbury in 1854, was extended to a separate terminus at right-angles to the Salisbury line at Templecombe, a connecting spur to facilitate the exchange of traffic being provided east of Templecombe station. The Dorset Central Railway was then in operation between Wimborne and Blandford, and the following year this was extended

northwards, passing beneath the S&Y main line to form an end-on junction with the Somerset Central. The famous Somerset & Dorset was born as a through route, and a considerable traffic was exchanged at Templecombe. A new west-facing curve was provided in 1870 together with an additional platform and other extended facilities at the L&SWR station. Thereafter it became the custom for S&D trains to use this – rather than their own station – despite the somewhat complicated working to which it gave rise – although the latter remained in limited use until 1887. The new curve rendered the original connecting spur redundant and it was severed in 1870. These alterations were made in good time to accommodate an even larger traffic, for the S&D's Bath Extension opened on 20 July 1874, and the number of wagons exchanged at Templecombe reached an enormous figure. Many new sidings had to be provided, and what had started out as a humble wayside station became an important and busy traffic centre.

The market town of Chard had long expected to be placed on a through route, and was less than pleased when the Exeter line passed some three miles to the south, thus enabling Axminster and Crewkerne to collar some of its trade. It had been intended to link Chard to the main line as soon as the latter was open, a consortium of local businessmen setting up the Chard Railway Company as early as 1859, but as with many such projects, matters did not go entirely smoothly and even the enthusiastic prediction that the branch would be ready for traffic by the end of 1861 proved wide of the mark! As the first sod had been cut with the usual ceremony on 1 November 1860 it should not have been impossible to achieve this target, but there were financial difficulties with the contractor which led to work ceasing in June the following year. Meanwhile the directors were attempting to reach an agreement with the L&SWR, it being the intention that the main line company would either purchase or lease the branch. At length the first option was taken up, the L&SWR buying the undertaking for £20,000 in March 1861 – although the Chard Railway Company remained in nominal existence until 1864. The short branch from Chard Road station to a terminus on the south-western edge of Chard opened on 8 May 1863, although Chard Road was not renamed Chard Junction until August 1872. There was no direct connection with the main line, branch trains using a separate dead-end platform on the opposite side of the station approach road to the main buildings. Goods wagons were exchanged via a very indirect spur line around the back of the goods shed, and this arrangement – which lasted throughout the existence of the line – did nothing to encourage any through working.

For a few years the L&SWR enjoyed a monopoly of Chard business, but the broad gauge branch from Taunton opened on 11 September 1866 and stole all but southbound passengers and freight consigned to standard gauge stations. It was not a 'through' route, as the Bristol & Exeter's terminus was situated some half mile north of the L&SWR station, and services were not designed to connect. However, matters were improved somewhat a few months later, the L&SWR opening a connecting line to the B&E station – which then became 'Chard Joint' on 26 November. The broad gauge was abolished on the Chard branch in July 1891, but despite this and the closure of the L&SWR terminus to passenger traffic on 30 December 1916, (after which all trains used the joint station) it was always worked as two separate branches. The next branch to attach itself to the Salisbury–Exeter line was never to be used by passengers. The Clifton Maybank line, which came into use on 13 June 1864, was constructed by the GWR as a means of relieving congestion at Yeovil Hendford station, hitherto the recognised transfer point for traffic between the broad and standard gauge companies. It left the Wilts, Somerset & Weymouth line at a point known as Clifton Maybank Junction, burrowed under the L&SWR main line, and climbed up to a site adjoining the 'down' platform at Yeovil Junction. A transhipment shed and double-sided platform were provided, broad gauge track being laid on one side and standard gauge on the other so that the contents of wagons could be quickly exchanged, and there were several sidings of both gauges. Earthworks were prepared for another curve in the direction of Weymouth, but no rails were ever laid. Although the resort of Seaton is a modern town which hardly existed for most of the 19th century, the independent Beer & Seaton Railway was promoted in the early 1860s with the primary intension of serving the ancient port of Axmouth and the lace-making village of Beer. This single line, which left the main line at Colyton station (promptly christened Colyton Junction), ran through Colyton itself, Colyford, thence alongside the Axe estuary to Seaton, opened on 16 March 1868. The local company was taken over by the L&SWR on 1 January 1888. In the meantime Colyton Junction had become 'Seaton Junction', but the branch carried only moderate traffic and the new owners did not see fit to improve the junction itself – which was only slightly more direct than that at Chard Road – which involved the exchange of wagons via a siding. There were improvements later, but they belong to the Southern Railway rather than the L&SWR and will be covered anon.

On 30 October 1871 a station was opened on the main line at Pinhoe. It handled passenger traffic only at first, but a solitary goods siding on the 'up' side was later added and it opened for freight on 3 April 1882. Today Sidmouth is well known as a 'Polite' resort, but in the early part of the 19th century it had ambitions as a port. In 1836 some £12,000 was spent on harbour works which included a length of railway (and a tunnel through a cliff) but the venture was abandoned. It was revived later in a modified form, the Sidmouth Railway & Harbour Company receiving its Act of Parliament in 1871. However, the harbour part of the project was soon dropped, and when the branch line

opened on 6 July 1874 the terminus was a mile inland as a disincentive to day trippers! The Sidmouth Railway met the main line at what was then called (after several changes of name) Ottery Road station. It had been opened as Feniton and its name was again changed to Sidmouth Junction for the occasion. Branch trains used a separate bay platform which gave reasonable passenger exchange facilities, but as with other junctions there was no direct connection. This was later improved, and in SR days it was possible to run through from Sidmouth to Exeter. Sidmouth has always attracted a fair number of 'superior' visitors, and the income generated by the resulting long-distance fares – many of them first class – enabled the independent company to survive until it was finally taken into the Southern Railway at the Grouping of 1923. Although it has no direct bearing on the subject of this book, it should be mentioned that Budleigh Salterton was reached by another branch from the Sidmouth Railway at Tipton St Johns in 1897, and that this was extended through to Exmouth in 1903, the existence of this route having some influence over traffic patterns on Summer Saturdays.

Lyme Regis was a port of some antiquity and as such became the subject of several early railway schemes, but nothing happened until the first sod of a branch line was cut in 1874. By that time good rail access to other harbours in the area had lost the town much business, but holidays by the sea were becoming sufficiently popular to offer it a future as a resort. Despite much optimism – this first project failed to mature, and as the century grew to a close, it seemed that Lyme would never get a railway. When it did arrive, it was built 'on the cheap' with sharp curves and severe gradients – although having regard to the nature of the country it would have been very costly to do otherwise. The Axminster & Lyme Regis Railway opened on 24 August 1903. Junction arrangements at Axminster were unusual – particularly for a 'light railway' and involved a flyover to carry the branch across the main line to its own bay platform on the 'up' side plus a separate connection to the 'down' goods yard for the exchange of freight. There was no signalling on the branch at first, but tablet working was introduced in 1906 to increase capacity. Again, there was no direct junction, and when the goods spur was removed in 1915, everything had to make several reversals via the 'up' siding. However, this did not discourage the SR from providing through Waterloo–Lyme Regis coaches in later years.

While the Lyme Regis branch was being built, much work was also going on at Salisbury. The 1859 station, which replaced that at Milford, consisted of just two staggered platforms of no great length – one on each side of Fisherton Street bridge – and by the turn of the century it was totally inadequate. Complete rebuilding was undertaken in 1902/3, six platforms – four of them suitable for through traffic – and greatly increased passenger and office accommodation being the result. At the same time, low-pressure pneumatic signalling of the latest design was installed.

With the opening of the Lyme Regis branch development of the Salisbury to Exeter line and its connections was virtually complete, future additions being of a minor character. In 1905 the military authorities opened a rifle range on the western edge of Honiton, with Roundball Halt – a simple wooden structure – being provided to serve it. This halt never had a public service, and with the outbreak of war in 1914 it fell into disuse and was later demolished. Of greater importance was the introduction in 1906 of a 'motor-car' service between Exeter Queen Street and Honiton which gave rise to several new halts in the immediate area of Exeter, namely Lions Holt (renamed St James Park in 1946) and Mount Pleasant – both between Queen Street and Exmouth

S15 4-6-0 No. 30844 (72A) stands alongside the signal box at Axminster with a 'down' stopping train for Exeter Central in 1960.

C. L. Caddy Collection

Junction – and Whipton Bridge between Exmouth Junction and Pinhoe. The first two were served by Exmouth branch trains as well as the Honiton locals. Tram, and later bus competition killed the service off during the inter-war period, Whipton Bridge closing on 1st January 1923 followed by Mount Pleasant on 2nd January 1928. Yeovil Junction station was rebuilt as two island platforms served by loops with two through fast lines in 1908-09, a large layout of sidings on the 'up' side being provided at the same time. Other stations on the line were to remain virtually unaltered, only three other major rebuildings taking place in the period leading up until World War II.

Urgently in need of attention was Exeter Queen Street; dirty, dingy, and fast becoming almost unworkable as traffic increased. This large task, started in 1927 but not completed until 1933, resulted in a station worthy of the important cathedral city, and one of which the Southern Railway could be proud. At that time holiday traffic was developing apace as working conditions and wages improved, and more and more families were able to afford a week by the sea. The Southern Railway, which had of course taken over all former L&SWR interests in the area in 1923, was very business-minded and ever looking out for the chance to create new traffic flows. In the London area this was done by sponsoring new housing estates, but elsewhere the best option was to expand an existing holiday resort or even build a new one as at Allhallows-on-Sea, Kent. Sidmouth was too 'Select' for this kind of treatment, but Seaton seemed willing to welcome visitors of all classes. The SR therefore decided to market the town as a 'Working Class' resort, and as this would mean that thousands of people would have to be accommodated on summer weekends some better facilities were deemed necessary. In 1928 Seaton Junction station was greatly enlarged, the platforms being served by long loops. The original office buildings on the 'up' platform were retained with a much extended canopy, but the 'down' side

was completely new. At the same time the physical connection to the branch was improved so that through trains from Waterloo could have access directly from the 'down' loop rather than having to shunt through the siding. As things turned out, the money spent at Seaton Junction was largely wasted, for although Seaton did develop along the lines envisaged by the Southern Railway, a holiday camp being constructed on a site adjoining the terminus, much of the traffic was road-borne. The unsuitability of Seaton for rail passengers with luggage travelling from any large centre other than London is obvious from a simple study of a railway map! The last station to be thoroughly modernised was the important junction at Templecombe, this work being carried out during 1937/38. In this case all of the original buildings were swept away and replaced by typical 'Southern' structures of the period, the platforms being much extended at the Salisbury end.

For the remaining inter-war years and again into the BR era the line was a busy one. Some local traffic was lost to the ever-expanding bus network, but otherwise holiday traffic boomed, long-distance passenger figures were well maintained, there was a rise in bulk milk transport as centralised dairies were opened adjacent to Chard Junction, Seaton Junction, and Semley stations, and there remained a healthy tonnage of general freight. The only loss was not significant, the Clifton Maybank goods line being closed on 17 July 1937. Thereafter all wagons for transfer between the Exeter and Weymouth lines travelled via Yeovil Town. The branch had really lost most of its value with the abolition of the broad gauge, and it is surprising that this economy had not taken place many years previously. Even in the late 1950s and early '60s there was sufficient optimism over the route for the Southern Region of British Railways to give serious consideration to electrification through to Exeter Central, and a lot of money was spent on signalling as a first step in this direction. There were no station closures during

13

this period, but reflecting the loss of local traffic, Sutton Bingham was reduced to halt status on 1 August 1960, followed by Milborne Port on 6th November 1961. Both stations were somewhat remote. There were no real worries over the future of the line until January 1963, when all former Southern lines west of Salisbury were transferred to Western Region control. It was immediately obvious that the new management intended to favour their own route to the West from Paddington via Westbury and Taunton rather than the former Southern line, and this intention was reinforced by the Beeching Plan published in March of that year (1963). This stated that only one line between London, Exeter and Plymouth could be justified.

Although there was little to choose between them when it came to intermediate traffic, the old Western line had the edge because it also carried a heavy through traffic from the Midlands and North – at least from Taunton down – and there was no way this could be worked onto the Southern line without a very long and slow diversion. Another aspect of the Beeching Plan was the elimination of both the rural branch line and the stopping main line service, the idea being to establish a few principal railheads serving a wide area and connect them with fast or semi-fast trains. This thinking was extended to freight traffic as well, local sidings being abolished and their traffic concentrated on main goods depots. The shedding of this 'unwanted' business would make further economies possible, and it was announced that whilst the Salisbury–Exeter line would stay – at least for the time being – it would carry only a limited service of semi-fast trains designed primarily to serve intermediate places and would be reduced to single track. The main flow of passengers and freight for the West of England was to be diverted away to the Western line. The summer of 1964 was the last to see busy weekends on the line with through expresses in many portions to serve the various North Devon and Cornish resorts, and thereafter there was a steady pruning of services and facilities. Through goods trains were withdrawn with the introduction of the Winter timetable, and many of the smaller goods yards were closed early the following year. An early casualty of the Beeching era –

although actually closed before the publication of his famous report – was the Chard branch, from which passenger services had been withdrawn on 10 September 1962. Its demise was not totally unexpected, since the line had previously closed for some five months during the fuel crisis of 1951 and traffic levels had never recovered. The section from Chard Junction to Chard Central remained open for goods – mostly private siding traffic – until 3 October 1966. The closure of the Lyme Regis branch on 29 November 1965 was an important event locally, but it was almost obscured by what was happening on the railways as a whole. Again, closure was not surprising as the only worthwhile passenger business was done on a few weekends during the summer. Local people had long since found the bus service more convenient.

The year 1966 was a truly black one for railways in the area as the full weight of the Beeching Plan began to be felt. On 7 March that year the stopping service on the main-line was withdrawn and many of the smaller stations closed completely, together with the Seaton branch. Plans to get rid of Sidmouth at the same time had to be shelved because of the difficulty of providing alternative bus services, but the much-loved Somerset & Dorset – already reprieved once for the same reason – finally met its fate. Stations closed on that date were: Wilton South, Dinton, Semley, Templecombe, Milborne Port, Chard Junction, Seaton Junction, Broad Clyst, and Pinhoe. An attempt had been made to close Yeovil Junction as part of the same rationalisation package, Sherborne being designated as the railhead for the district, but the ferocity of local opinion caused this to be reconsidered. As if to get even with the vociferous residents of Yeovil, the railway management dealt them another blow later in the year. On 2nd October the Town station was closed and the shuttle service diverted to Pen Mill – very useful for passengers changing trains – but less so for serving the town proper, as Pen Mill station was right on the eastern outskirts. Perhaps because of its reduced utility, the shuttle service was not destined to last long. It was finally withdrawn on 5 May 1968, although the connecting line has survived.

Despite this depressing catalogue of closures, things had

'Battle of Britain' class 4-6-2 No. 34054 *Lord Beaverbrook* approaches Yeovil Junction from Yeovil Town with the 9.35 am Yeovil Town–Exeter Central on 6 September 1964.

Gerald T. Robinson

Class U 2-6-0 No. 31793 arrives at Salisbury with a local passenger train from Basingstoke on 27 August 1963. Another superb class of mixed traffic locomotive on which I and many other Southern footplatemen spent our working days and nights.

Rodney Lissenden

still not reached rock bottom. This was achieved on 6 March 1967 when passenger services over the Sidmouth branch, together with its connecting line from Tipton St John's to Exmouth, were withdrawn and the station at Sidmouth Junction closed. An occasional goods train visited Sidmouth for the next couple of months, but the branch closed completely on 8th May. The situation at the commencement of the 1967 Summer timetable can be summarised thus: all of the branch lines had gone and the erstwhile main line was down to a basic service of one train in each direction every two hours, most of which called at all remaining stations. These were: Tisbury, Gillingham, Sherborne, Yeovil Junction, Crewkerne, Axminster, Honiton, Whimple, and Exeter Central. Sutton Bingham, already reduced to a halt and little used, had been closed almost furtively on 31 December 1962. Most trains terminated at Exeter St Davids, the one exception being the daily Brighton–Plymouth service. St James Park Halt remained open, but was served only by Exmouth trains. There were actually rumblings concerning the Exeter–Exmouth branch, but in the end the passenger figures were just too impressive even for a Beeching-style management to ignore. Had this line also closed, one wonders what would have become of Exeter Central station if it was left with just the two-hourly London service. As it was, this once busy main station was reduced to something only slightly better than an unstaffed halt, all the offices and facilities being transferred down the hill to St Davids where they were, of course, well away from the city centre.

With traffic at this level the time was ripe for implementing the next phase of the economy drive – reducing the line to single track. The manner in which this was done was both very costly and extremely ill-considered, and it is difficult to resist the unworthy suspicion that the line was deliberately being made unattractive in order to expedite closure at an early date. The first sections to be singled were Wilton South to Gillingham (where a passing loop was retained) and Gillingham to Templecombe, these being dealt with over the weekend 1-2 April 1967. Templecombe to Sherborne was allowed to remain double track, although a complication was introduced by signalling what had been the

'up' line for bidirectional working. The next phase was truly astonishing and involved the creation of one single-line section from Sherborne all the way to Chard Junction, this coming into use on 7 May. On 11 June the Chard Junction–Honiton and Honiton–Pinhoe sections were singled and the former main line finally reduced to a very secondary route with such a limited capacity that even the basic two-hourly service could only be handled efficiently if everything ran strictly to time! Of course, this was unlikely to happen, a combination of engine failures and problems with the new signalling ensured that delays were very substantial indeed. Within a few months even the railway authorities were forced to concede that rationalisation had been a little too hearty, and following the derailment of a newspaper train at Sherborne they were obliged, at great expense, to restore the double line between that point and Yeovil Junction, this being done on 1 October the same year.

One only has to look at the map to grasp the strangeness of this resignalling plan. To start with, crossing places were not evenly spaced out – either in time or distance. Many stations which remained open for business were unable to regulate traffic in any way, whilst places which had disappeared from the passenger map – frequently stopped trains for regulating purposes – Wilton South, Templecombe, Chard Junction, and Pinhoe all being potential points of delay. The year 1967 can be seen as representing the lowest ebb on the Salisbury–Exeter line; a period of unreliable services and a disgruntled public which made closure seem a certainty. But the line did not prove easy to kill off, and within a few years there was some indication of rebirth. A large housing development was taking place adjacent to the site of Sidmouth Junction station, and there was a concerted effort to get it reopened. This took time, but eventually the campaigners were rewarded by being given a train service from 3 May 1971 when the station reopened as Feniton. At first, tickets were issued from the gate box at the level-crossing, but in 1974 the crossing controls were moved into a building on the platform and tickets were then sold from there. Shortly after this the eastern end of the route, between Salisbury and Yeovil Junction, found itself again

Class 50 No. 50046 *Ajax* in large logo livery arrives at Templecombe on 10 July 1991 with the 11.55 Exeter St Davids–Waterloo. The train has arrived from the double track section that links Templecombe with Yeovil Junction and is now entering the single line section to Gillingham. The comparison with former days couldn't be greater with the once vast Upper Yard to the right beyond the signal box now occupied by trees and scrub.

John Scrace

administered from Waterloo, and services on this part of the line began to increase slightly. Doubtless encouraged by this, the Templecombe Station Promotion Group was set up in 1982 to campaign for the reopening of that station which, it was claimed, would act as the railhead for a large area including the growing town of Wincanton – once served by the S&D. Only the platforms and signal box survived of this once large station, all of the buildings having been demolished around 1968, so the railway management needed some convincing. To demonstrate the potential, the Promotion Group, organised three party excursions in the summer of 1982, and these were so well supported that further agitation succeeded in obtaining a temporary reopening for a trial period of three years from 3 October 1983. The initial service was not brilliant, but enough business resulted for the trial period to be extended indefinitely, and since then Templecombe has been an undoubted success. The temporary arrangement adapted part of the signal box as a ticket office and this continues to the present day, but in 1990 a new waiting room and footbridge

were added and a landscaped garden laid out at the back of the platform. The same year also saw the reopening of Pinhoe station on 16 May. This was given a basic service of three or so trains each way daily designed purely to cater for Exeter commuters, and its use is therefore very limited and certainly nothing on the scale of Templecombe, but it does represent a step in the right direction.

It is most unlikely that many of the other stations closed in 1966 will ever reopen, as most of them remain in very rural settings and offer no great passenger potential. Possible exceptions are Wilton South, where it is thought that a reintroduction of train services would ease road traffic problems in Salisbury and the site for a new station has actually been surveyed, and Chard Junction where there have been several suggestions to provide a 'Parkway' station to cater for Chard and Ilminster. If the Seaton Tramway could be extended over the remainder of the old branch to Seaton Junction it would again become possible to enter that resort by rail, but as the formation on the approach to the Junction station has been destroyed perhaps this is a little ambitious.

Class 33s in tandem – Nos 33102 and 33114 power away from Yeovil Junction hauling the 12.26 Exeter St Davids–Waterloo on 4 April 1992. The leading locomotive is on the bridge carrying the main line over the ex GWR line from Yeovil Pen Mill to Weymouth.

John Scrace

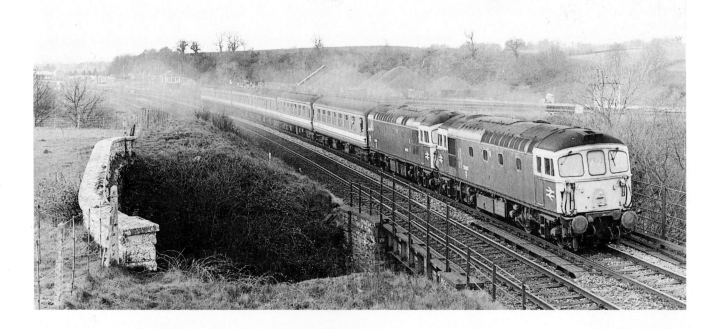

Signalling and Signal Boxes

When the line first opened it was single throughout with crossing loops at the stations, the signalling conforming to the standards of the time. Traffic was regulated by 'policemen' who worked the points and signals by means of adjacent levers, interlocking still being a thing of the future. The priority of trains over the single-line sections was dictated by the working timetable, amended as necessary by written train orders. Cook & Wheatstone's electric telegraph was installed, the instruments being housed in the station offices, and this allowed last-minute adjustments to be made to the working. The signals themselves were of the revolving disc type designed by Albinus Martin, and generally – two were provided at every station for each direction – a 'Stop' and an 'Auxiliary'. The latter acted more or less as a repeater for the former, its clearance allowing the driver of an approaching train to put on enough steam to run right into the crossing loop. Starting signals were not provided, authority to proceed into the section ahead being given by the policeman, either verbally or by presentation of a train order.

Doubling of the line made little difference at first, although the train orders were no longer necessary and a 'Time Interval' system was adopted. The telegraph was useful for organising special traffic or advising of delays, but it was not used in the process of routine train running. However, during the early 1870s the L&SWR was busy installing the Absolute Block system on all its lines, and the Exeter line received attention in 1875. Signal boxes were erected at all the stations and at one or two intermediate locations, these being to a standard design now classified by the Signalling Record Society as Type One. The lever frames and outdoor signals were supplied by Stevens & Son, already established as the main contractor to the L&SWR, the block instruments being of the Preece one-wire pattern. Much of this equipment was destined to have an extraordinarily long working life! Boxes installed as part of the 1875 signalling were: Wilton, Dinton, Tisbury, Semley, Gillingham, Templecombe, Milborne Port, Sherborne, Yeovil Junction No. 1, Yeovil Junction No. 2, Sutton Bingham, Crewkerne, Chard Road, Broom Gates, Axminster, Colyton Junction, Honiton, Sidmouth Junction, Whimple, Broad Clyst, Pinhoe, Exmouth Junction, and Exeter Queen Street 'A', 'B' and 'C'. It is not known whether the intermediate boxes at Abbey Ford, Hardington, and Honiton Incline were part of this original signalling package, as no photographs of the first two have been located and their style of building is therefore unavailable to furnish a clue, and Honiton Incline was so totally non-standard that it cannot be dated. Hardington may well be a later addition, as it was the only box on the line to contain a Saxby & Farmer lever frame, but no opening date for it has been located.

As traffic increased, experience showed some of the block

Left: Salisbury 1972 at the west end of the station, showing the lattice mast bracket signal with the inner home arms guiding trains into the 'up' platform line (left arm) or the 'up' through platform (right arm); the distant signal arms are fixed permantly at caution. Tracks to the far left are from Westbury, and from Exeter on the far right while the tracks in between were once used as carriage sidings.

Adrian Vaughan Collection

Right: The latticed mast lower quadrant 'down' starting signal at Exeter Central in September 1975.

Adrian Vaughan Collection

The interior of Salisbury West signal box in 1972 – no signal levers here banging in the frame – just sets of pull out slides, working the signals and points on the compressed air system.

Adrian Vaughan Collection

sections to be too long, and in 1892 some additional boxes were opened at level crossings. These were of a ground-level type classified as Type Five, the construction being all-timber with a slate roof and much larger windows than the Type One. Tisbury Quarry and Tisbury Gates opened on 4 June 1892 and Wyke and Axminster Gates followed later that Summer. Mystery surrounds the provision of a signal box at Hewish Gates (between Crewkerne and Chard Junction) since it would appear to fit in with the general pattern of the 1892 scheme yet was of the Type Four design – a style not introduced until 1895. Again no opening date has been found.

At the turn of the century the L&SWR became interested in power signalling, and whilst the rural Salisbury–Exeter line might seem an unlikely place to find such advanced equipment at an early date, the eastern end of it became one of the first sites in Britain. In connection with the rebuilding of Salisbury station two new boxes – Salisbury East and West – opened in November 1902. All the points and signals were worked by low-pressure compressed air, and instead of lever frames the boxes contained sets of pull-out slides which were mechanically interlocked in the conventional way. This pneumatic system was so successful that two years later it was used on the busy four-track section between Woking and Basingstoke. The installation at Salisbury was, however, an isolated step into modernity for the line which otherwise remained resolutely old-fashioned. Apart from those signal boxes added in 1892 about the only development since the original signalling had been the provision of a few ground signals at points which were either frequently used or too far from the controlling box for the signalman to see that they were properly over before

giving a handsignal for a movement. In most cases these additional signals were added without extending the boxes, either by adding a couple of levers, by converting some of them to push-and-pull working, or by cramming in a few 'Russell' levers. The latter were found exclusively at the eastern end of the line; Wilton, Dinton, Tisbury, Semley, and Gillingham all being so fitted during the mid '90s but west thereof the preference seemed to be for the push-and-pull lever. Thereafter signalling arrangements on the line remained almost untouched until it was taken into the Southern Railway fold in 1923, the only changes being:

AXMINSTER – August 1903: Lever frame extended by three levers in connection with new branch to Lyme Regis. Latter to be worked by train staff under 'One Engine in Steam Regulations'.

AXMINSTER – July 1906: Lever frame again extended from 17 to 30 levers for the introduction of Tablet Working with full signalling on Lyme Regis branch. Original box structure retained with suitable extension.

HARDINGTON – January 1909: New sidings for milk traffic on 'up' side. Spare levers used up, and two levers added to existing Saxby frame.

YEOVIL JUNCTION – 1909: Station rebuilt and track layout remodelled. No. 2 box renamed Yeovil Junction West and retained with altered locking. New East box with 60-lever Stevens pattern frame replaced old No.1 box.

AXMINSTER GATES – 5 April 1913: Abolished as Block Post but retained under the control of a crossing keeper.

DINTON – 1915: New sidings on 'down' side together with War Department branch to Fovant Camp. Spare levers 5, 6, and 7 brought into use.

Signalman Jim Maidment stands in the doorway of the former L&SWR signal box at Sherborne as No. 35015 *Rotterdam Lloyd* sweeps through heading the Brighton–Plymouth in the late 1950s.

B. J. Charlwood – courtesy of Jim Maidment

ABBEY FORD – 31 January 1918: Signal box abolished and Gillingham to Templecombe made one Block Section.
BROOM GATES – 1 June 1919: Ballast pit sidings on 'down' side and crossover road abolished. Old lever frame removed and replaced by new 6-lever frame in existing box.

Once the Southern had taken control there were quite a few changes which were a mixture of expansion and contraction. Traffic was increasing, but the use of more powerful engines was giving higher average speeds and several of the intermediate block posts were proving unnecessary. Almost immediately both Quarry Gates and Tisbury Gates were downgraded to crossing keeper's positions and the instruments removed, and in 1924 the additional sidings provided at Dinton (1915) were taken out. Crannaford Gates (between Broad Clyst and Whimple) was likewise downgraded to a gate box on 15 September 1925. On the other hand, within a few years a lot of improvements were being introduced in the Exeter area. The decrepit Queen Street station was an urgent candidate for rebuilding, and some preparatory work was done in 1925 when a new 'C' signal box was provided. This was of the Type Four design and contained a 35-lever back-to-traffic frame of the Stevens type supplied by Tyer & Co. The main construction work started in 1927, a new 'A' box with 90 levers opening on 15 November that year to replace the old 'A' and 'B' boxes.

Block instruments, polished brasswork, shining levers, a ticking clock and constantly ringing telephones – of such sights and sounds are signal boxes remembered. Signalman Jim Maidment is seen in the old L&SWR box at Sherborne in the late 1950s.
Courtesy Jim Maidment

This frame was also supplied by Tyers. At the same time the engine shed layout at Exmouth Junction was enlarged, the signal box there being greatly extended although in this case

The 'down' platform starter at Chard Junction formed of an ex L&SWR signal post (complete with finial) fitted with a Southern Railway upper quadrant arm, seen here on 3 August 1957.

Courtesy of Ron Lacey

rounded corners, wings of equal length to house batteries and relay equipment, and an internal staircase. Boxes of this type – classified as Type Thirteen – became familiar to all who travelled widely on the Southern as layouts were altered in connection with electrification schemes, but Templecombe was to be the Western extremity of the design. Having completed Templecombe the Signal Engineer prepared a scheme for Yeovil Junction which envisaged doing away with the old West Box and placing the whole layout under the control of East, into which a new 70-lever back-to-traffic frame would be installed. However, before any real progress could be made World War II broke out, and the idea had to be shelved 'for the duration' – which resulted in nothing being done. One new box that did appear before the war was that at Chilmark (between Dinton and Tisbury). The RAF had taken over an old quarry for storing bombs and ammunition, connecting it to the main-line by a siding which trailed into the 'up' line. A signal box was opened on 10 July 1938, and this too had a Westinghouse frame – but only of 14 levers. There was no attempt to introduce modern architecture to this isolated isolation, a derivative of the old Type Four design being used instead. Being close to Dinton, Chilmark was of little use as a break-section box and was switched out of circuit when access to the RAF siding was not required.

Throughout the period so far discussed the original Preece instruments had remained unchallenged except for on the Exeter Queen Street–Pinhoe section, where Syke's Lock & Block had been installed in 1908. This situation changed a little in 1938, when the new SR three-position block was introduced between Sidmouth Junction and Axminster – this amount of conversion being necessary because the intervening boxes at Honiton, Honiton Incline, and Seaton Junction were fitted with closing switches and did in fact regularly close, so all the instruments had to be changed to make them compatible. At about the same time the Syke's equipment at Pinhoe, Exmouth Junction, and Exeter Central 'A' was likewise replaced by three-position. There were to be no further inroads into the old Preece's empire until well into British Railways days. The Second World War did, of course, suspend many planned improvements, but in fact the conflict made only a small impact on the signalling of the area. The most notable was at Dinton where large Government depots sprang up around the station which made it necessary to provide additional sidings and goods loops. The scale of these alterations made it impossible to adapt the frame in the old box, so a new one with a 32-lever Westinghouse frame was opened on 8 November 1942. This box was a typical wartime structure of reinforced concrete and blast proof brick with a flat roof, and is classified as Type Fourteen.

For the remaining years of the war and for a considerable period afterwards, Dinton handled an enormous traffic in Government supplies, and the money spent on extending the layout was amply justified. The only other alteration attributable to wartime traffic was the provision of a long loop suitable for both passenger and freight trains at Hewish Gates, which was brought into use on 4 October 1942. The existing box was retained, but the lever frame was enlarged from nine to 16 levers. There was virtually no further amendment to the signalling arrangements on the line until well into British Railways days. In the late 1950s the Southern Region embarked upon a programme of signal box

the original basic structure was retained. The next place to receive attention was Seaton Junction, remodelled on a lavish scale to cater for what the company hoped would be a large increase in traffic over the Seaton branch. The new layout employed the Southern's favourite device of through fast lines with loops to serve the platforms, and the siding accommodation was also greatly expanded. In connection with these works the old Type One box which had started life as Colyton Junction was closed and a large new Seaton Junction box with 55 levers opened on 3 April 1928. Again the lever frame was of the Stevens pattern, but it is believed to have been supplied by the Railway Signal Company who were doing a fair amount of work for the SR at the time. The building itself has been classified as a Type 4a – similar in many respects to the standard Four but having more windows to give the signalman an all-round view suitable for an island site.

Templecombe was another ramshackle box dating from the 1875 signalling, and had suffered through having the lever frame extended to the extent that the interior was very cramped. This was remedied on 15 May 1938 when, in connection with the general rebuilding of the station, a new 60-lever box was provided on the 'up' platform. The new Templecombe box was the first departure from traditional designs to be seen on the Exeter line, and it was also the first appearance in the area of a Westinghouse frame. Architecturally it was the very latest thing, with flat roof,

Signalman Ralph Bartlett gets to grips with the signal levers in the newly opened (1960) box at Sherborne.

Courtesy Ralph Bartlett

renewals, and the Exeter line, upon which most of the equipment was elderly, received plenty of attention. Plans for electrification were still on the drawing board, so it seems likely that much of this work was seen as leading towards that end. All of the boxes erected over the next ten years were built to a common design with only minor differences in detail. Classified as Type Sixteen they were of all-brick construction with flat concrete roofs, external stairs, large sliding plate-glass windows (tinted to eliminate glare) and every modern convenience for the signalman. They were also very spacious, and must have seemed truly enormous to a man accustomed to being cooped up in a tiny Type One box. Westinghouse 'A3' lever frames and illuminated track diagrams were also common to all the new boxes. The first one to open was at Gillingham on 28 April 1957 (30 levers) hotly pursued by Honiton (24 levers) on 16 June. On 12 October the following year a new box was opened at Tisbury (24 levers), and 1958 also saw the replacement of more of the old Preece instruments with three-position equipment.

In 1959 Hardington box was closed, which left a rather long section from Sutton Bingham to Crewkerne, but otherwise the signal engineer was fully employed in the area installing new boxes. Exmouth Junction received a new 64-lever box on 15 November that year, and towards the close of 1960 two more came on stream – Crewkerne (24 levers) on 6 November, and Sherborne (30 levers and gate wheel) on 18 December. Several others were planned, including Axminster, Whimple, and Broad Clyst, but in the end only one more was completed – Semley (28 levers), which came into use on 29 January 1961. By then, there was already some underlying uncertainty about the long-term future of the route, and further large projects were put aside. Not that modernisation was cancelled entirely, for over the next two years most of the distant signals were replaced with two-aspect colour lights, multi-aspect signals even appearing at Tisbury and Crewkerne, and the British Railways Automatic Warning System (AWS) was installed throughout.

The Western Region took operational control of everything West of Wilton in January 1963, and they inherited a very mixed bag of signalling equipment ranging from the antique to the very modern. At the time of the takeover – the situation can be summarised thus:

Signal box	Year	Lever frame type	Remarks
Salisbury East	1902	Low-pressure pneumatic	
Salisbury West	1902	Low-pressure pneumatic	
Wilton South	1875	Stevens	
Dinton	1942	Westinghouse 'A2'	
Chilmark	1938	Westinghouse 'A2'	
Tisbury Quarry Gates	1892	Stevens	Not a block post
Tisbury	1958	Westinghouse 'A3'	
Tisbury Gates	1892	Stevens	Not a block post
Semley	1961	Westinghouse 'A3'	
Gillingham	1957	Westinghouse 'A3'	
Templecombe	1938	Westinghouse 'A2'	
Milborne Port	1875	Stevens	
Sherborne	1960	Westinghouse 'A3'	
Wyke	1892	Stevens	GF since 1960
Yeovil Junction 'A'	1909	Stevens pattern	
Yeovil Junction 'B'	1875	Stevens	
Sutton Bingham	1875	Stevens	
Crewkerne	1960	Westinghouse 'A3'	
Hewish Gates	c1897	Stevens	Altered 1942
Chard Junction	1875	Stevens	
Broom Gates	1875	?	New frame 1919
Axe Gates	1949	?	Replacement
Axminster Gates	1892	Stevens	Not a block post
Axminster	1875	Stevens	Extended 1906
Seaton Junction	1928	Stevens pattern	
Honiton Incline	?	Stevens ground level	
Honiton	1957	Westinghouse 'A3'	
Sidmouth Junction	1875*	Stevens	*Later additions
Whimple	1875	Stevens	
Crannaford Crossing	?	Stevens ground level	Not a block post
Broad Clyst	1875	Stevens	
Pinhoe	1875	Stevens	
Exmouth Junction	1959	Westinghouse 'A3'	
Exeter Central 'A'	1927	Tyer, Stevens pattern	
Exeter Central 'B'	1925	Tyer, Stevens pattern	

Furthermore, the SR standard three-position block was now in use throughout the line, and all the newer boxes had illuminated diagrams. The non-block level crossings were fitted with relay bells and repeater block indicators. Taken over all, the signalling was reasonably modern – as even most of the 1875 survivors had colour-light distants – but the Western Region engineers had little experience with either Stevens or Westinghouse frames, and they must have wondered what they had taken on! Within a couple of years they were going to be in a position to sweep most of it away as the plans published by Beeching down-graded it to a secondary line and made singling possible. Many of the smart new signal boxes erected at great expense by the Southern were destined to have remarkably short working lives. It took a couple of years for the new owners to get to grips with a planned series of economies, the first stage being the withdrawal of goods facilities from most of the smaller stations in 1965. As this made the sidings redundant – it was no longer necessary to retain the boxes which controlled them, so several were closed in advance of the main singling scheme. The boxes closed in this first wave during 1965 were: Sutton Bingham on 6 May (the signal arms and lamps had actually been removed on 14 February), Milborne Port on 21 June, Broad Clyst on 12 December, and Semley – then only fours old – on 21 December. Honiton

Incline box was abolished on 6 March 1966, after which there was a stay of execution until work commenced on the main resignalling scheme the following year.

For some time, the Western Region had made it known that they intended to single the line, but when the plans were published and the full extent of the rationalisation became public knowledge, they caused widespread dismay. It was obvious that line capacity was going to be barely sufficient to handle a very basic service, and there was certainly no spare pathways to allow for excursions, freight, or any future increase in frequency. Many feared that it was a prelude to total closure, despite denial by the railway management. Some boxes were closed just ahead of the task of singling to make the job a little easier. The singling itself was carried out in several stages, starting at the Salisbury end. From Salisbury to Wilton – the part still administered by the Southern Region – double track was retained, but single-track was introduced from Wilton to Templecombe over the weekend 1-2 April 1967. On this long section, only Gillingham box was retained, that station becoming the only passing place. The next phase, carried out on 7 May, was very complicated. Double track was allowed to remain between Templecombe and Sherborne, but the 'up' line was reversible so that Templecombe box could be switched out at slack times. Single track then extended from Sherborne to Chard Junction, and all the intermediate boxes were abolished except Yeovil Junction 'A' where the layout was simplified to the extent that it controlled only movements from the branch into the bay platform. A ground-frame was provided at Yeovil Junction to work a connection between the single line and the Yeovil branch, but it was impossible to cross trains there. The final stretch came into service on 11 June, and this involved Chard Junction to Pinhoe with an intermediate box and loop at Honiton. From Pinhoe into Exeter double-track was retained. The single-line sections were controlled by the (then) rather controversial 'Tokenless Block' system, and the fact that neither the signal engineers nor the signalmen had any experience of it led to a series of failures which played havoc with the train service. At completion of the 1967 singling project the only signal boxes remaining in use were: Wilton South, Tisbury Gates (as a ground frame), Gillingham, Templecombe (reduced from 60 to 16 levers), Sherborne, Yeovil Junction (formerly 'A' with no control over the main line), Hewish Gates (as a ground frame), Chard Junction, Broom Gates (as a ground frame), Axe Gates Ground Frame, Axminster Gates (as a ground frame), Honiton, Sidmouth Junction Crossing Ground Frame, Crannaford Gates Ground Frame, Pinhoe, Exmouth Junction, and the two Exeter Central boxes. Over the next few months most of the intermediate level crossings were automated and the ground frames abolished, Axe Gates on 6 August, Broom Gates (20 August), Hewish (30 August), and Crannaford on 22 November.

Experience soon showed the inadequacy of the arrangements, and following the derailment of the newspaper train on the points leading onto the single line at Sherborne – double track was restored between that location and the east end of Yeovil Junction station on 1 October 1967. Because such a mess had been made of Yeovil Junction box, it was easier to fit a new lever frame than tinker about with the old one, the Reading signal works supplying a replacement 44-lever 5-bar VT frame. Yeovil Junction box was out of use from 10 September to allow the new frame to be installed, a temporary ground frame being provided. Even the 'new improved' layout at Yeovil Junction was far from ideal, and it was altered again in March 1975 so that the former bay line could become a loop. Sherborne box survived for a while after the re-doubling to control the

Pinhoe signal box (pictured here on 8 July 1959) opened in 1875 by the L&SWR – and closed by BR in 1988 – a tribute to Victorian engineering.

H. C. Casserley

level crossing, but it eventually closed on 4 January 1970 when the station staff were given charge of the barriers. Another signalling casualty of 1970 was Exeter Central 'B' which closed on 23 February following simplification of the track layout. What remained in use was concentrated on the former 'A' box in which the frame was reduced from 90 to 50 levers. A closing switch was also fitted so that on nights and Sunday mornings the block section could be worked as Exeter West–Pinhoe. There matters rested until 1973, when there was a major development at the eastern end of the line. On 28 October a new double junction between the Exeter and Westbury lines was brought into use at Wilton, the new layout being controlled from the existing Wilton South signal box (of 1875 vintage). Although the points were motor-operated and all the signals were colour lights, no attempt was made to introduce a panel, the Stevens frame being reconditioned and re-locked. This connection enabled the separate former GWR line between Wilton and Salisbury to be closed except for a short goods spur to Quidhampton Siding. The only other notable event that year was on 16 December, when the box at Axminster Gates was abolished and control of the barriers transferred to the station office with the aid of CCTV.

During the period 17 to 28 August 1981 a new panel box was commissioned at Salisbury, the East box closing on the 19th followed by the West box on 21st. This work also included some simplification of the layout. The panel finally took control of Wilton Junction – and the entrance to the Exeter single line on 29 November that year, Wilton South box being abolished. By this time the Southern Region had regained control of the line as far west as Yeovil and were anxious to improve the train service. In the end it was decided to lay in a new passing loop at Tisbury, worked of course from Salisbury panel, and this came into service on 23 March 1986. Unfortunately the 'down' platform at Tisbury had already been sold off to the neighbouring

agricultural engineer, so it was not possible to position the loop in the station. The need to stop trains virtually in the middle of nowhere probably reduces the appeal of using Tisbury loop, but it is available at times of disruption or for special traffic. The 1980s saw several other panel projects besides the one at Salisbury. The box at Chard Junction which dated from 1875 was finally deemed 'life expired' and was closed on 11 September 1982, temporary switches being provided until a proper mini-panel was opened in a new building on the site of the original box on 11 December. There were no alterations to the track layout.

Finally we must look at the Exeter end of the line, where many alterations were being made later in the decade in connection with the Exeter Power Box scheme. Exeter panel is situated adjacent to St Davids station, and its main area of concern is the former GWR main line between Taunton and Totnes, but on 6 May 1985 it assumed control of what was left at Exeter Central and the old 'A' box closed. Exmouth Junction remained untouched for a while, but the lever frame was removed on 30 January 1988, the points being barred over by hand until 13 February when a small panel in the same building was commissioned. At the same time Pinhoe signal box was closed, the level crossing being fitted with CCTV and worked from Exmouth Junction. With the closure of Pinhoe – the last Type One box disappeared from the line after 103 years of service – a tribute indeed to the quality of Victorian engineering.

Plans exist for the provision of crossing loops at such places as Axminster and Crewkerne which will permit an hourly interval service to be run to Exeter, but nothing is likely to happen until the line is signalled from a new super signalling centre at either Eastleigh, Basingstoke, or Woking. The future of the line is probably more secure than it has been for the last 35 years, but it remains low priority when it comes to matters of capital investment, and it might be many years before there are any further alterations to the infrastructure.

Salisbury

The London & South Western Railway constructed the 21 miles 78 chain double-track branch (although single was contemplated at first under Section 108 of the 1844 Act) from Bishopstoke (Eastleigh) on the London–Southampton main line to a terminus at Milford – situated on the south-eastern fringe of the Cathedral City. On 21 January 1847 a special train arrived from London carrying officials from the L&SWR and "all the London Newspapers". Coal traffic started a few days later on 27 January and this was followed on 23 February by the inspection of the line by the Board of Trade. The necessary approval being granted and public services started on 1 March of the same year.

The terminus consisted of a single platform 350 ft long, with a collection of timber built structures. A goods shed and warehouse were also provided. Trains ran to and from Bishopstoke where they connected with services to London, Southampton, and Gosport. A two-road locomotive shed was also established from the start – constructed of brick, and measuring 150 ft x 38 ft. A 25 ft turntable was also provided. Meanwhile on the other side of the city the Great Western Railway, via its Wilts, Somerset, & Weymouth branch from Westbury, opened a terminus on the west side of Fisherton Street in 1856 – to mineral traffic on 11 June, and to passenger traffic on 30 June. The GWR had been dragging its feet over construction of the broad gauge branch, (the section from Westbury to Warminster had opened as early as 9 September 1851), and was convinced that the line could never be made to pay, but under pressure from legal action by the local populace, and the threat of penalties, eventually completed the 19½ miles from Warminster as a single line. The GWR terminus was constructed in the Brunellian style with an overall roof with glazed ends covering two platform roads, and two centre sidings, and a goods yard was opened to the north of the station. A two-road broad gauge engine shed and turntable opened in April 1858. Salisbury was now served by two rival companies of differing gauges, and London could be reached via Eastleigh (L&SWR) 95.6 miles, or via Westbury and Swindon (GWR) 136.3 miles.

The direct London line (L&SWR) reached Salisbury from Andover and opened to public traffic on 1 May 1857 and as the new station at Fisherton (L&SWR) was not ready, trains went direct to Milford, setting back into the terminal. The new station at Fisherton was opened to public traffic on 2 May 1859. It was a one-sided affair, with a single platform (including a bay) some 800ft in length, on the south side of the line extending over Fisherton Street (where it recessed to form a bay) and was claimed at the time to have been one of the longest platforms in England. This was concurrent with the opening of the first section of the Salisbury & Yeovil Railway from Salisbury to Gillingham, the trains being worked by the L&SWR, and from this date all L&SWR trains ran into and out of Fisherton. The terminus at Milford was closed to passenger traffic from the opening of the new station with the services to and from Andover and Bishopstoke transferring to the new station. The old terminus remained open for goods traffic, and eventually became the principal depot for Salisbury. The station building at Fisherton Street was completed in time for the inaugural train carrying officials of the L&SWR and other notables from London to Exeter on 18 July 1860 in a serpentine length train of 20 coaches hauled by three locomotives – a Joseph Beattie 6ft 6in 2-2-2, No. 151 *Montrose*, (built 1857) and two of John Gooch's 7ft 2-2-2s, (1852/53), Nos 115 *Vulcan* and 122 *Britannia*. The whole

The road ahead is clear – and rebuilt 'West Country' class 4-6-2 No. 34037 *Clovelly* bound for Waterloo, departs from Salisbury on 27 August 1963.

Rodney Lissenden

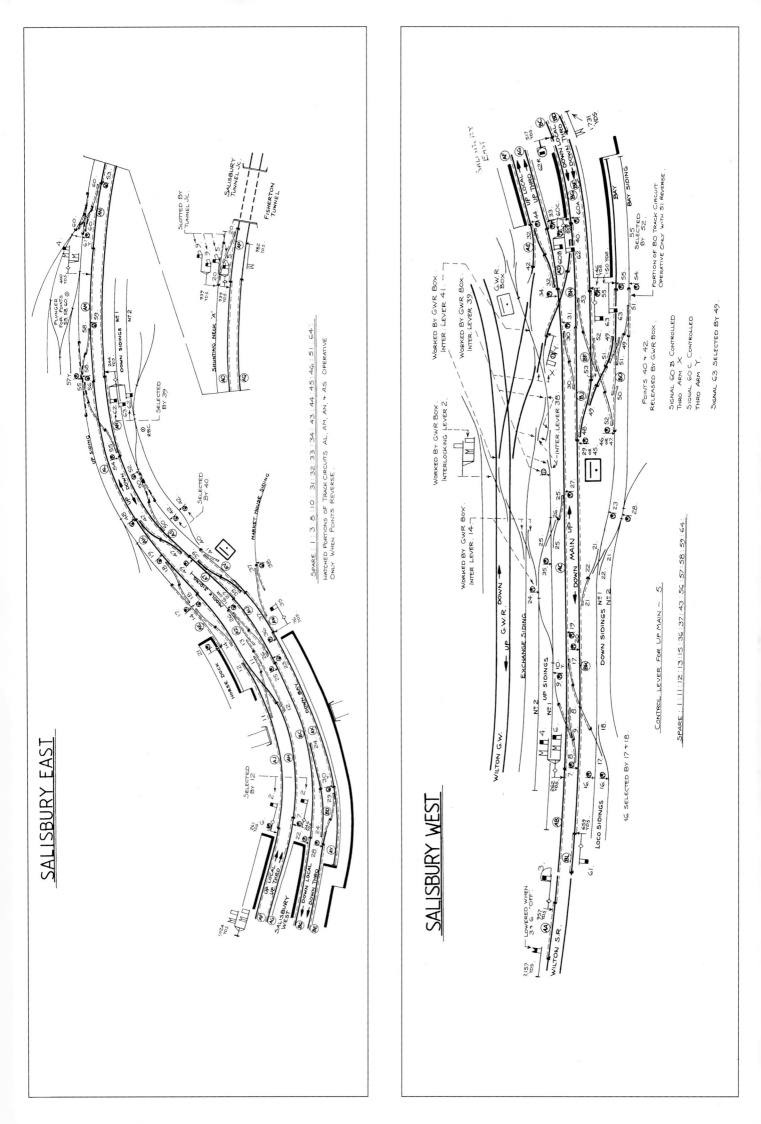

SALISBURY EAST

SALISBURY WEST

'Battle of Britain' class 4-6-2 No. 34063 *229 Squadron* departs from Salisbury with the 11.15 am Exmouth–Waterloo on 31 July 1965.
S. C. Nash

journey to Exeter Queen Street took a lengthy seven hours. The line to Exeter was opened to public traffic on the following day, the 19th. Timetables for November 1860 show that the first train 'down', starting from Salisbury at 5.55 am, arrived at Queen Street at 9.20 am, followed by four trains departing from London at 6 am, 9 am (EXP), 10.15 am, and 2 pm. Trains from Exeter departed at 7.30 am, 10.30 am, 1.15 pm (EXP), 2.45 pm, and 6 pm, the latter terminating at Salisbury. Sunday services for November 1860 comprised two 'up' trains departing from Exeter at 7.30 am and 1.35 pm, and one 'down' train, the 9.15 am from London. A 'down' train started from Yeovil (Hendford) at 7.20 am. Also in 1860, a goods transit shed for the exchange of traffic between the two gauges was opened, the

shed having a single track of each gauge with a platform between. Most of the transfer traffic between the GWR and the L&SWR took place at Basingstoke, where mixed gauge track had been in place since 1856. Situated on the boundary between the two differing systems and west of the two stations, the shed was in use until the gauge conversion of the Wilts, Somerset & Weymouth branch in June 1874. A long footbridge connected the two stations.

A connecting siding was brought into use between the GWR and the L&SWR in February 1878, each side paying 50% of the estimated cost of £80. It was not used for through working as a reversal was necessary. The L&SWR station, as previously mentioned, consisted of one platform on the 'down' side surmounted by an overall roof supported by iron

Bulleid Pacific 4-6-2 No. 34057 *Biggin Hill* pulls away from Salisbury with a Plymouth–Brighton train on 27 August 1963.
Rodney Lissenden

pillars and open on the 'train' side. The platform could hold 'up' and 'down' trains simultaneously, the problem being that the 'up' services could not run direct into the platform. The usual practice, was for trains to run to a ticket platform beyond the station, make a lengthy stop, and then set back into the station where the impatient and unhappy passengers could at last alight. A ticket platform on the 'down' line was also in use until 1893. Traffic was expanded further when the cross-country branch from the Eastleigh line to the Southampton & Dorchester, the 18½ mile-long single line from Alderbury Junction to West Moors Junction (the Salisbury & Dorset Junction Railway Company, incorporated on 22 July 1861) opened on 20 December 1866, and was worked throughout by the L&SWR.

By 1876, with congestion and delays being widespread at Salisbury with its awkward layout, the L&SWR traffic committee created plans for the enlargement of the station "in concert with the G.W. Co.". But to put it mildly, relations between the two companies were rather strained due to the connivance between the L&SWR and the Midland Railway, in snatching the Somerset & Dorset Railway away from the GWR the previous year. Undaunted, the L&SWR formed an alternative plan for a new separate 'up' platform, which was constructed on the curve east of the main station and separated from it by Fisherton Street bridge. This new 'up' station, with a platform of 683 ft, and a bay at the eastern end, was furnished with a booking office, waiting rooms and refreshment room, all of which were constructed in timber – painted and sanded to look like stone. The new premises opened on 19 August 1878. On 1 July 1896, the through Portsmouth–Cardiff services were officially initiated, the services calling at the L&SWR station, and a new 'direct siding' was laid by the GWR for the passenger service enabling access to the WS&W line. This was a temporary connection, subject to the major station changes that were to occur later, the new connection being controlled at the GWR end by a ground-frame, and subject to a 4 mph speed restriction.

The L&SWR considered that, because of the ever-increasing traffic, both passenger and freight from both companies, passing through Salisbury in its role as an important and expanding trunk route, a major remodelling of the congested station premises was necessary. One factor in this was the opening of the Severn Tunnel in 1886, and the growing demand for coal transported through Salisbury via the GWR as steam replaced sailing ships at Southampton and Portsmouth. After extensive and prolonged discussions between the GWR and the L&SWR, a formal agreement was eventually reached between the two parties, dated 28 January 1898. The big 'fly in the ointment' as far as the L&SWR was concerned, with regard to station expansion was the former broad gauge GWR engine shed, but this was demolished. A new GWR Dean pattern locomotive shed (opened 1899) was constructed at the expense of the L&SWR in a position west of the GWR terminus, an exchange of land took place, and the L&SWR gained enough land to construct three additional platforms, two 'up' and one 'down', opposite the original single platform west of Fisherton Street. The six platforms of the new station measured thus: No. 1 ('up' local) 662 ft. No. 2 ('up' main) 665 ft. No. 3 ('down' local). No. 4 ('down' main) 695 ft. No. 5 ('down' bay) No. 6 (loop bay east of No. 4). With the L&SWR moving its own engine shed, the original single platform was extended westwards, and a new set of station buildings constructed adjoining the original (1860) offices. The new buildings, built in red brick, comprised an entrance hall, booking offices, buffet and waiting rooms. The first of the new platforms (No. 1) was brought into use on the morning of Sunday, 6 April 1902. The separate 'up' platform (closed the previous night) was replaced by a marshalling and transfer yard of 16 roads. The GWR through trains were restricted to platforms Nos 1 and 3, and were made freely accessible to GWR trains and staff at all times. Under the agreement of 28 January 1898 the GWR put in a permanent double-junction to the L&SWR's platforms Nos 1 and 3, which allowed direct running to or from these platforms only, and constructed a 93-lever signal box which opened on 27 May 1900. Although the GWR had gained a foothold in

Salisbury East bay on 19 July 1924, and 4-4-0 No. E113 has just arrived – stopping just short of the 'blocks' with the 4.25 pm from Portsmouth.

H. C. Casserley

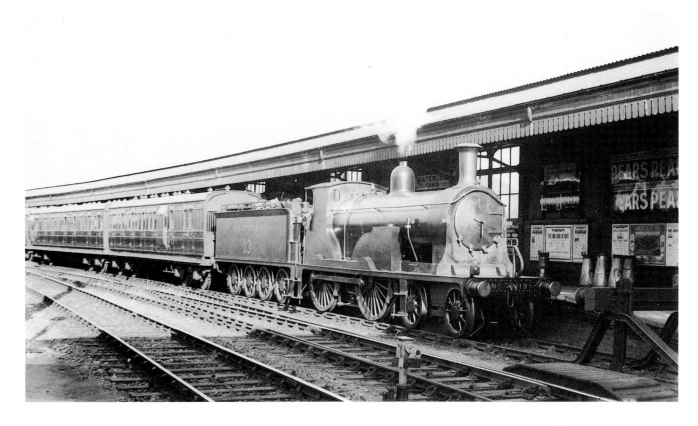

A view taken during a quiet interlude on the main 'down' platform at Salisbury complete with W. H. Smith's bookstall to the left from which a *Guide to Stonehenge* could be obtained amongst other publications.

the new L&SWR station, it was to be another 30 years before the old GWR terminus would close to local passenger services. Also under the 1898 agreement, GWR crews and locomotives worked through to the East yard on freight or coal trains destined for the L&SWR, and in the opposite direction L&SWR engines and crews worked onto the GWR, handing over in Fisherton yard.

The Market House Railway opened in 1859 and made a trailing connection east of the station on the 'down' side off the Bournemouth bay. This line was built for the Salisbury

Station pilot M7 0-4-4T No. 30254 'skulks' alongside the 'down' bay at Salisbury on 9 April 1964. This is one of the Drummond M7s that was not fitted with the auto push-and-pull gear unlike the two M7s allocated (Nos 30129 and 30131) to our shed at Yeovil Town (72C). The auto-fitted tanks were known as the 'motor tanks' amongst Southern crews. The Salisbury station pilots were kept very busy with carriage shunting, and attaching and detaching stock from main line trains.

Barry Eagles

Railway & Market House Company (incorporated on 14 July 1856) for the total sum of £1,501 8s 8d by Thomas Brassey, although the actual market house itself was built (by other contractors) for over £5,000. Traffic consisted of grain for Main & Sons the local seed merchants, a builders yard, and coal for the local electricity company. The 1943 working appendix shows the following engines that were restricted from working on the branch: Nos 330-335, 443-478, 482-524, 736-755, 763-806, 823-837, 850-865, 900-914 and 1816, Z class 0-8-0 shunting tank engines and all engines fitted with 8-wheel tenders.

In 1900 the L&SWR was accelerating its services to the West with the best expresses taking 3 hrs 55 mins and 5 hrs 44 mins to reach Exeter and Plymouth respectively, these being:

Down
10.50 am Waterloo–Exeter (3 hrs 35 mins) Plymouth 5 hrs 44 mins.
11.00 am Waterloo–Exeter (3 hrs 57 mins).
 3.00 pm Waterloo–Exeter (3 hrs 45 mins)
 5.50 pm Waterloo–Exeter (4hrs 15 mins).
Up
10.20 am Exeter–Waterloo (4 hrs 20 mins).
12.00 pm Exeter–Waterloo (3 hrs 40 mins).
12.40 pm Exeter–Waterloo (4 hrs 20 mins).
 4.15 pm Exeter–Waterloo (4 hrs 6 mins).

The timings of the fastest services were just 25 minutes longer than the best GWR expresses to Plymouth – still at that time using the Swindon and Bristol route. Salisbury (like Exeter) was a major engine change-over location for the Plymouth expresses with as long as ten minutes being allowed (12 mins at Exeter) for the operation. This timing was whittled down over the years until five minutes became the average for a change-over. The 1912 timings show the still-accelerating services, most of which were powered by the superb T9 class 4-4-0s.

Down
10.50 am Waterloo–Exeter (3 hrs 12 mins).
11.00 am Waterloo–Exeter (3 hrs 15 mins).
11.10 am Waterloo–Exeter (3 hrs 14 mins).
 3.30 pm Waterloo–Exeter (3 hrs 15 mins).
Up
10.17 am Exeter–Waterloo (3 hrs 30 mins).
12.00 pm Exeter–Waterloo (3 hrs 15 mins).
12.55 pm Exeter–Waterloo (3 hrs 33 mins).
 2.10 pm Exeter–Waterloo (3 hrs 50 mins).

In the 1930s, all but two of the cross-country GWR services from Westbury worked to and from Southampton. It was therefore more cost effective to close the GWR terminus and switch all their trains to the Southern Railway station with effect from 12 September 1932, the former broad gauge terminus was then relegated to goods traffic.

Three serious accidents have occurred at Salisbury over the years; the first, on 6 October 1856 when a double-headed, 35-wagon train from Westbury carrying heifers, oxen and sheep – hauled by *Virgo*, a 2-4-0 of the 'Leo' class and *Bergion*, an 0-6-0 of the 'Premier' class, ran away when approaching Salisbury – and crashed into the buffers of the GWR terminus, killing the driver and fireman of *Bergion*. The second accident, also involving the GWR, happened on 5 August 1873 at Bemerton bridge (where the A30 crosses the railway) when the 1.30 pm passenger train from Bristol headed by *Homer*, a 4-4-0 saddle tank, collided with *Gladiator* hauling the 4.35 pm mixed train to Chippenham on the then single-line section. The guard and driver of the 1.30 pm ex Bristol were killed, the driver of the Chippenham bound train escaping with a broken leg while seven passengers were seriously hurt. The third and most disastrous accident occurred at the L&SWR station on 1 July 1906 when a Drummond L12 class 4-4-0, No. 421, hauling an 'up' boat express containing passengers from the RMS *New York* overturned on the intricate trackwork and curves immediately east of the station, colliding with a milk train in the process. 28 deaths resulted from the accident. Of the 43 passengers, 24 were killed together with the driver and fireman of the express, and the guard and fireman of the milk train also perished. Many of the surviving passengers were seriously injured.

Trains at Salisbury – 1932 working timetable London–Exeter. Times are taken from the weekday working time table and are the departure timings from individual stations in arrival order at Salisbury.

Down

Time		Route / description
12.00 am	(MO)	Salisbury–Templecombe *Light Engine*.
9.32 pm	(NMM)	Nine Elms–Plymouth *Freight*.
10.10 pm	(NS)	Nine Elms–Torrington *Freight*.
10.47 pm	(NS)	Nine Elms–Exmouth Jcn Sidings *Freight*.
9.50 pm	(NMM)	Waterloo–Yeovil Junction *Empty Churns*.
1.50 am	(NM)	Eastleigh–Yeovil Town *Passenger and Mail*.
1.30 am		Waterloo–Plymouth & Ilfracombe *Newspaper*.
3.15 am		Salisbury–Yeovil Town *News and Mail*.
4.30 am	(NM)	Salisbury–Exmouth Jcn *Freight*.
11.53 pm	(NMM)	Feltham–Exmouth Jcn Sidings *Freight*.
7.20 am		Salisbury–Templecombe *Freight*.
12.10 am	(MO)	Nine Elms–Exmouth Jcn Sidings *Freight*.
3.08 am		Waterloo–Seaton Jcn *Parcels, Churns, Horse Boxes*.
7.58 am		Salisbury–Plymouth *Passenger*.
4.15 am		Victoria–Sherborne *Empty Churns*.
7.47 am		Basingstoke–Exeter Passenger.
8.40 am		Waterloo–Plymouth–Ilfracombe *Passenger*.
10.53 am		Salisbury–Exeter *Passenger*.
3.12 am	(MO)	Feltham–Exmouth Jcn Sidings *Freight*.
10.45 am	(Q)	Waterloo–Exeter *Passenger*.
11.00 am		Waterloo–Exeter *Passenger*.
12.46 pm		Salisbury–Exeter *Passenger*.
12.52 pm		Salisbury–Yeovil *Passenger*.
12.00 pm	(FO)	Waterloo–Lyme Regis–Seaton–Ilfracombe *Passenger*.
12.20 pm	(Q)	Waterloo–Padstow *Passenger*.
11.30 am	(MFOQ)	Brighton–Plymouth *Passenger*.
11.30 am	(TWTH)	Brighton–Plymouth *Passenger*.
12.40 pm		Waterloo–Plymouth–Ilfracombe *Passenger*.
2.47 pm		Salisbury–Exeter *Passenger*.
3.10 pm		Salisbury–Yeovil Junction *Freight*.
3.00 pm		Waterloo–Ilfracombe–Plymouth *Freight*.
4.45 pm		Salisbury–Barnstaple Junction *Passenger*.
3.05 pm	(FO)	Waterloo–Ilfracombe *Passenger*.
4.51 pm		Salisbury–Yeovil Junction *Passenger*.
5.00 pm	(FO)	Salisbury–Yeovil Junction *Passenger*.
11.36 am	(NTue)	Clapham Junction–Yeovil Junction *Empty Churns*.

Rebuilt 'Merchant Navy' class 4-6-2 No. 35013 *Blue Funnel* takes water at Salisbury on 18 April 1964 before heading for Waterloo with the 'Atlantic Coast Express'. Footplatemen were based on the 'up' and 'down' platforms during the busy summer workings to assist with shovelling coal forward on locomotives that were working through on duties which were not booked to exchange engines. As a young engine cleaner I was sent on loan to Salisbury shed from Yeovil, and spent many a happy day shovelling coal forward and putting the 'bag' in the tender. All this was spent with smoke drifting from the locomotive and the safety valves roaring away, then when we had accomplished our task in the short time allowed (6 minutes only), the locomotive would leave with an almighty slip on the ever greasy rails, and we would retire to the locomen's cabin on the platform for a brief spell to have a cup of tea before the next arrival.

Hugh Ballantyne

Rebuilt 'West Country' class No. 34095 *Brentor* clanks into Salisbury with the 'down' 11.5 am Waterloo–Padstow relief 'ACE' on 24 August 1964. Only 4½ minutes were allowed here for crew changeover, take on water, and shovel coal forward; this is the reason that spare crews were kept on the station to assist enginemen. Class 5MT No. 73119 *Elaine* stands in the 'down' bay to the right in readiness to follow the 11.5 am with the 12.36 pm stopper to Exeter Central.

Hugh Ballantyne

The fireman of No. 34038 *Lynton* shovels coal forward at the west end of Salisbury station in readiness for the leg to Westbury, of an RCTS special to Swindon on 5 May 1960. Members of the aforesaid society *swan* around on the platform as Class 4MT 2-6-0 No. 76060 (70D) 'fresh off shed' trundles light engine through the station. Note the freight traffic in the massive West yard to the left, and also in the former GWR sidings to the right.

Derek Phillips Collection

T1 0-4-4T No. 10 whiles away a quiet moment in Salisbury West yard on 29 August 1940. The locomotive is in unlined Maunsell green, with Bulleid lettering and bunker side numerals – a livery which had been applied at Eastleigh Works in March of the same year.

H. C. Casserley

'King Arthur' class 4-6-0 No. 451 *Sir Lamorak* in superb external condition, reverses onto its westbound train at Salisbury in 1939.

C. L. Caddy Collection

11.35 am	(Tu.O)	Clapham Junction–Yeovil Junction *Empty Churns.*	8.25 am	Plymouth–Waterloo *Passenger.*
5.00 pm		Waterloo–Exeter *Passenger.*	10.37 am (Q)	Exeter–Portsmouth and Brighton *Passenger.*
6.00 pm		Waterloo–Plymouth *Passenger.*	12.50 pm	Templecombe–Salisbury *Passenger.*
8.06 pm		Salisbury–Yeovil Junction *Passenger.*	9.00 am	Ilfracombe–Waterloo *Passenger.*
8.30 pm	(Q)	Salisbury–Meldon Quarry *Stone Empties.*	10.30 am	Ilfracombe–Waterloo *Passenger.*
			9.40 am	Padstow–Waterloo *Passenger.*
9.25 pm	(MO&Q)	Salisbury–Templecombe *Light Engine.*	11.05 am	Plymouth–Portsmouth *Passenger.*
5.00 pm		Basingstoke–Exmouth Jcn Sidings *Freight.*	10.15 am (FO)	Padstow–Waterloo *Passenger.*
			2.30 pm	Yeovil Town–Salisbury *Passenger.*
10.40 pm	(NS)	Salisbury–Templecombe *Freight.*	12.20 pm	Ilfracombe–Waterloo *Passenger.*
Up			2.55 pm (FO)	Sidmouth Junction–Waterloo *Passenger.*
5.00 pm	(NM)	Wadebridge–Salisbury *Freight.*		
4.15 am		Templecombe–Salisbury *Freight.*	4.05 pm (FO)	Yeovil Town–Salisbury *Passenger.*
7.00 am		Yeovil Town–Waterloo *Passenger.*	4.10 pm	Yeovil Town–Salisbury *Passenger.*
7.37 am		Yeovil–Salisbury *Passenger.*	2.05 pm (FO)	Ilfracombe–Waterloo *Passenger.*
7.20 am		Exeter–Waterloo *Passenger.*	2.20 pm	Ilfracombe–Waterloo *Passenger.*
6.30 am		Exeter–Waterloo *Passenger.*	3.50 pm	Plymouth–Waterloo *Passenger.*
8.35 am		Yeovil Junction–Salisbury *Freight.*	4.25 pm	Templecombe–Salisbury *Freight.*
9.35 am	(MO)	Exeter–Waterloo *Passenger.*	4.50 pm	Sherborne–Victoria *Milk.*
9.55 am		Yeovil Junction–Salisbury *Milk and Horse Boxes.*	4.35 pm	Exeter–Woking *Passenger.*
			6.05 pm	Sherborne–Waterloo *Milk.*
5.52 am		Plymouth–Salisbury *Passenger.*	4.43 pm	Exeter–Waterloo *Milk and Parcels.*

With the Southern Railway circlet around the smokebox door and throwing smoke and cinders high into the sky. 'Merchant Navy' class No. 21C14 *Nederland Line* leaves Salisbury and heads West with the Waterloo–Ilfracombe 'Atlantic Coast Express' on 21 September 1946.

Ken Nunn Collection LCGB

6.55 pm	Exmouth Jcn Sidings–Salisbury *Freight.*	12.45 pm	Torrington–Nine Elms *Freight.*
		11.00 pm (MOQ)	Templecombe–Eastleigh *Freight.*
7.30 pm (NS)	Exeter Goods Yard–Nine Elms *Freight.*	5.18 pm	Plymouth–Nine Elms *Freight.*
4.45 pm	Ilfracombe–Eastleigh *Passenger and Mails.*	7.54 pm (Q)	Okehampton–Salisbury *Stone.*
		4.52 pm	Torrington–Salisbury *Freight.*

Bulleid 'West Country' class No. 21C120 *Seaton* enters the outskirts of Salisbury and runs down the bank towards the station whilst heading the 8.15 am Plymouth–Waterloo on 21 September 1946.

Ken Nunn Collection LCGB

Salisbury 25 September 1991. Class 47/7 No. 47709, working the 11.00 Waterloo–Exeter St Davids, stands alongside Class 155 'Sprinter' No. 155306 forming the 11.10 Portsmouth Harbour–Cardiff.

John Scrace

Maunsell class N 2-6-0 No. 31821 (70C) with a pair of WR 'Toad' brakevans coupled to the tender, leaves Salisbury with a freight train bound for Basingstoke on 27 August 1963.

Rodney Lissenden

Below: The S15 class 4-6-0s, or 'Blackuns' as they were known by Southern footplatemen, gave stirling service over the South Western main line on freight and mixed traffic duties. Here, a stalwart of the class – No. 30841 – arrives at Salisbury from the South West with a heavy freight train on 27 August 1963.

Rodney Lissenden

The above workings are just those applicable to the Exeter line and do not include the Southern Railway services to Bournemouth, Southampton, Eastleigh, etc., the many local trains radiating eastwards, the light engine movements to and from the shed, or the trip workings between the East and West yards and the carriage shunters. In addition, there were the GWR services, including the long trains of coal from South Wales (and the returning empty wagons) trundling through on the cross-country route – hauled by the large 42xx and 72xx tank engines, making this station very busy indeed right up until the end of steam. Two 64-lever signal boxes 'A' (East) and 'B' (West) controlled the area in conjunction (to a lesser extent) with the GWR box. Southern trains used the 'up' and 'down' through platforms (2 and 4) and the GWR services the 'up' and 'down' local platforms (1 and 3). Local trains to the West departed from the 'down' bay (5), and the bay at the east end of the 'down' platform (6) was used by local trains to Bulford & Amesbury, Romsey, Bournemouth, and Southampton. This was perpetuated until the end of steam, although some 'up' services from Exeter would use the 'up' local platform. The large 17-siding East yard, busy day and night, handled freight traffic from the GWR en route to the Southern, and the equally busy West yard dealt with goods traffic heading down the line to Exeter and beyond. Traffic for the GWR was mainly shunted at the 'up' (Fisherton) sidings and these practices continued throughout nationalisation until the end of steam.

Today, the station with its buildings standing almost unaltered, is still a major cross-country intersection, with the Class 159 'Turbos' operating on the Waterloo–Exeter trains, and Class 158 'Super Sprinters' on the Portsmouth–Cardiff services. The clanking of buffers from the freight yards is no longer heard, but stone trains from Westbury are a common sight, hauled by the General Motors Class 59s of Messrs Foster Yeoman and ARC now under the banner of Mendip Rail. Colour light signalling now controls the area being controlled by Salisbury Panel, housed in the former parcels office of the original station building. At one time the WR and SR routes westwards ran on separate parallel tracks, however, from 27 October 1973, two miles of the former WR line into Salisbury were abandoned, and a new connection – Wilton Junction – was installed with trains using the Westbury route to and from Salisbury now travelling over the former L&SWR main line for two miles. However, part of the former WR route has been retained to gain access to the ECC quarry's sidings at Quidhampton where chalk slurry is loaded and conveyed in tank wagons to Port Elphinstone near Aberdeen.

Footplate comments

From Wilton the ex GWR line had run parallel with our mainline, giving us the chance sometimes to run alongside with those 'Western blokes' with a bout of whistling and hand gestures! We would usually run into Salisbury with the fire banked up and the footplate swilled down in readiness for our relief, or if the engine had to come off and go to shed, then the fire would be run down in readiness for squaring up on the ash pit. We would run down the bank with the engine shed to the right with smoke drifting everywhere and the sound of steam escaping from safety valves. To our left would be the carriage sidings packed with coaches. The West yard to our right would be packed with freight wagons. We would clank in to the 'up' through platform, squeal to a halt, gather our kit together, and place it on the platform. Our relief would be there, and they would swing the bag around to refill the tender. I would assist the relief fireman to push some coal forward, they would pull away towards London and my mate and I would enter the enginemens' cabin on the platform to have a cup of tea and a 'Woodbine' before relieving a Nine Elms crew on a 'down' train and head home.

Salisbury Shed

With the opening of the new station at Fisherton a new brick-built three-road locomotive shed was instituted at the west end of the station in the summer of 1859. A 45 ft turntable, coal stage, small shed office surmounted by a

No. 34054 *Lord Beaverbrook* powers its way up the incline from the station with the 11.30 am Brighton–Plymouth on 6 February 1960.

S. C. Nash

'Battle of Britain' class 4-6-0 No. 34057 *Biggin Hill* stands in the 'down' bay at Salisbury on 5 September 1964 with a local stopping train for the South Western main line.

C. L. Caddy

water tank, stores, water columns and inspection pits supplemented the building. Various improvements to the facilities took place over the years including lengthening of the shed by approximately 40 ft, provision of a 50 ft turntable, and extending the coal stage to 160 ft, but traffic growth meant more locomotives, needing more space, and in 1885 an additional three-road wooden shed was constructed measuring 200 ft x 50 ft. The building was positioned adjacent to the former shed. However, by 1895 the L&SWR was again seeking locomotive accommodation and a site to the far west of the station was chosen.

The superb brick-built ten-road shed with a five-span slate roof was opened in December 1901, the two earlier sheds falling victim to the remodelling of the station. A huge, 100,000 gallon water tank surmounted a brick built dormitory adjacent to the 55 ft turntable. A large elevated wooden coaling stage from which engines could be coaled from either side also stood near the turntable. Turntables

Class U 2-6-0 No. 31632 on the outskirts of Salisbury hauling set No. 613 on the 12.42 pm Templecombe–Salisbury 27 August 1963.

Rodney Lissenden

Southern locomotives predominate the scene at Salisbury shed in this view taken on 20 September 1947; a long rank of locomotives await their turn for disposal and turning on the right, and the atmosphere is full of smoke and steam.

H. C. Casserley

Class Z 0-8-0T No. 957 with Bulleid lettering on the tank side, stands in Salisbury shed yard on 9 July 1945.

H. C. Casserley

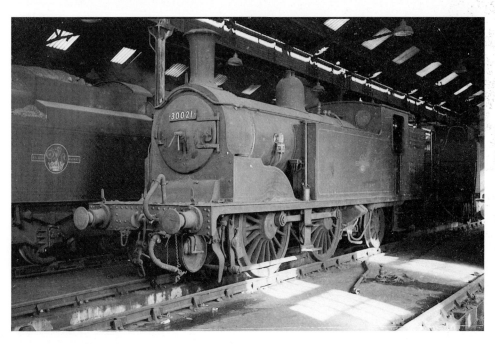

M7 0-4-4T No. 30021 sits quietly inside Salisbury shed on 8 March 1964 (in fact right by the pedestrian entrance and shed 'gaffers' office) contemplating the fact that the end of her days are nigh.

Hugh Ballantyne

were replaced over the years, the early version being replaced by a 65-footer in 1912, and a 70 ft table was installed in 1956. As with Exmouth Junction, the shed was well known for its stud of the magnificent 'King Arthur' class of which the doyen of the series, No. 453, was based here for many years. The GWR locomotive shed was closed on 26 November 1950 (although engines were still stabled there for a time) with the WR engines being serviced at the Southern shed. Salisbury shed finally closed at the end of steam on 9 July 1967, and lingered on as a signing-on point until February 1969. The shed became well known as the gathering point for withdrawn steam locomotives awaiting their call to the scrapyards.

Allocation 1934
4-6-0: 330/2/3/4, 450-7, 749/50/4, 828-32
4-4-0: 121, 285/92/6/7, 382/9, 405/70/1/2, 586, 684, 713/27/9.
0-6-0: 306/17/68. 689/91/6, 3441.
2-6-0: 1413/4, 1851.
0-4-2: 606/21/49/50/2/4.
0-8-0T: 957.
0-4-4T: 17, 75, 326/5.

0-6-0T: 275, 349/51.

Allocation 1945
4-6-2: 21C6-10.
4-6-0: 330-5, 448-57, 475/6, 744/5/6.
4-4-0: 117/22, 285/8, 310/2/3/4, 882/8/9, 405/21/32, 709/15/21/7/9.
0-6-0: 315/7, 355, 690/1, 3441.
2-6-0: 1612/8/26/30/6. 1839/46/8/72/3.
0-4-2: 644/9/52/54.
0-8-0T: 957.
0-4-4T: 10/3, 41, 60, 243, 361, 675.
0-6-0T: 237, 279.

Allocation 1950.
4-6-2: 34022/23/32/42/43, 35006/7/8/9.
4-6-0: 30448/9/50/2/53//4, 30739/44/48/53, 30826-32.
4-4-0: 30122, 30288/89, 30301, 30421, 30709/19/24/5/7/30.
0-6-0: 30315/17/55, 30577, 30690-91.
2-6-0: 31612/18/26, 31836/46/72/73.
0-8-0T: 30957.
0-4-4T: 30023/41, 30127, 30243, 30675.
0-6-0T: 30238.

Sunlight streams through the roof of Salisbury shed during the last days of steam on 2 July 1967. No. 34060 *25 Squadron* stands in company with No. 34098 *Templecombe*, a DMU of lesser rank and pedigree than the two Pacifics stands to the left.

Hugh Ballantyne

Urie H15 class 4-6-0 No. 487 in L&SWR livery was only two months old when this view was taken on the ash pit at Salisbury shed on 18 April 1914. This was Robert Urie's first locomotive design, and the doyen of the class, No. 486, had emerged from Eastleigh Works in January of the same year.

Ken Nunn Collection LCGB

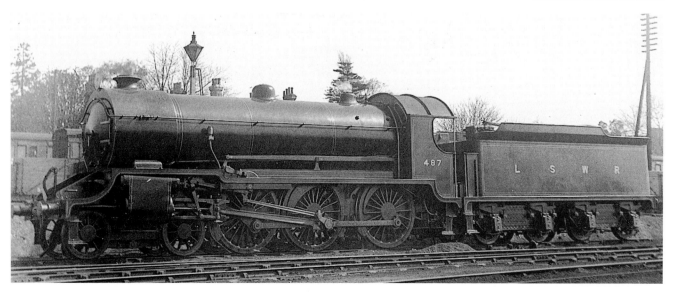

Drummond 4-6-0 No. E0449 (former No. 449) seen here at Salisbury shed on 26 October 1925 was fitted experimentally with superheater and 135° crank phase giving eight exhausts per driving wheel revolution in anticipation of the coming 'Lord Nelsons'. The locomotive went on the duplicate list (until withdrawn in 1927) as No. 0449 in 1925 upon the appearance of No. 449 *Sir Torre* one of the new 'King Arthurs'.

H. C. Casserley

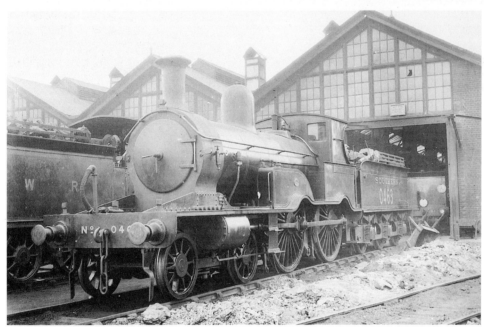

Adams 0460 class 4-4-0 No. E0463 of the 1884 series, stands outside Salisbury shed on 19 July 1924. The locomotive (previously No. 463) – went into the duplicate list in March 1912 upon the appearance of the D15 class. No. E0463 was painted Maunsell green and received the suffix 'E' in May 1924. Previously based at Exmouth Junction (1890), Northam (1896), Eastleigh (1911) the locomotive was allocated to Salisbury in 1924.

H. C. Casserley

Adams 0460 class 4-4-0 No. E0466 stands on the ash pit alongside the coaling stage at Salisbury shed on 26 October 1925.

H. C. Casserley

Allocation 1959

4-6-2: 34049/50/51/52/53/54/55/59, 35004/6/7.
4-6-0: 30331/35, 30448/49/50/51/52/53, 30823/24/25/26/
27/28/29/30/31/32/47
4-4-0: 30301/13, 30729.
0-6-0: 30309/15/, 30692.
2-6-0: 31813/14, 76005/6/7/8/9.
0-8-0T: 30954.
0-4-4T: 30673/74.
0-6-0T: 30266.

Allocation 1965

4-6-2: 34005/6/7/12/13/15/26/32/48/51/52/56/57/59/63/66/
89/100/108.
2-6-0: 76005/7/8/17/67.

Salisbury was issued with shed code 72B from 1950 to 1962 and then became 70E from 1962 until closure in 1967.

Footplate comments

This was a superb shed in every sense of the word. Packed with rows of locomotives in the shed yard, engines on the coaling line, piles of clinker and smokebox ash. The interior of the shed was also alive with noise, hammering and banging as boilers were washed out, and locomotives being attended to by the fitters. The enginemens' cabin with its smell of tobacco smoke, full of footplatemen from sheds far and wide, playing cards, arguing, or just gossiping away – with the ever boiling kettle singing away on the stove. During my first summer as an engine cleaner at Yeovil Town I was sent on loan with another cleaner to Salisbury for firedropping duties – or 'squaring up' as it was known. After reporting to the shed office, my mate and I were directed to the disposal pits situated by the coaling stage . . . what a sight met my eyes! The whole length of the pit was packed with engines of all types, Bulleid Pacifics, 'King Arthurs', T9s, and from Cardiff and Bristol on the Western Region – 'Halls', 'Castles', and the 28xx freight engines known as 'Long Toms'. We were allocated an engine each with instructions to be as quick as possible, and as each engine was finished, to move it down the rank to be coaled and watered. The shed enginemen would take them down to the turntable and over to the shed roads to await their next turn of duty.

Now, we cleaners had only a few turns of squaring up back at Yeovil, but here we were thrown in the thick of it though, on reflection, it was the best way to learn. My first engine to square up was a 'Hall' and there was so much clinker in the firebox it was falling out of the firehole door onto the cab floor! The first step was to cut up the clinker with the long handled dart, and then the sweat started to pour off me as I dug the clinker shovel into the firebox and threw the glowing clinker out over the side of the cab. The only answer on this engine was to throw the whole lot out and light her up again with some cut up sleepers and oily rags. As she was in steam it didn't take long for the fire to pull through after relighting with the assistance of the steam blower. After cleaning the fire, it was time to clean out the smokebox, so armed with the firing shovel, I climbed up onto the bufferbeam, unscrewed the smokebox clip and opened the door. The hissing of the blower grew louder and the fine char flowed out. Shovelling the hot ash was no easy task, it was so light it would blow almost everywhere and as usual I managed to get some down my neck. But by far the most unpleasant task on squaring up an engine was the ashpan. Clutching a long handled rake I jumped into the pit with its piles of hot clinker and pools of water, trying to avoid burning the soles of my boots on the clinker and only succeeding in filling them with water. The ashpan was jammed full and as I raked it out, the air in the pit filled with clouds of choking grey dust. And so it went on until the line of engines had dwindled and it was time for a welcome break.

H15 4-6-0 No. 30331 and Light Pacific No. 34048 *Crediton* stand on the ash pit at Salisbury shed on 30 August 1956. The heaps of clinker and smokebox ash strewn along the side of the pit bear witness to the many locomotives calling in for engine requirements.

Terry Gough

'Battle of Britain' class 4-6-2 No. 34055 *Fighter Pilot* in immaculate condition is pictured here on the turntable at Salisbury on 25 July 1962. I have been on this 'table' many times and have fired this particular engine which was one of the best. The turntable at Salisbury was the scene of more than one locomotive dropping into the pit when the 'table' had not been positioned back to the coaling line.

Barry Eagles

The more modern engines like the Bulleids and the Standards were made easier by the design of their rocking grates which cascaded the fire straight down into the pit, but with their enclosed cabs the heat thrown back by the fire was almost unbearable in the hot summer. Tank engines were the worst to square up – there I would be, delicately balancing a piece of clinker on the end of the shovel when 'bang', the top end of the shovel handle would hit the cab roof and the clinker would drop back into the firebox! Or, swinging the long-handled clinker shovel carefully around the cramped cab I would bark my knuckles on the reversing lever or the handbrake handle. The Drummond tanks were

particularly tricky, but like all jobs you soon learnt the best way of doing things. They were long days at Salisbury. We arrived on the early train and returned on the 8.41 pm from Salisbury at night, but after a few weeks of squaring up we were recalled by our home shed, and by now (in our view) we had become 'old hands' and had learnt another part of our footplate training. I worked to Salisbury many times as a fireman and was always impressed and proud of the place, and this shed – plus my old shed at Yeovil Town and Exmouth Junction are always in my memory of days gone by – we shall never see their like again.

With Salisbury 'B' box in the background. 'Modified Hall' No. 7902 *Eaton Mascot Hall*, having arrived from the Western Region on a cross-country service on 9 April 1964, reverses towards the locomotive shed (in the distance) for engine requirements and turning.

Barry Eagles

Wilton South to Buckhorn Weston Tunnel

Wilton South

The station, at first known as Wilton, came into public use on 2 May 1859 (receiving the suffix South on 26 September 1949) when the section from Salisbury to Gillingham opened. Initial services when the line opened to Yeovil in 1860 consisted of four trains from Salisbury, and five from Yeovil on weekdays, with two each way on Sundays. The main station buildings and station master's house were located on the 'up' platform. Sidings were positioned to the east of the station on the 'up' side serving the goods shed and dock, with sidings also located behind the 'down' island platform. A platform mounted signal box was situated at the Salisbury end of the 'up' platform. Up

until closure passenger services at the station consisted of a mixture of trains that either terminated or started at Salisbury/Templecombe/Yeovil Town/or Exeter Central. A total of 2,480 passenger tickets was issued in 1928, compared with a total of 917 tickets issued in 1936 – reflecting the competition offered by the nearby bus services to and from the City of Salisbury. Two 'down' and three 'up' weekday freight trains called (1932 working timetable) to pick up and set down wagons.

On 16 June 1947 the Southern Railway instigated the all-Pullman 'Devon Belle' from Waterloo to Ilfracombe and Plymouth. As the train was not booked to pick up or set down passengers at Salisbury, and to save platform occupation it

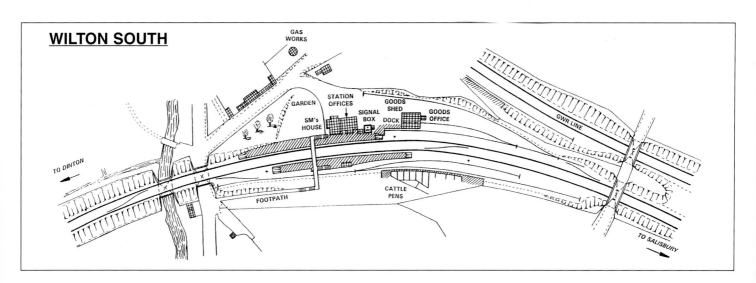

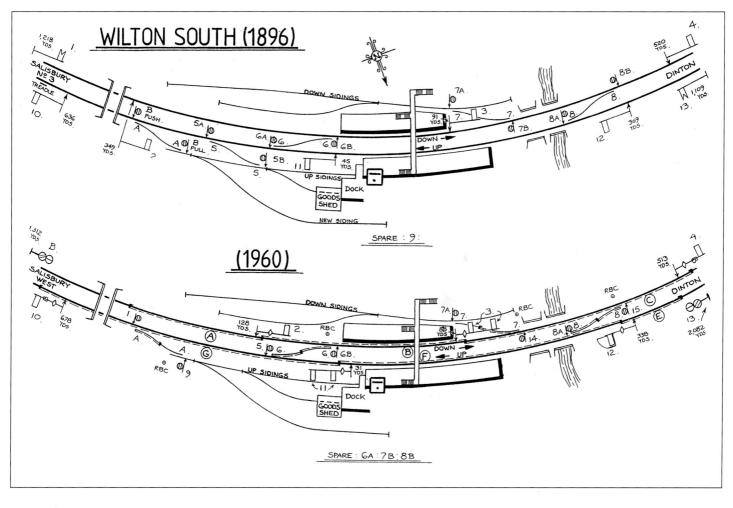

No. 34003 *Plymouth* arrives at Wilton South with the 2.55 pm (SO) Yeovil Town–Salisbury on 5 September 1964. A look with a glass at the fireman, shows him to be none other than one of my fellow footplateman from Yeovil Town – Vic Rigden.

C. L. Caddy

was decided that the engine changeover (of both 'up' and 'down' trains) would take place at Wilton. So at 1.47 pm, the station was treated to the superb spectacle of a Bulleid 'Merchant Navy' Pacific carrying the 'Devon Belle' nameboard not only on the bufferbeam but also on the smoke deflectors – heading a splendid train of Pullman vehicles in their distinctive livery – complete with an observation car at the rear, coming to a halt with a squeal of brakes. Six minutes only were allowed for the engine changeover before the 'Devon Belle' would set off to the West. At first the 'Belle'

was run at weekends only, but in the summer of 1949 it ran five days a week in each direction, at times hauling 14 Pullman cars. The service was withdrawn at the end of the 1954 season. Freight services ceased on 6 July 1964, with the station closing on 7 March 1966. The line west of the station was singled in 1967, the signal box soldiered on controlling the nearby Wilton Junction until 29 November 1981, when the layout came under the control of Salisbury Panel. Happily, the box has survived and can be seen working at Medstead & Four Marks station on the Mid-Hants Railway.

No. 35007 *Aberdeen Commonwealth* sweeps westwards through Wilton South on 18 August 1964 heading the 9am from Waterloo.

Terry Gough

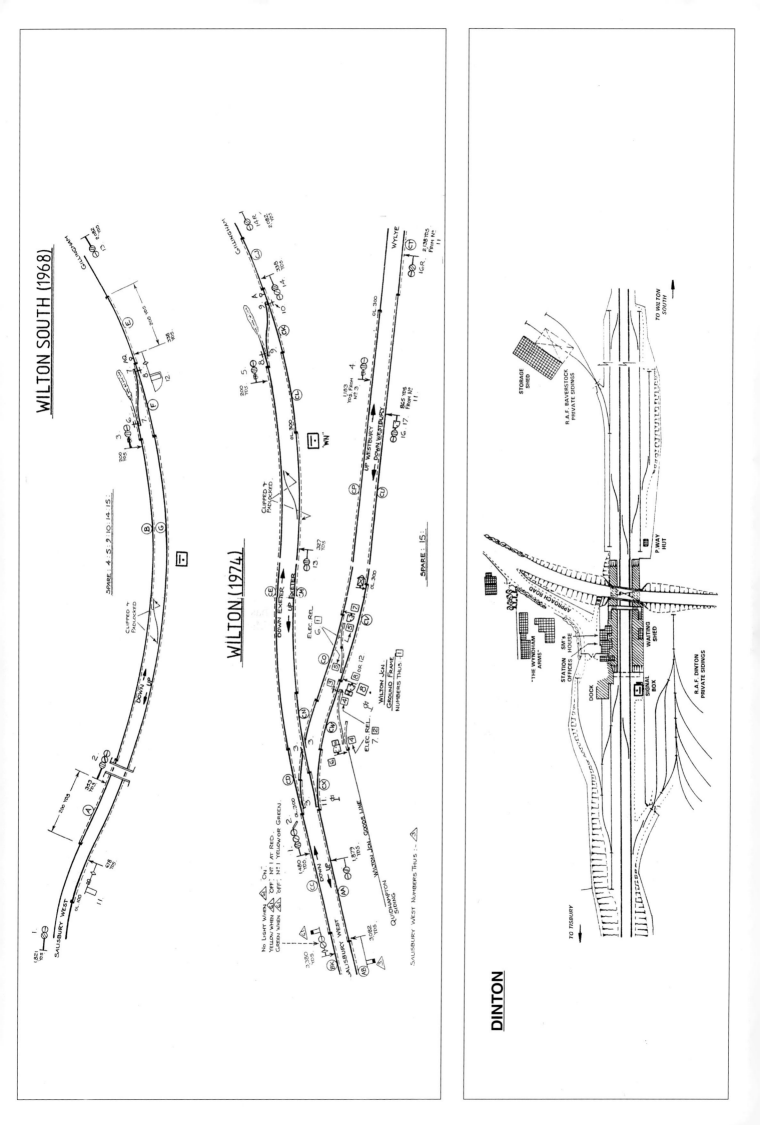

Dinton looking west c1930, taken from the footbridge with the 'down' platform in the foreground and the main station buildings situated on the 'up' platform to the right. The small building on the 'up' platform is reputed to have been the original signal box which in turn had been replaced by the box at the end of the 'down' platform. The small goods yard, shed, and crane serving the local traders stands adjacent to the 'up' main line.

Brunel University: Mowat Collection

Footplate comments

Two things strike me about Wilton, one being, if we were working an 'up' train, then relief was not far away at Salisbury, and the chance of a cup of tea and a bite to eat in the shed would be welcome, especially if a rough trip was the order of the day. If we were heading west, this meant that half of our shift would be over, and it would be home to mother for tea, or breakfast!

Dinton

Serving the village sited approximately a half-mile to the south, this was a small way-side station with its main buildings comprising the booking office, waiting room, etc., and station master's house grouped on the 'up' platform. The ubiquitous brick-built waiting shelter was positioned on the 'down' platform. A small goods yard complete with a corrugated iron goods shed was sited west of the station

Dinton looking east on 5 September 1964. The main station buildings are grouped on the 'up' platform with a brick-built shelter on the 'down' platform.

C. L. Caddy

Dinton looking west showing the third signal box to have been in use. It is pictured here standing with signal arms removed and in use as a ground frame. Dinton was at the hub of services radiating to military camps and depots in the area.

C. L. Caddy

alongside the 'up' main line. With the massive build up of military camps in the area during the First World War a two mile long branch (Dinton & Fovant Military Railway), much of it graded at 1 in 35, was constructed to Fovant Camp situated south of the station. The military line was in use from 1916 intermittently until 1924. An Adams 0415 4-4-2T, No. 0424, was purchased for the sum of £800 in June 1916 from the Woolmer Instructional Railway for use on the line. This locomotive was replaced in October 1917 by *Westminster*, an 0-6-0 Peckett saddle tank. *Hampshire* and *Woolmer* were also used on the line. A 'down' siding was instituted east of the station, and sidings established west of the station, also on the 'down' side leading to the WD depot.

Sidings for military traffic were also established east of the station alongside the 'up' main line. Dinton has had three signal boxes in its lifetime, the first a platform-mounted box (1875) still stands to this day on the former 'up' platform. A second box was constructed on the Tisbury end of the 'down' platform, controlling not only the signalling and entrance to the goods yard, but also two crossover-roads, one situated 203 yards from the box on the Wilton side, and another 47 yards from the box on the Tisbury side. This box was in turn replaced by the third and final box (32 lever) on 8 November 1942 situated off the end of the 'down' platform, the new box controlling access to the New sidings south of the station serving the Dinton depot of the RAF which was laid on part

With steam cascading from the safety valves, No. 34101 *Hartland* heads for Salisbury with a lightweight three-coach stopping train from Dinton on 18 July 1964.

Colin Caddy Collection

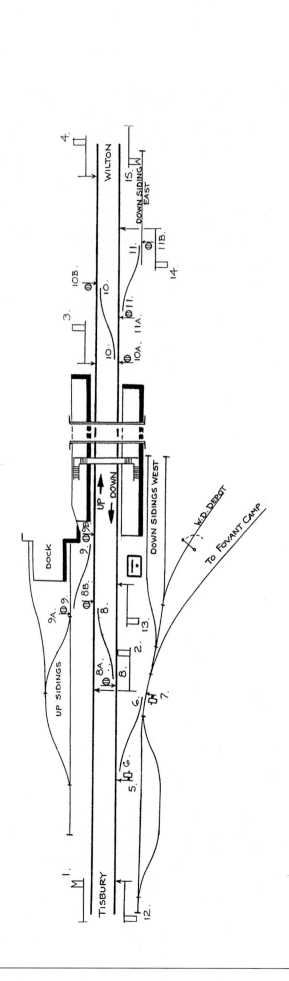

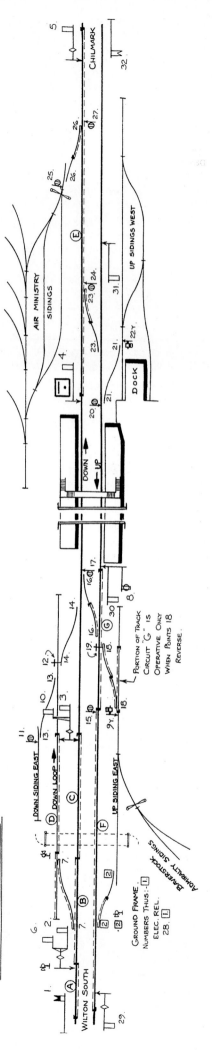

DINTON (1915)

DINTON (1944)

of the formation of the former Fovant Military Railway, and included exchange sidings with the 2 ft gauge internal system to the depot. The large Baverstock Depot to the east of the station was also controlled by the new box, a 'down' loop being laid east of the station for the military traffic.

The station, as with other stations along the route, dealt with milk traffic with a total of 55,956 churns being forwarded in 1928 alone. Local produce including watercress was also sent by rail. The station closed to passengers on 7 March 1966 and to general goods on 18 April the following year. When the main line was singled a portion of the former 'up' line was retained and used as a long siding between Chilmark Depot (to the west) and Baverstock Depot (to the east). Access to the main line was gained by a crossover, and to Dinton Depot via a ground-frame from the running line. The MoD, which took control of the depots from the Air Ministry in 1964, had standard gauge shunters which were used in the depots, and narrow gauge diesel locomotives saw regular use on the internal system. Following the closure of the station, a senior railman was kept here to deal with the MoD traffic. Dinton West ground-frame to Dinton Sidings (MoD Air) are now out of use with the last train, the 11.40 to Didcot, being hauled by No. 47347 on 2 November 1994. Dinton East ground frame to Chilmark Siding (MoD Air) also closed on the same date. Today, the station still retains its former 'up' platform, complete with its original signal box, the station buildings are in private ownership and are fenced off from the platform. The 'down' platform has been demolished.

Footplate comments

The station had an impressive layout when approached from Salisbury – running past the 'down' loop and coasting to a stop at the platform with a passenger train. The station in my day never had much passenger support, due to good bus services to and from Salisbury which was more convenient for the local population. The military sidings to the south of the siding always looked mysterious – with tracks leading into various buildings behind closed doors. The route westwards from Dinton climbs all the way to Semley and from here the fireman has to bend his back whilst tending to the needs of the firebox. The 'up' line here witnessed some considerable speeds as trains not booked to stop at Dinton would accelerate down the bank heading for Salisbury. I was on a light engine once from Yeovil Town to Salisbury, this was a special working and not advertised in the working

timetable, as the engine an ex LMS 2-6-2 tank from Exmouth Junction was en route to Eastleigh for repair. We were booked home 'on the cushions' so it was a case of working to Salisbury, leave the engine on shed, return home by the next available train and book off, no hanging about, straight there and back. For a fireman, a light engine working is a doddle of a job; I had banked the fire up at Yeovil, and apart from tending to the needs of the boiler, and the odd shovel of coal, it was a case of sitting down, lighting a 'fag' or two, and keeping a lookout ahead. We rattled down the bank – through Tisbury under clear signals at a good rate of knots, rounding the curves on the way to Dinton, when all of a sudden there was a movement of bodies on the line ahead of us, as the local permanent way gang were struggling to get a jack off the track. They achieved this (just), as we flashed past with a long blast on the LMS hooter. What had happened was this. The local track gang had decided to do a bit of packing, etc. – between the normal booked trains. Nothing wrong with this; it was normal procedure. They had the look-out men posted in accordance with the rules, it was just tough luck that as soon as they had the jack on the track the rails started quivering with our approach, and they had to get their kit moved fast, as our little light engine, with rods and wheels revolving so fast, they were just a blur, appeared around the curve, going like stink and blowing a blast on the hooter like the *Queen Mary*!

Teffont Mill Crossing

The crossing, complete with gateman's cottage, is situated half a mile west of Dinton. When the portion of the 'up' line was retained between Dinton and Chilmark Siding upon the singling of the main line trains approaching the crossing from Dinton en route to Chilmark had to stop to enable a member of the train crew to press a plunger to operate miniature red and green lights on the road. Main line trains on the single line alongside operated the lights automatically.

Chilmark Siding

The disused limestone caves near Chilmark became one of the largest bomb storage depots in the country when chosen by the RAF in 1937. During the Second World War thousands of tons of munitions were stored here imported and exported by rail. The sidings were connected to the 'up' main-line by a trailing connection. A 14-lever signal box (coming into use on 10 July 1938) was erected alongside the

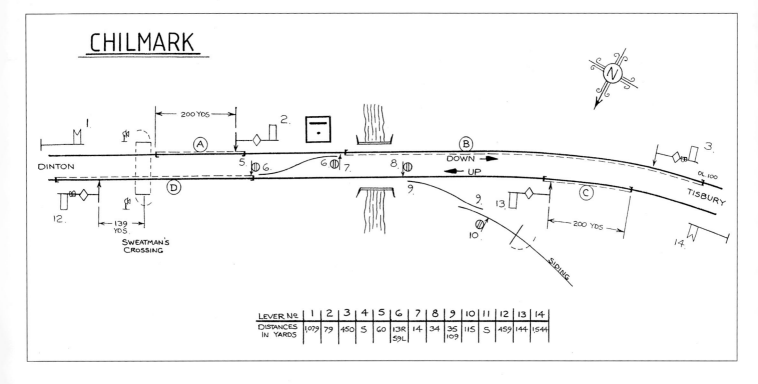

LEVER No.	1	2	3	4	5	6	7	8	9	10	11	12	13	14
DISTANCES IN YARDS	1,079	79	450	5	60	13R 59L	14	34	35 109	115	5	459	144	1,544

The 'up' platform at Tisbury in 1952 with its former L&SWR signal box, slate-hung station master's house and distinctive long platform shelters. The signal box was replaced by a new box which opened on 12 October 1958.

Adrian Vaughan Collection

'down' main-line, controlling the signalling, points to the siding, and cross-over road between the 'up' and 'down' main lines. The former 'up' line from Dinton was slewed into the depot in 1967 (lifted eastwards to Gillingham), thus forming a long siding. The last service train having departed to RNAD Glen Douglas on 2 November 1994, there was an official closing ceremony at Chilmark on 27 January 1995.

Tisbury

The station, with its distinctive long waiting shelters on both platforms, has its main station buildings, station master's house, etc., grouped on the 'up' platform. Sidings existed here on both sides of the layout west of the station. With the goods shed, feed stores and coal pens being positioned on the 'up' side, and a trader's store, coal pens, weighbridge, and a crane in the 'down' sidings. A gas works (on the 'down' side) was also served by the railway at one time. As with other stations on the line, milk was a prime scource of

revenue, with 57,827 cans being forwarded in 1928. Coal was another important traffic with 6,278 tons delivered by rail in the same year. The following freight trains were booked to call here in the 1932 working timetable:

7.20 am Salisbury–Templecombe, 3.10 pm Salisbury–Yeovil Junction, 4.15 am Yeovil Junction–Salisbury, 4.25 pm Templecombe–Salisbury. The L&SWR signal box which stood on the Semley end of the 'up' platform was replaced by a new 24-lever brick-built BR(S) Type 16 box on 12 October 1958, the new box standing adjacent to the former box – but positioned off the end of the 'up' platform. The 1932 weekday passenger service consisted of eight 'down' and nine 'up' services, plus the following milk trains, etc., in the same year:

9.55 am Yeovil Junction–Salisbury. *Milk and Horse Boxes.*
4.50 pm Sherborne–Victoria. *Milk.*
6.05 pm Sherborne–Waterloo. *Milk.*

Old van and coach bodies were once a common sight around the yards of the railway system and here, an old L&SWR van is pictured at Tisbury on 5 September 1964. The faded word 'Luggage' can be seen near the right-hand front end.

C. L. Caddy

TISBURY (1963)
"WDB"

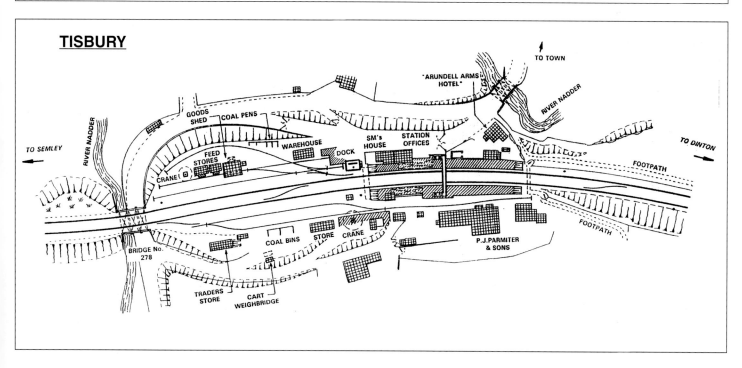

RED TO YELLOW BY TISBURY GATES.
YELLOW TO GREEN BY TISBURY.

RED TO YELLOW BY TISBURY
YELLOW TO GREEN BY QUARRY GATES.

1703 YDS.

250 YDS.

227 YDS.

UP SIDINGS

190 YDS.

RBC.

752 YDS.

SEMLEY

UP

DOWN

CHILMARK

574 YDS.

411 YDS.

250 YDS.

1,816 YDS.

RBC

DOWN SIDINGS

RED TO YELLOW BY TISBURY.
YELLOW TO GREEN BY TISBURY GATES.

RED TO YELLOW BY QUARRY GATES
YELLOW TO GREEN BY TISBURY

SPARE : 13 :14 :15

TISBURY

TO TOWN

"ARUNDELL ARMS HOTEL"

RIVER NADDER

GOODS SHED

COAL PENS

WAREHOUSE

SM's HOUSE

STATION OFFICES

DOCK

FOOTPATH

TO SEMLEY

RIVER NADDER

FEED STORES

CRANE

TO DINTON

BRIDGE No. 278

COAL BINS

STORE

CRANE

FOOTPATH

P.J.PARMITER & SONS

TRADERS STORE

CART WEIGHBRIDGE

'Merchant Navy' class 4-6-2 No. 35007 *Aberdeen Commonwealth* is pictured here passing Tisbury at speed with an 'up' train to Waterloo on 5 September 1964.
C. L. Caddy

S15 4-6-0 No. 30825 works an Exmouth Junction–Salisbury pick-up goods on 21 August 1958 and, having left part of the train on the 'up' main line, pulls out of the goods yard at Tisbury with a lengthy raft of wagons. Above the cab of the locomotive can be seen the roof of the new signal box (opened 12 October 1958) with the old box on the right. Tall repeater signals such as the 'down' starter to the left were once a common sight on the Salisbury–Exeter line.

Hugh Ballantyne

The balancing empty milk workings comprised the following;

  3.08 am Waterloo–Seaton Junction.
  4.15 am Victoria–Yeovil Junction.
11.35 am Clapham Junction–Yeovil Junction.

Freight facilities were withdrawn from the station on 18 April 1966, the 'down' line and sidings were lifted in 1967, the signal box closing in the same year on 5 February. The

'down' platform and footbridge was demolished following the singling of the main line and the area sold off, and is now occupied by Messrs Parmiter's – suppliers of agricultural machinery, etc. Today, all trains use the former 'up' platform with the 'new' signal box of 1958 standing gaunt and unused at the end of the platform. In order to improve timekeeping and provide crossing facilities in the case of emergency on the long single-line section between Wilton and Gillingham, the Tisbury loop, lying east of the station (installed here because previously available railway land at the station had

Tisbury looking east on 19 September 1988 showing the now singled main line with the former 'up' platform and station buildings to the left. The new signal box, dating from 1958, was closed on 5 February 1967 being in use for only nine years, which was just a fraction of the life span of the former L&SWR box it replaced. The MAS signal at the far end of the platform controls the entry to the Tisbury Loop opened on 24 March 1986 to improve timekeeping over the long single line section between Gillingham and Wilton.

John Scrace

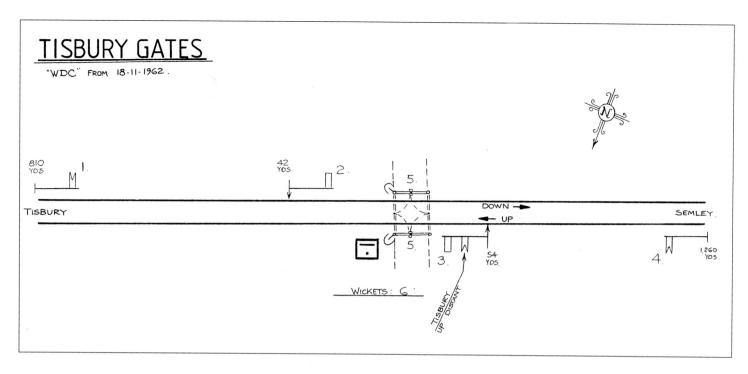

TISBURY GATES

"WDC" FROM 18-11-1962.

810
YDS. |.   1.

42
YDS.   2.

5.

TISBURY   DOWN ➡
                                      ⬅ UP   SEMLEY.

5.

3.   54
YDS.

4.   1,260
YDS.

WICKETS : 6

TISBURY
UP DISTANT

been sold off) was opened on 24 March 1986, and was built at a cost of £435,000, and is under the control of Salisbury Panel. Tisbury Gates, situated one mile west of the station, had a signal box installed in 1892 which was subsequently reduced to a ground frame in 1922, coal and stores were delivered via the 7.20 am 'down' freight from Salisbury, the level crossing gates have now been replaced by AHBs and the box, now privately owned, has been moved from its original position.

Footplate comments

Salisbury Duty No. 471 was shared by Salisbury and Yeovil men and involved us in booking on at Yeovil Town at 2.30 am, travel light engine to Yeovil Junction, turn the engine (one of the faithful S15 4-6-0s) and work the 3.40 am Yeovil Junction–Salisbury freight. This was a particularly heavy train which we worked to Tisbury and changed over with Salisbury men who would be working Salisbury Duty No. 503 – this being the 5 am Salisbury–Yeovil Town. We would clank into Tisbury and reverse our train into the 'up' sidings and await to changeover with our mates from Salisbury. The station master at Tisbury used to complain about the noise erupting from an engine's safety valves early in the morning. The problem on my side was, that with a very heavy train

and the box full of fire needed to bring us up the Semley bank, then running down to Tisbury with the regulator almost closed, we would arrive with a very hot engine. I used to shut the dampers whilst running through Semley, and keep the water in the boiler as low as I dared without dropping a lead plug, although some drivers that I have had, didn't give a fig for the station master. Their view being, that as we were awake at that hour, so should he! Of course, the fire had to be kept banked up for the onward trip to Salisbury and it was touch and go sometimes as the gauge would gradually creep forwards to the red line. We would changeover on the platform at 5.25 am when the Salisbury train arrived and worked the train to Sherborne. There we would changeover with Yeovil men (Yeovil Duty No. 514) who had been on the Templecombe upper shunter all night. At Sherborne we would shunt the yard until 10.10 am when we would set off light engine for Yeovil Town Loco, and leave the engine on the pit for the P&D men.

Semley

At one time the running-in boards proclaimed 'Semley for Shaftesbury'. The station at the summit of the climbs from Tisbury and Gillingham was an important centre for rail-borne milk traffic. The L&SWR had, from 1874,

The occupant of the crossing keeper's cottage keeps a wary eye on the photographer from an upper window as Bulleid Pacific No. 34076 *41 Squadron* rattles through Tisbury Gates with the 6.15 am Plymouth–Salisbury on 21 August 1956.

Hugh Ballantyne

'Merchant Navy' class 4-6-2 No. 35013 *Blue Funnel* sweeps through Semley with the 8.15 am Plymouth–Waterloo on 21 August 1956. Here, as at other stations on the route, a typical L&SWR platform-mounted signal box can be seen on right.

Hugh Ballantyne

provided facilities for a wholesale milk depot here serving the nearby milk factory of United Dairies. Until 1931 churns were the prime mover of milk by the railway (83,165 cans from Semley in 1928) until replaced by rail-tankers (4,780,186 gallons in 1936). The rail-tankers were marshalled into a dock siding alongside the 'up' platform at the west end of the station. A gantry carried the pipework from the milk factory across the nearby road from which the

rail-tanks were filled. The factory produced its own electricity, thereby using coal brought by rail. However, with the factory buying electricity from the grid from 1932 this brought a decrease to the inward coal traffic, milk traffic lasting until 1980. The main station buildings were grouped on the 'up' platform, with a waiting shelter complete with canopy adorning the 'down' platform. A signal box was located on the London end of the 'up' platform, complete

Standard Class 5MT 4-6-0 No. 73085 *Melisande* rolls through Semley with the 9.10 am Torrington–Waterloo in 1962. The locomotive is carrying the name from a withdrawn 'King Arthur' class. The gantry to the right carries the pipework from the nearby creamery, from which rail borne milk tankers were refilled at this station.

C. L. Caddy

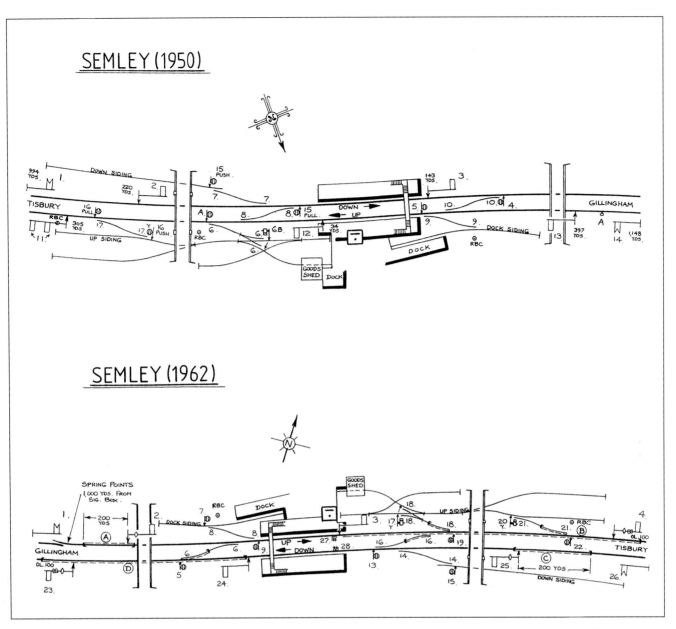

SEMLEY (1950)

SEMLEY (1962)

Semley looking west on 29 May 1928. The L&SWR lower quadrant 'down' starter signal arm, with its tall repeater arm, is 'off' indicating the passage of an Exeter bound train. The station running-in board to the right announces 'Semley for Shaftesbury'. Churns abound on the 'up' platform, and milk vans await loading in the siding beyond the end of the platform. Rail tankers mostly replaced the churn traffic from 1931.

H. C. Casserley

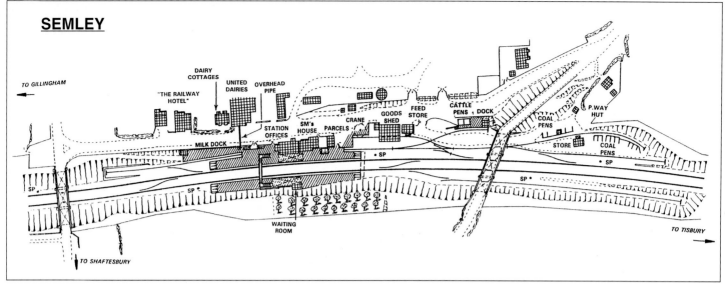

SEMLEY

with a superb L&SWR lower quadrant starting signal – which I remember well from my firing days. Unfortunately the signal box and lower quadrant were replaced by a new, 28-lever box and upper quadrant 'up' starter on 29 January 1961. The goods yard, goods shed, feed store, coal staithes and cattle pens were situated east of the station on the 'up' side and there was a siding located east of the station on the 'down' side.

The 1910 *Bradshaw* shows a weekday service of twelve 'down' and ten 'up' weekday services. This was a situation that altered little during the stations existence. In the 1963 Summer working timetable the following trains were booked to call at Semley on weekdays:

Down

3.20 am Salisbury–Yeovil Town. *News and mail.*

Up

6.45 am Yeovil Town–Salisbury

1.50 am (MX) Basingstoke–Yeovil Town. *Empty milk.*
8.10 am Salisbury–Ilfracombe.
6.33 am Woking–Templecombe.
11.04 am Salisbury–Yeovil Town.
12.46 pm Salisbury–Exeter Central.
3.05 pm Salisbury–Exeter Central
4.54 pm Salisbury–Templecombe.
4.48 pm Basingstoke–Yeovil Town.
3.54 pm (SX) Clapham Junction–Exeter Central. *Milk empties.*
4.04 pm (SO) Clapham Junction–Exeter Central. *Milk empties.*
8.41 pm Salisbury–Yeovil Town.

Semley looking east from the road overbridge on 7 September 1959. A bunch of cows glance over the fence on the left to see what all the noise is about as 'Merchant Navy' class No. 35012 *United States Lines* streaks through with the 'down' 'Atlantic Coast Express'.

Adrian Vaughan Collection

'King Arthur' class 4-6-0 No. 30449 *Sir Torre* tackles the climb from Gillingham with ease, nearing the Semley inner home signal with an 'up' train, bound for Waterloo in August 1958. This locomotive represented the Southern Railway when it took part in the Darlington railway celebrations in 1925.

Kenneth Leech

A stranger to the South Western main line in the shape of 9F class 2-10-0 No. 92209 runs through Semley on the 'down' main line with a Southern Counties Touring Society special train on 8 March 1964. The tour comprised: 'Britannia' No. 70020 *Mercury* from Waterloo to Salisbury including the Ludgershall branch, and No. 92209 Salisbury–Templecombe–Hamworthy Junction–Bournemouth, No. 70020 for the return trip from Bournemouth to Waterloo. The 9F is carrying WR headlamps being one of the batch allocated to that particular region. Although rare to the Salisbury–Exeter line proper, the 9Fs could often be seen at Templecombe on the Somerset & Dorset line.

S. C. Nash

A superb L&SWR lower quadrant signal arm, complete with finial-mounted post, (Semley 'up' starter) stands at danger, as 4-6-0 S15 No. 30830, with steam shut off, rattles in with a three coach 'down' stopping train in August 1958. Empty cattle wagons, stand in the 'up' sidings to the far left.

Kenneth Leech

No. 35009 *Shaw Savill* nears the top of the climb from Gillingham heading the 'up' 'ACE' in August 1958. Note the ex LNER coach behind the locomotive. The signal to the right is the Semley 'up' inner home and I, like many other footplatemen, when pounding up the bank with a heavy freight, and perhaps down the pan for steam, would sigh with relief on spotting this signal as it meant that the worst part of the journey was over.

C. L. Caddy Collection

8.20 am Semley–Salisbury.

6.40 am Exeter Central–Waterloo.

6.15 am Plymouth–Salisbury.

12.42 pm Templecombe–Salisbury.

1.10 pm Exeter Central–Salisbury.

4.28 pm Gillingham–Salisbury. *School train.*

4.06 pm Yeovil Town–Salisbury.

4.35 pm Exeter Central–Salisbury.

6.15 pm Axminster–Clapham Junction. *Milk and parcels.*

8.23 pm Yeovil Junction–Waterloo. *Milk and parcels.*

The station closed to general goods traffic on 5 April 1965, and to passenger traffic on 7 March of the following year. Today, the single-track main line runs past the remnants of this once busy wayside station. The main station building survives as a private residence. The goods shed also survives, with the goods yard now in use as a scrap yard for agricultural implements. The old L&SWR signal box (closed in 1961) until 1993 at least, still stood in the nearby car breaker's yard on the Shaftesbury road.

Footplate comments

The Semley 'up' distant signal (as with Milborne Port) situated at the summit of the ascent, would be a welcome sight to footplatemen struggling up the bank from Gillingham with an engine that was doing badly for steam – knowing that the run down to Tisbury would be enough to rally an engine around. The same also applied to 'down'

trains climbing up from Tisbury, for as soon as the end of the platform at Semley was reached, there was a four-mile downhill stretch to Gillingham which would push the steam pressure gauge up to a healthier pressure!

Gillingham

On a very cold, wet and windy 3 April 1856 the first sod of the Salisbury to Yeovil line was cut here by Miss Seymour, sister of the Chairman (Henry Danby Seymour Esq) of the Salisbury & Yeovil Railway Company. Three years later the first section of the line from the new L&SWR station at Salisbury (Fisherton) to Gillingham opened on 2 May 1859 to great celebrations. The town was gaily decorated with arches and flags, over 2,300 people including working people and their wives were regaled in large marquees, the sick and infirm were supplied with beef and beer. As Gillingham was the temporary terminus of the line it was found convenient to erect an engine shed here, housing the locomotives working the trains to and from Salisbury, and importing materials for the construction of the line westwards. The two-road shed, measuring 83 ft x 36 ft, was erected west of the station on the 'down' side, but with the opening of the line to Exeter in 1860 the shed would have found its importance diminished and by 1916 the building had not been used for many years by the operating department. It eventually became the premises of a private trader. The station (the first in Dorset as approached from Salisbury) has its impressive William Tite main station

S15 4-6-0 No. 30833 pauses at Gillingham whilst heading the 4.35 pm Exeter Central–Salisbury on 13 August 1964.

Terry Gough

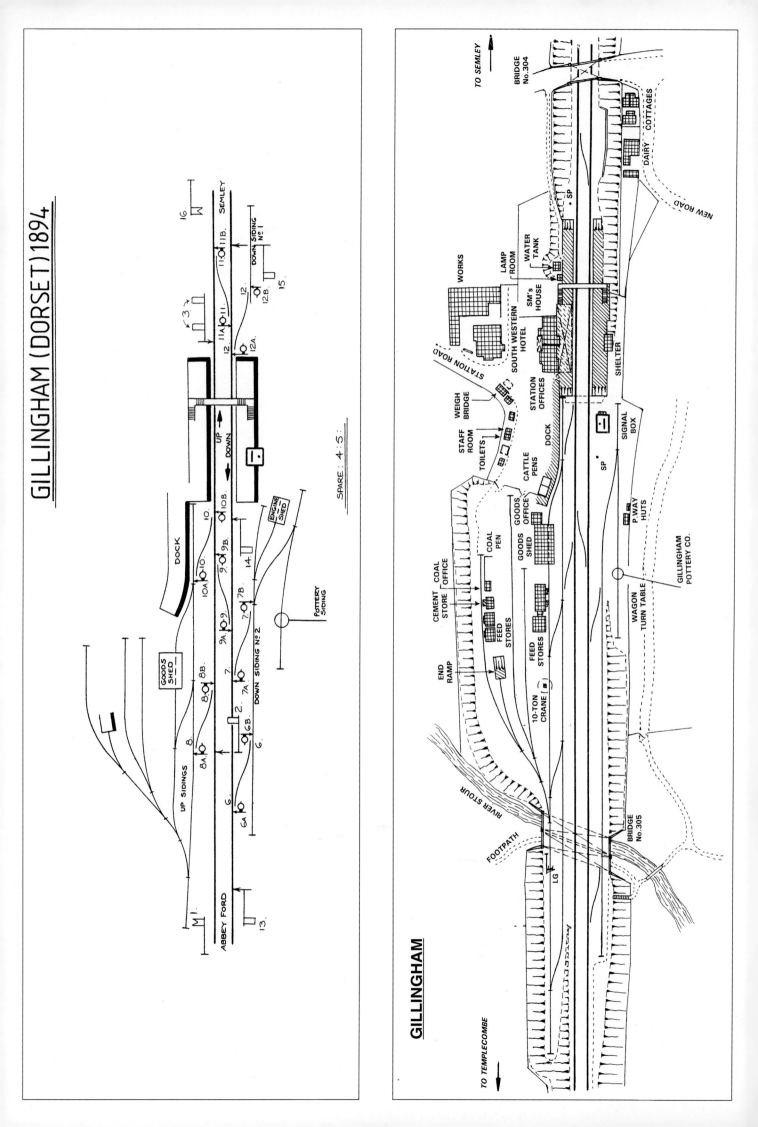

GILLINGHAM (DORSET) 1894

SPARE: 4 : 5 :

ABBEY FORD

SEMLEY

DOCK

UP SIDINGS

GOODS SHED

ENGINE SHED

POTTERY SIDING

DOWN SIDING No 2

DOWN SIDING No 1

UP

DOWN

GILLINGHAM

TO SEMLEY

BRIDGE No. 304

DAIRY COTTAGES

NEW ROAD

WORKS

LAMP ROOM

WATER TANK

SM's HOUSE

SOUTH WESTERN HOTEL

STATION ROAD

WEIGH BRIDGE

STAFF ROOM

TOILETS

CATTLE PENS

GOODS OFFICE

STATION OFFICES

DOCK

SHELTER

SP

SP

SP

COAL PEN

GOODS SHED

CEMENT STORE

COAL OFFICE

FEED STORES

FEED STORES

END RAMP

10-TON CRANE (■)

SIGNAL BOX

P. WAY HUTS

WAGON TURN TABLE

GILLINGHAM POTTERY CO.

RIVER STOUR

FOOTPATH

LG

BRIDGE No. 305

TO TEMPLECOMBE

Gillingham station on 21 August 1958 and No. 34036 *Westward Ho* stands at the 'up' platform with the 12.42 pm Templecombe–Salisbury local train.

Hugh Ballantyne

Gillingham on 5 September 1964 with the 'up' platform to the left, and the 'down' platform with waiting shelter on the right. As with most stations on the line, the main buildings are grouped on the 'up' platform. The signal box replacing an earlier box of L&SWR design came into use on 28 April 1957 and was still operational in 1996.

C. L. Caddy

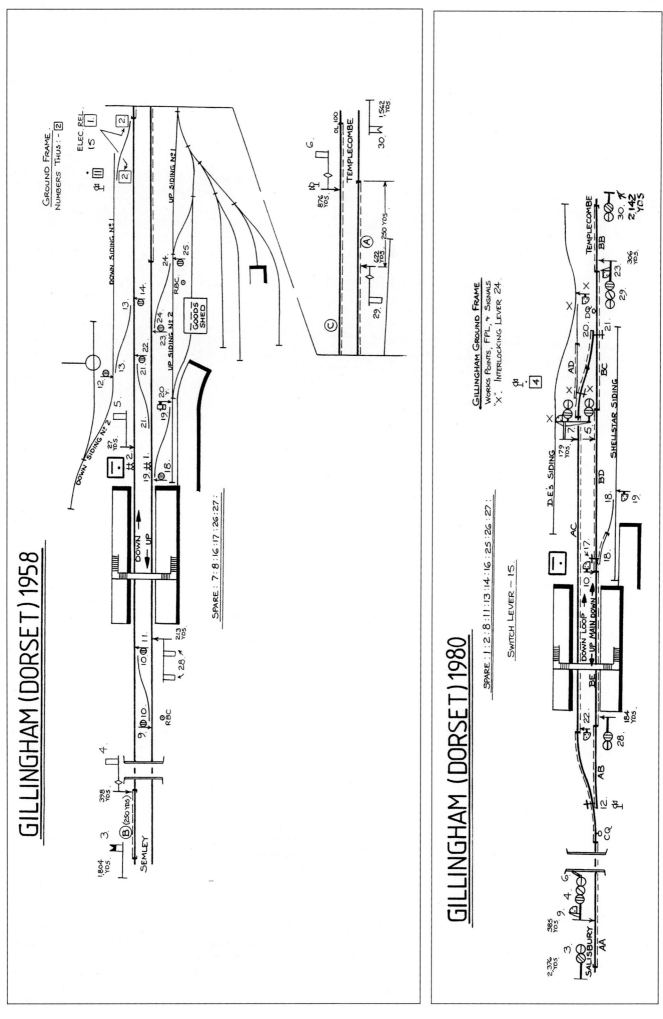

GILLINGHAM (DORSET) 1958

GROUND FRAME.
NUMBERS THUS :- 2

ELEC. REL.
15

DOWN SIDING Nº 1

UP SIDING Nº 1

DOWN SIDING Nº 2

UP SIDING Nº 2

GOODS SHED

RBC

SPARE : 7 : 8 : 16 : 17 : 26 : 27 :

SEMLEY

1,804 YDS.

B (200 YDS.)

DOWN

UP

213 YDS.

27 YDS.

398 YDS.

3

4

A

C

TEMPLECOMBE

876 YDS.

1,562 YDS.

622 YDS.

250 YDS.

30.

6

GILLINGHAM (DORSET) 1980

GILLINGHAM GROUND FRAME.
WORKS POINTS, FPL, & SIGNALS
"X" INTERLOCKING LEVER 24

4

SPARE : 1 : 2 : 8 : 11 : 13 : 14 : 16 : 25 : 26 : 27 :

SWITCH LEVER — 15

D.E's SIDING

SHELLSTAR SIDING

DOWN LOOP

UP MAIN DOWN

DE'S SIDING

AC

AD

BD

BC

BE

AB

CQ

AA

SALISBURY

2,376 YDS.

385 YDS.

3

9. 4. 6

TEMPLECOMBE

30.

2,142 YDS.

306 YDS.

179 YDS.

184 YDS.

BB

buildings situated on the 'up' platform, with a waiting shelter located on the 'down' platform. The running-in boards carried the suffix 'Gillingham change for Mere' for many years under the L&SWR, and the said company operated a bus service to Mere, Zeals and Shaftesbury from the station. Founded in 1865, the brickworks, situated west of the station, on the 'down' side, provided tiles, bricks and other pottery items, not only for local distribution, but also nationally via the rail system to which it was connected. Goods wagons gained access to the works via a 12 ft 2 in turntable off the brickworks own siding. Right up to the late 1930s horse power was utilised for shunting purposes here as at many other stations, as shown in this extract from the 1934 working appendix . . . Gillingham Pottery Company's Siding – *Connection to this private siding is provided by means of a turntable situated in the Railway Company's siding running alongside the Pottery Company's premises. Wagons are placed by the Railway Company's horses into the Pottery Company's siding as required, to enable that Company to load or unload traffic into or from the wagons over the boundary fence. Wagons for the works are placed on the turntable and worked to and from the private siding by the Pottery Company's employees. In the event of an engine being employed in shunting into the Railway Company's siding, such engine must not be permitted to pass over the turntable leading to the Pottery Company's siding.*

The goods shed and yard were situated west of the station on the 'up' side of the layout. The well known bacon factory of Oake Woods situated in the station yard itself, made good use of the railway by sending much of its produce to London. Milk from the surrounding farms went to London and its suburbs via the railway, (in 1928, 25,810 milk cans went from this station alone) and not only milk, but other dairy products; eggs, cheese, and butter were also sent by rail. The Salisbury, Semley & Gillingham Dairy (later absorbed by Wilts United Dairies), Shute Brothers – Victorian Butter Factory, and Blackmore Vale Cream – were all involved in exporting their products to the Capital. Tomatoes and watercress from the local areas of Mere and Zeals were also sent from the station. Hudson & Martin had an extensive timber mill in Station Road from which pit props and chair seats, etc., were sent by rail. Tractors and other agricultural implements were imported by rail for Messrs Braddicks or Stricklands, and coal was brought in for three companies: J. H. Rose & Sons, The New Rock, and Maloneys.

The signal box standing off the 'down' platform (the only operational box in use in 1996 between Salisbury and Templecombe) came into use on 28 April 1957 replacing an earlier L&SWR box which had stood on the Templecombe end of the 'down' platform. The footbridge was removed in 1967 and replaced by a concrete version from Dinton station. The station today (1996) is a passing loop on the single-line section between Tisbury loop and Templecombe. The 'up' loop is signalled for bidirectional working. The station buildings have hardly altered over the years, and with a growth in the local population, passenger traffic has increased, making it the busiest on the line today. Freight services were withdrawn on 5 April 1965, but one of the 'up' sidings was left intact. The old goods shed was demolished and replaced by a rail served fertiliser depot in 1968. With the withdrawal of freight traffic from Blandford (on the former Somerset & Dorset route) on 6 January 1969, Gillingham became the railhead for fertiliser distribution in the local area. The Shellstar Fertiliser Depot (later UKF Fertilisers) was served by a weekly pallet train from Ince & Elton in Cheshire, with part of the train

remaining at Andover. However, this service ceased on 15 April 1993.

Footplate comments

We had a turn at Yeovil which involved shunting at Gillingham with an S15 4-6-0. One of the things that I remember about the place was the terrible smell from the nearby glue factory in Station Road which used animal bones as part of the process. Messrs Oake Woods shop near the station always served the most delicious faggots and bacon – always a favourite with hungry footplatemen. I used to make a point of visiting the shop if we were booked there shunting, and return home to mother with my diddy box packed full with bacon and sausages, etc. Starting from the platform end, 'up' trains are faced with the four-mile Semley bank, a formidable obstacle for steam locomotives with its gradients of 1 in 130 and 1 in 100. The 'down' line also climbed from here to Buckhorn Weston Tunnel, but was never as harsh as the climb to Semley.

Buckhorn Weston Tunnel

Situated 2¼ miles west of Gillingham – the 742 yd long tunnel (the second longest between Salisbury and Exeter) is on a gradient of 1 in 100, and steam footplatemen on 'up' trains had a job on, especially if the locomotive wasn't steaming too well. However, once the summit was breasted east of the tunnel there was a long run down to Gillingham, which was long enough to rally an engine around before the ascent to Semley. This tunnel has always given problems to the operating department, as the bore is constructed under a natural spring, and water is always dripping down from the roof and on to the rails, and if an engine was going to slip, then you can bet your boots, that she would slip there. At times, I have known the sure-footed S15s to slip as they barked their way through on the 'up' line. The 'down' services had no problem as they would swoop down through the tunnel, accelerating for the climb to Templecombe.

Emergency Telephones – *Cupboards, painted with black and white diagonal stripes, are fixed on the up side of the line at each end of Gillingham Tunnel and contain telephones connected with the Salisbury–Templecombe signal box circuit. When the handle fixed to the door of the cupboard is turned to enable the door to be opened the telephone will be automatically switched into circuit. These telephones are available for Trainmen to communicate with the Signalmen in case of emergency . . .* 1934 Working Appendix.

Footplate comments

I well remember one unforgettable trip through the tunnel on a winter's night with No. 34104 *Bere Alston* on an Exmouth Junction–Salisbury freight train. Now, don't get me wrong; like all Southern men, I loved the Bulleid Pacifics on passenger trains, but they were not popular on freight trains, being too high in the wheel for goods work, plus their tendency to slip could create problems. We had relieved the crew at Yeovil Junction, and they informed us that they had been slipping badly coming up Chard bank. We had a full load on, with a class of engine that was prone to slipping, the sandboxes were almost empty, and it was pouring down with rain. This was going to be one of those trips! But apart from a brief period of slipping whilst pulling away from Yeovil Junction, we had no problems at Sherborne – and arrived at Templecombe with no problem, where we dropped off, and picked up more wagons. With the rain still lashing down, and the night sky as dark as a 'cows guts' we set off again, rolling down the bank towards the tunnel, which at that time was reduced to single-line working for the benefit of the

'Battle of Britain' class 4-6-2 No. 34077 *603 Squadron* bursts out of the eastern portal of Buckhorn Weston Tunnel heading towards Salisbury with the 'up' 'Atlantic Coast Express' on 13 August 1964.

Terry Gough

Standard Class 4MT 2-6-0 No. 76018 rattles out of Buckhorn Weston Tunnel and heads west with the 11.4 am Salisbury–Yeovil Junction on 5 September 1964. This is Salisbury Duty No. 479 and the Salisbury crew will be relieved by Yeovil Town men at Yeovil Junction. The Yeovil Town crew will then use the locomotive on the pick-up goods to Crewkerne, Chard, Axminster, and return to Yeovil Junction. The Salisbury crew will return to their home ground working Salisbury Duty No. 478 – the 4.6 pm Yeovil Town–Salisbury.

C. L. Caddy

'Battle of Britain' class 4-6-2 No. 34054 *Lord Beaverbrook* accelerates westwards from Buckhorn Weston Tunnel with a 'down' train on 5 September 1964.

C. L. Caddy

Double heading between Salisbury and Exeter was comparatively infrequent compared with other routes, and to have a pair of Bulleid Pacifics on a train was rare indeed. No. 34106 *Lydford* pilots No. 34079 *141 Squadron* on the 8.25 am Plymouth–Waterloo, seen here on the approach to Buckhorn Weston Tunnel, 5 September 1964.

C. L. Caddy

contractors re-lining the tunnel roof. A temporary signal box named after a signal box which once stood between the west end of the tunnel and Templecombe (Abbey Ford) was erected at the western end of the tunnel and this controlled the crossovers at either end and the signalling. The dim amber glow of the 'up' distant glimmered out of the darkness as we approached, this was to be expected as they were 'fixed' distants standing permanently at caution. I had hoped that we would get a clear road through, but no such luck, as the outer home signal remained at danger. My mate blew the whistle hard to call the signalman's attention, but the signal remained at danger and with a loud curse, my mate closed the regulator and applied the vacuum brake.

I climbed down from the locomotive and made for the temporary signal box in accordance with Rule 55. The signalman told me that he had accepted the 'down' newspaper train which had to clear the tunnel before we could proceed. Walking back to the locomotive was quite an experience, the whole area was lit by arc lamps and there was the sound of generators and pumps working away. There were large huts on the embankment, which were the navvies' sleeping quarters, as the work was continuous night and day. The electric headlights on our engine were shining brightly, and the engine was wreathed in steam with the safety valves roaring away, as if to say that she was ready to go. I climbed back into the warm cab with the rain still lashing down outside and told my driver the news, and to say he wasn't too happy about it would be putting it mildly, but it was no good blaming the signalman. The newspaper train had priority over our freight train, and he had no option but to stop us. I had the firebox stacked full ready for the off, the safety valves were lifting, and the steam generator powering our cab and headlights was whining away, our warm cab being an oasis of comfort against the elements outside. A few minutes later an eerie whistle indicated the presence of the 'down' train as she crawled from the tunnel, obeying the severe speed restriction. As the train passed us, headed by a rebuilt Bulleid Pacific, the driver opened up as he entered the double track and sped away on his run to Exeter.

Now it was our turn, and we had a climb of 1 in 100 through the tunnel and beyond. The signal in front turned from red to green. I gave a long blast on the whistle to alert the guard far behind us in his brakevan, my mate opened the large and small ejectors and gently opened the regulator. At the same time the sand lever was opened to help with the adhesion, the engine moved forward then, with a huge roar she slipped, then stopped and started again, then another slip, as a huge shower of steam and sparks flew into the dark night air. At the third attempt, she managed to pull away and the regulator was opened wider as we neared the tunnel mouth – with my mate blowing a long blast on the whistle to warn the workers in the tunnel of our approach. The interior as we entered was lit by the glare of electric lights. The workmen by this time had stopped work at the sound of our approach and were standing in groups on the closed 'down' track to our right. The noise from our exhaust was deafening, and sparks from our chimney showered down from the tunnel roof. We were in full forward gear and the regulator was wide open as the engine dragged our heavy train up the bank, and then it happened – she slipped. The workmen dived for cover as smoke and sparks flew everywhere, four times she slipped and regained her feet, by which time we had lost a lot of momentum due to the slipping and were moving at walking pace. Although the sand lever was still open I had the feeling that the sand-boxes were empty, and if she slipped once more we would be in real trouble. The fire had been stirred up with all that slipping and the pressure gauge had been knocked back to about 180 lb and half a glass of water in the boiler gauges, but slowly, ever so slowly, we gained the exit from the tunnel and out into the fresh air as we cleared the top of the bank. She picked her heels up, and started to run down to Gillingham. We had no more trouble that night as we climbed the Semley bank but I was proud of that locomotive, it was she who had won, my mate and I had just helped her along. I fired this engine many times, and she was one of the best of the class.

Templecombe to Crewkerne

Templecombe

The station opened on 7 May 1860 when the portion of line from Gillingham to Sherborne (to Yeovil from 1 June) was brought into use. The section from Salisbury to Gillingham had opened the previous year, on 2 May – construction difficulties with the 742 yd long Buckhorn Weston Tunnel had resulted in delaying of the opening to Templecombe and Sherborne. The station, which was just a wayside halt on the Salisbury & Yeovil line, increased in importance when the northern section of the Dorset Central Railway (from Templecombe) connected with the eastwards extension of the Somerset Central Railway (from Glastonbury) near Cole (Bruton). For this a third rail was laid on the SCR, the section being formally opened on 18 January 1862, and opened to public use on 3 February the same year. The DCR station at Templecombe opened on the

same date, the section from Cole to Templecombe being worked by the Somerset Central Railway. In his history of the Salisbury & Yeovil Railway of 1878 Louis Ruegg described the SCR as a company "Going from nowhere to nowhere" until the two companies amalgamated on 1 September of the same year to form the Somerset & Dorset Railway. The remaining 16 miles between Blandford and Templecombe opened on 31 August 1863 (Wimborne to Blandford had opened on 1 November 1860) giving the S&D a total of 61½ route miles between Burnham-on-Sea to Wimborne.

The important extension from Evercreech to link up with the Midland Railway at Bath was opened in 1874, completing the route from Bath to Wimborne and onwards to Poole under running powers granted by the L&SWR. Extensive sidings were installed on the 'up' (L&SWR) side

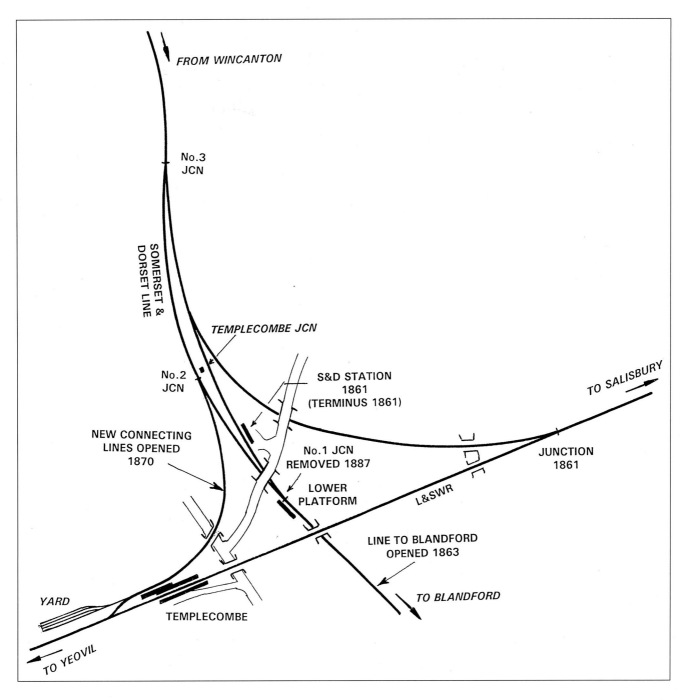

TEMPLECOMBE

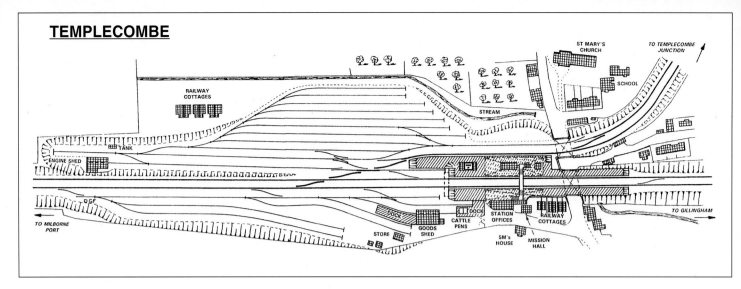

at Templecombe allowing for the expected interchange of freight traffic. Financial difficulties led to the 999-year lease of the line jointly to the Midland and London & South Western Railway (one of the best moves ever made by the L&SWR) from 1 November 1875 – with the rescued company being known as the Somerset & Dorset Joint Railway. Louis Ruegg wrote in 1878 that at Templecombe Junction, "the best paying line in the Kingdom (the L&SWR) is brought into connection (and contrast) with the worst" (the S&D).

In the early years, connection between the two lines diversified considerably. After calling at the lower DCR station which was served by a variety of through and terminating services, trains reversed, and then travelled via an easterly spur to a junction with the S&Y, half-a-mile east of Templecombe station. They then reversed into the S&Y (upper) station – or Templecombe Junction as it was

sometimes known. The S&Y had agreed to lay an extra line from the junction to the S&Y station as long as their (S&Y) line remained single and the DCR had to provide a third line if it was so doubled. A shuttle service was operated by the L&SWR between the two stations from 1862 until 1870. From 1867 some of the through S&D trains ceased to call at the lower station, stopping only at the upper station. This was a time-consuming and costly practice, involving four changes of direction for each train! This was not possible however for trains from Blandford as a double reversal would have been necessary.

Increased traffic on both the S&D and S&Y, plus the proposed doubling of the Salisbury–Exeter line, led to a new connecting line being constructed – a 67-chain westerly double-track spur, authorised under the Salisbury & Yeovil Railway Act of 1866. Constructed as a separate 'Templecombe Junction Railway' it came into operation in

'Merchant Navy' class 4-6-2 No. 35005 *Canadian Pacific* runs into Templecombe heading the 3.54 pm Clapham Junction–Exeter Central empty milk tanks on 23 August 1952. Note the running-in board to the right, 'TEMPLECOMBE change for Somerset & Dorset Line Bournemouth, Bath, Bristol, Birmingham & The North'. Long gone are the days when the station could offer trains to destinations such as this via the S&D.

R. E. Toop

TEMPLECOMBE (1950)

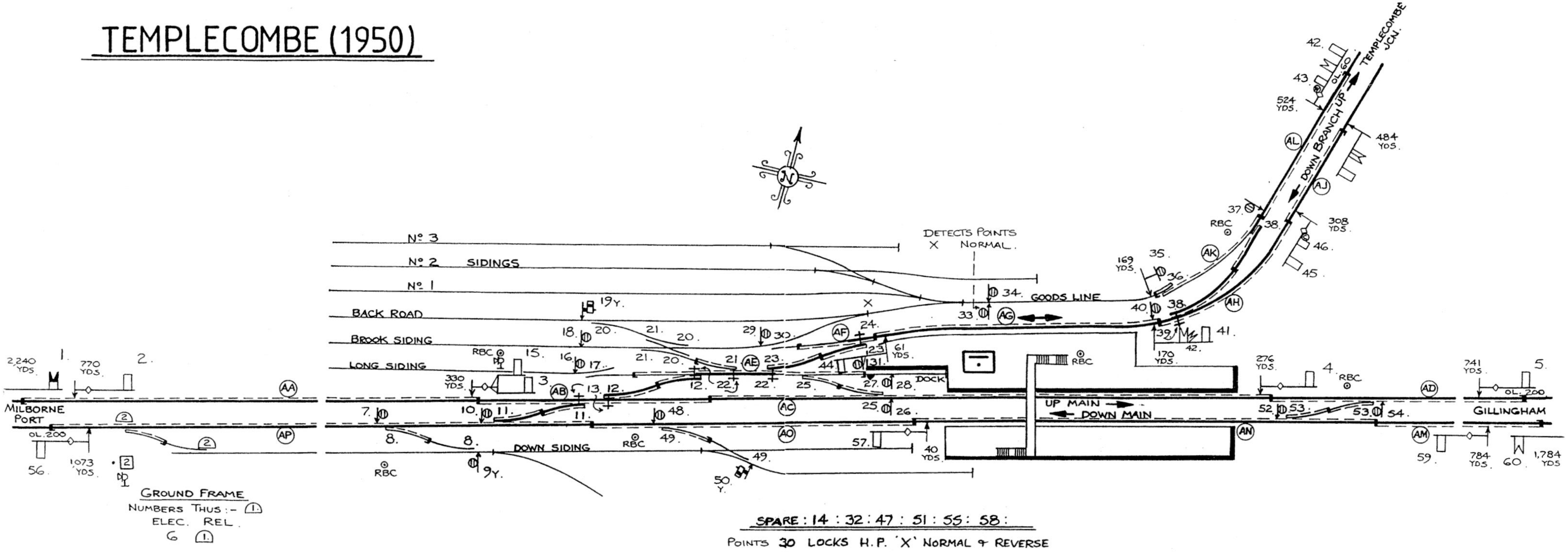

DOWN BRANCH UP → TEMPLECOMBE JCN.

No. 3   No. 2   No. 1   SIDINGS

BACK ROAD

BROOK SIDING

LONG SIDING

GOODS LINE

UP MAIN

DOWN MAIN

DOWN SIDING

DOCK

DETECTS POINTS X NORMAL.

GILLINGHAM

MILBORNE PORT

GROUND FRAME
NUMBERS THUS :— ①
ELEC. REL. ⓛ
G ⓛ

SPARE : 14 : 32 : 47 : 51 : 55 : 58 :
POINTS 30 LOCKS H.P. 'X' NORMAL & REVERSE

2,240 YDS.   770 YDS.   1,673 YDS.   OL.200

741 YDS.   784 YDS.   1,784 YDS.   OL.200

484 YDS.   308 YDS.   524 YDS.   OL.60

(1968)

GILLINGHAM

DOWN UP

DOWN MAIN

DOWN SIDING

SHERBORNE

AA   AB   BC   BB

SWITCH LEVER — 10
SPARE : 3 : 7 : 8 : 9

2,242 YDS.   727 YDS.   20 YDS.   IG. 2,084 YDS.

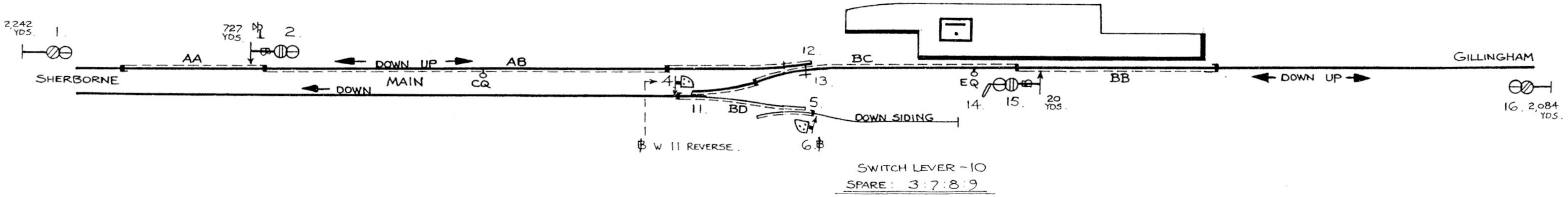

Maunsell Z class 0-8-0T No. 30953 engaged on station pilot duties, stands on the 'down' main line at Templecombe. A westbound train has left empty milk tanks and the shunter (standing by the locomotive) is awaiting the crossover ground signals to clear. The locomotive will then move forward via the crossover and then reverse its train along the 'up' main line in the foreground and into the upper yard.

Bob Barnard

March 1870 and was the only branch line authorised under the auspices of the Salisbury & Yeovil. The new spur ran north to west leaving the Somerset & Dorset line next to Horsington level-crossing (later known as No.3 Junction) and running southwards and at a higher level to the original Dorset Central Railway track before curving away to the S&Y station. This afforded all 'down' S&D trains calling at Templecombe to run directly into and reverse out of an enlarged upper station before continuing their travels – and vice versa for 'up' S&D services. This arrangement, with

engines being utilised at both ends of trains to and from the lower junction, lasted until the closure of the Somerset & Dorset line and Templecombe. The new curve also gave L&SWR trains direct access on to the Somerset & Dorset and vice versa. The easterly connection was closed from the opening of the new curve, but remained in use as a siding for 97 years, until July 1967. The Dorset Central Railway station was closed in 1887 (although it had been largely abandoned with the opening of the new westerly curve in 1870 and was later integrated into the Somerset & Dorset

The 9 am Waterloo–Exeter (Nine Elms Duty No. 5) runs into Templecombe for its three-minute station stop (arr 11.30 am, dep 11.33) headed by No. 34101 *Hartland* in the summer of 1962.

C. L. Caddy Collection

The massive bulk of a 9F 2-10-0, No. 92226 (82F), stands alongside the Somerset & Dorset platform at Templecombe on a passenger service from the S&D main line on 6 June 1964.

Barry Eagles

engine shed yard), with a new Lower Platform (situated slightly south) coming into use the same year. The Lower Platform was little used except by the occasional express not booked to call at the upper station, and by the daily last train from Bournemouth.

Massive exchanges of freight traffic took place at Templecombe with over 10,000 tons being exchanged per month at this major crossroads between the two companies. Two signal boxes, 'A' (L&SWR) and 'B' (S&D) were situated at the upper station. The 'B' box closed in 1933 with its work being absorbed by the 'A' box which had to be extended. A goods shed was situated on the 'down' side of the South Western main line, west of the station. Freight sidings existed west of the station alongside the 'up' and 'down' main lines, with the main upper yard largely used for exchange of wagons. The station and track layout was re-built in 1938 and the platforms extended to cater for 14-coach length trains. A new footbridge (replacing the old subway) connected the 'down' main line platform to the 'up' island platform which served the Exeter–Waterloo trains on its inner face and the S&D trains on the outer face. A new 60-lever signal box was situated on the Sherborne end of the 'up' platform, replacing the former 'A' box. Interchange of passenger traffic was also excellent with passengers travelling north or south via the Somerset & Dorset, and east and west via the Southern Railway route.

An air raid occurred on 5 September 1942 and of the four bombs dropped two landed in the area of the station, one landing behind the buffet, and the other opposite the signal box on what is now the car-park. Extensive damage was caused to the station buildings, and also to two trains which had just arrived, with many people being wounded by shrapnel. Thirteen local people were killed, including five railway workers. (An air raid at the junction of the Weymouth and Taunton lines at Castle Cary on the GWR had occurred two days previously on 3 September, with three people killed and ten injured.) An ambulance train

was stationed in the 'down' sidings at Templecombe upper during the war. This was a twelve-coach train, complete with operating theatre and US Army medical staff. The train was hauled by an LNER 2-6-0 fitted with a Westinghouse brake, and crewed by two pairs of North Eastern men who worked twelve hours on and twelve hours off. The engine was kept in steam night and day, ready to move off at short notice, and a special truck of coal was stabled with the locomotive at the lower yard. The train was used to travel to Southampton to collect American servicemen wounded in action, taking them to various hospitals, and many operations were carried out on the train itself. One of the steam-raisers' jobs in Templecombe shed during the war was to warn villagers of an air raid by blowing a fluctuating whistle on an engine in steam, with one long blast for the 'all clear'.

A small wooden engine shed was opened in 1863 at the Somerset & Dorset lower station, which was shared by the two companies. However, there seems to have been a disagreement in 1867 which led to a request from the S&D to the L&SWR – and in fact forcibly ejecting the L&SWR tank engine from the shed. The L&SWR, not to be outdone, constructed a timber-built single-road shed at the end of the headshunt from the upper yard to house their shunting engine, together with a hand coaling stage, water tower, engine pit and small mess room. This was an out-station of Yeovil Town shed from which the engines were supplied and maintained. G6 class 0-6-0 tanks Nos 238/240/266/276/351 were allocated to Yeovil Town over the years, and representatives of these locomotives were outstationed at Templecombe at various times. Other locomotives working off various trains would visit the shed for water and servicing. The small shed had been demolished by 1936 – but locomotives continued to be stabled here, using the water and coaling facilities. With the expansion of the upper yard during the Second World War the coal stage was re-erected on a spur off the new headshunt, complete with pit

Collett 0-6-0 No. 2218 (83G) waits for the station staff to finish loading the parcels vans before proceeding to buffer up to its train at the S&D platform at Templecombe on 11 June 1964.

Barry Eagles

and water column, and an old coach body was used as a combined mess room/store. In my firing days during the 1950s and '60s the pit and column were still in regular use, and I have more than once watered an engine and cleaned a fire 'up the neck' as it was called. The Templecombe upper shunter remained under Yeovil control until June 1950 when G6 No. 30274 was transferred to the lower S&D locomotive

shed. No. 30274 was replaced by a Z class 0-8-0T, No. 30953, in December 1954.

Templecombe was unique as here, in the heart of rural Somerset, Southern Railway locomotives could be seen standing alongside their counterparts from the LMS and its constituent companies for many years. And I well remember sitting in a 'West Country' Pacific in the upper yard (waiting

S15 4-6-0 No. 30832 pulls briskly away from Templecombe with a two-coach set forming the 3.34 pm Templecombe–Exeter Central on 24 August 1963.

S. C. Nash

Two locomotives – years apart in design and capabilities – stand side-by-side in the upper yard at Templecombe on 8 August 1960. 4F 0-6-0 No. 44557 is ready to pull into the S&D platform with the 12 noon train to Bath Green Park, and Bulleid 'Battle of Britain' class 4-6-2 No. 34069 *Hawkinge* whiles away the time before working the 12.42 pm stopper to Salisbury. Just part of the immense freight traffic dealt with in the upper yard can be seen; shunting was performed in this yard day and night.

Terry Gough

to leave with the 12.42 pm Templecombe–Salisbury stopper for example) and standing alongside us would be one of the Fowler 4F 0-6-0s – with the crew awaiting their turn – before working the 12 pm Templecombe to Bath Green Park. The massive freight yards which had echoed to the sound of clanking buffers for donkey's years, eventually closed to goods traffic on 5 April 1965. With the run-down of the Somerset & Dorset and its eventual closure in 1966, the station closed on 7 March of the same year – the last service train to call being the 18.45 Exeter–Eastleigh mail train.

All the station buildings (except for the signal box) were demolished, the line being singled from Gillingham to a point west of Templecombe station where the double-track section to Yeovil Junction begins. However under the auspices of British Rail, Somerset County Council and the Templecombe Station Working Committee, the station was re-opened on 3 October 1983. The first train to *officially* call was the 09.10 Waterloo–Exeter headed by No. 50023 *Howe* which did the honours by breaking through a large banner proclaiming 'Templecombe' – for the benefit of the many people who had turned out to witness the event. (The first

Templecombe looking east on 10 July 1991, a glorious summer's day, with the single (former 'up') line stretching away to Gillingham. Tickets are obtained from the signalman (the box is still operational). Hanging baskets and flower tubs enhance the station. Further down from the signal box is the platform shelter dating from 1988 which had the addition of a new waiting room and toilet in 1990. The superb footbridge in the background was re-erected in 1990 and came from the former LB&SCR station at Buxted in East Sussex.

John Scrace

During the 1950s a series of diesel trials took place on the Western Section of the Southern Region involving the SR/BR prototype 1 Co-Co 1 locomotives Nos 10201-10203. Pictured here is No. 10201 approaching Templecombe with the 1 pm from Waterloo. The locomotives were extensively used and were capable of making two return trips between Waterloo and Exeter per day. The two LMS/BR prototype Co-Cos Nos 10000 and 10001 appeared on the route to accompany the Southern diesels in 1953 – working express trains including the 'ACE'. When the LMS locomotives were moved back to the London Midland Region in 1955, the Southern diesels were transferred with them.

Bob Barnard

'West Country' class 4-6-2 No. 34023 *Blackmore Vale* runs into Templecombe with 6.10 pm (SO) Salisbury–Yeovil Junction on 5 July 1959.
C. L. Caddy Collection

train to actually stop that day was the 05.47 Exeter–Waterloo.) Officials for the event included the Chairman of Somerset County Council and the Divisional Manager of the South Western Division of British Rail. The station today is a great credit to everyone who has been involved in its resurrection. Trains stop at the former 'up' platform where tickets can be obtained at the signal box which, since the re-opening of the station, has doubled as a waiting room/ticket office. A waiting shelter was added in 1988, with other facilities being provided later, the most striking feature being the erection of a lattice footbridge (removed from the former LBSCR station at Buxted, East Sussex) connecting the car park alongside the old abandoned 'down' platform with the one now in use. Hanging baskets, well-tended flower beds, an attractive statue (commissioned by British Rail) on the lawn, have won the station many awards – and rightly so; it is well worth a visit. The initial service from Templecombe comprised six services each way, with the addition of one more in either direction in 1984. Three locomotives have been named *Templecombe* over the years: 'West Country' class 4-6-2 No. 34098, No. 33112 which was named at the station on Saturday, 17 October 1987, and No. 47708 carried the name from June 1991. Also, Class 159 'Super Sprinter' car No. 57875 was named *Templecombe* at a ceremony held at the station on 3 October 1993.

Footplate comments

I have many memories of Templecombe in my footplate days. The freight traffic dealt with in the upper yard was very heavy with goods trains arriving and departing at all hours. The Yeovil U class 2-6-0s were used on all types of train, freight or passenger, and one turn in particular involved night shunting in the upper yard. The 'Dorset' men crewed the day and back shifts with a Midland tank engine. One of their drivers was a bookie, and would put a bet on for any of the crews, on Grand National day. Yeovil Town Duty No. 514 involved riding passenger to Templecombe on an 'up' freight and changing over at 1.00am with the crew (Yeovil men) on the U class which was already in the process of shunting at the top of the yard. The engine had arrived at Templecombe earlier on the 4.54 Salisbury–Templecombe (Yeovil Duty No. 513, worked by Salisbury men) and had been involved in carriage and freight shunting since then. Knowing that this was a busy yard to shunt, we would put up the tender sheet to keep out the cold night air, and our faggots and onions were placed behind the hot pipes in the cab to warm up for supper later on. I would usually add to the good fire left by my comrades by building up a large amount under the firedoor, but the boiler level was kept down, to keep the engine quiet. The shunters were on the driver's side of the engine, and there would be four or five men on duty – leaving the fireman not much to do except keep the fire topped up and have a fag or two whilst looking at the comings and goings on the main line. The 'down' West of England newspaper train would be quite a site streaking up the bank with a shower of sparks emitting from the chimney, or the 'up' perishable trains tearing down through the station. Anyway, enough of this distraction, back to the shunting. There would be a whistle and a green light from the leading shunter, and we would back down on to the rows of wagons waiting to be re-marshalled. The yard was on a severe slope, and we would cough our way up to the shunting neck with about 40 or 50 wagons at a time, and roll gently back as the wagons were cut out and assembled into trains. This went on all night, except for a short break to enjoy the faggots and onions, washed down with a mug of tea in the shunters' cabin.

4F 0-6-0 No. 44422 (83G) (now preserved) stands in the dock at Templecombe on 31 August 1964 before her next trip over the S&D. Templecombe Upper Yard was a unique place where Bulleid Pacifics and other Southern engines could be found standing alongside many variants of the former LMS classes. Just a portion of the once heavy freight traffic in the Upper Yard can be seen in the background.

John Scrace

'Battle of Britain' class 4-6-2 No. 34087 *145 Squadron* approaches Templecombe with the 12.46 pm Salisbury–Exeter Central on 31 August 1964.

John Scrace

Templecombe was a fascinating place at night after the last evening passenger train had gone, and the freight trains had started their wanderings; milk trains standing side by side, non stop freights thundering through, and many freight trains calling to pick up and detach wagons. Our shunting would finish as the first rays of light pierced the cold dawn sky, when the Midland tank engine would arrive from the 'Dorset' shed to start the day's shunting. And we would pull up to the far end of the yard and reverse into the small engine spur where the water column and ash pit were situated – these being the remnants of the old Yeovil Town sub depot. Whilst the 'bag' was in the tender, most firemen (myself included), took the chance to clean the fire, pull the fire around and shovel coal forward on the tender, ready for the climb out of Templecombe. My mate would be oiling the rods and straps, and the lamps would be extinguished and replaced on the smokebox door by the white route discs. Meanwhile I would be banking up the fire, cleaning down the footplate, and at the same time filling the bucket with hot water to wash off the night's coal dust, and freshen up a bit. Now it was time to reverse down on to our freight train, the 5.30 am Templecombe–Yeovil Junction, and after coupling up, the guard would arrive, give us the load, take the driver's name and engine number, and walk back to the brake van.

The ground signal which gave us the exit from the upper yard was difficult to see, especially with 60 or more wagons on our tail, so the guard, on seeing the 'dummy' come off, released his brake. This in turn tightened the couplings and the movement was felt on the engine. Up on the footplate, all was ready – the vacuum gauge quivering with the twin needles at 21 inches, the fire was roaring away, and the locomotive pulsating with power. Great care had to be taken as we reversed down the yard and on to the 'up' main line. With so many wagons a hasty brake application could snap a coupling, and then we would have a runaway on our hands. We came to a halt alongside the 'up' platform near the signal box with a clanking of buffers from our train.

Now was the time to stir up the fire with the pricker. Up ahead of us, the ground signals were clearing as the points were set to guide us on to the 'down' main line. All 'down' trains starting from Templecombe are faced with a 1 in 150 gradient, so with a blow on the whistle to alert the guard, we pulled slowly away, the regulator is opened, slowly at first, to take the strain on the couplings, a loud cough from the chimney, then another, each beat growing louder as the regulator was opened wider and the engine got into its stride. We lurched to the left as the crossovers guided us on to the 'down' main line, the advanced starting signals giving us a clear road with their upper quadrant arms rising high into the air. It was time to open the firedoors and start shovelling coal as we barked up the incline, the firedoors banging with each massive blast from our chimney, smoke and steam rising high into the air. As the engine strained and struggled, gaining ground by the minute, still firing, I concentrated on the back corners of the firebox and under the firedoor. At the top of the bank our speed increased and the beat from our exhaust softened as the regulator was eased and the reverser wound back; the Milborne Port 'down' distant was clear, and we rattled through the small station. The injector was on to top up the boiler, and there was time to spray down the tender and footplate, the regulator was now closed and the engine given a touch of brake to hold our train, just in case the road was against us at Sherborne. We rolled down the bank and around the curves, our long train of wagons snaking along behind us. If the Sherborne 'down' distant signal was clear the brake would be released and we would swoop over the level crossing with our whistle blowing. The regulator was opened for the continuation of our journey (booked arrival at Yeovil Junction 6 am), but not for long as the Yeovil Junction distant signal stood at caution looming ahead of us at Bradford Abbas. We ran in and reversed our train into the down sidings where we uncoupled. At 6.20 am we would departed tender-first for Sherborne and indulged in shunting the yard until 7.28 am when we changed over to Salisbury Duty No. 503. This was was the 5 am Salisbury–Yeovil Town milk. The train was a varied assortment of vans and GUVs etc., and carried fish and all sorts of odds and ends and was worked on this trip by

Milborne Port looking east on 29 July 1962 from the 'up' platform with its brick-built waiting shelter. The main buildings and signal box are located on the 'down' platform to the right.

C. L. Caddy

another Yeovil crew. Having left our U class engine in the 'up' yard we waited on the 'down' platform as they bowled in, as usual with a 'King Arthur', or sometimes an S15. It would be fair to say that, at this point in our duty, both crew members would be tired and looking forward to a spot of breakfast and some sleep. Anyway, after a bit of banter with our comrades, we set off, and after running around our train at Yeovil Junction, we arrived at Yeovil Town and were relieved by another Yeovil crew at 8.10 am who were

involved in shunting the train, and squaring up the engine on shed. As for my mate and myself, we booked off, had a wash in the enginemens' cabin, I set off home to mother, and returned again the same night to repeat the performance all over again.

Milborne Port

This small way-side station was located 1¼ miles from the village bearing the same name so passenger traffic was

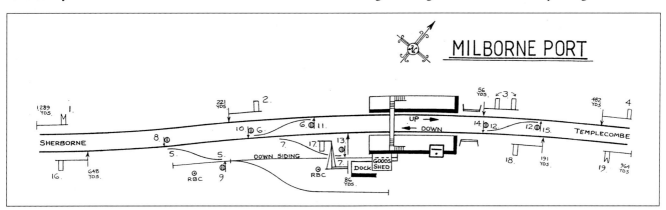

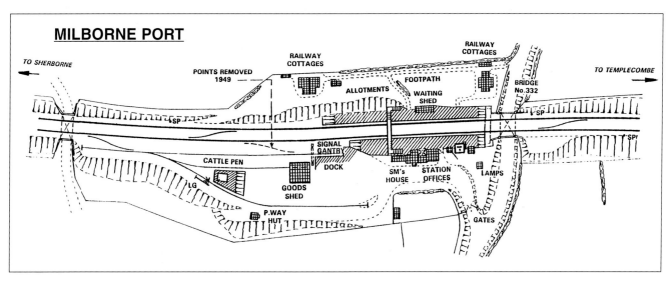

Sherborne looking east on 10 May 1964. The level crossing gates in the distance can be seen closed to rail traffic. Here again, the main station buildings are grouped on the 'up' platform, with a canopied shelter serving passengers' needs on the 'down' platform.

C. L. Caddy

never heavy, particularly as the village was situated on the A30 trunk road with its adequate bus services, etc. The main station buildings, including the station master's house were positioned on the 'down' platform. A footbridge connected the two platforms and a small brick-built waiting shelter adorned the 'up' platform. The small L&SWR signal box stood on the east end of the 'up' platform. A crossover road was positioned 194 yards from the box on the Sherborne side, and another (opened 9 September 1896) was located 86 yards on the Templecombe side of the box. A small goods yard with a goods shed containing a 40 cwt crane and a cattle loading dock with pens was situated west of the station on the 'down' side. The station closed to goods traffic on 6 November 1961 and was reduced to an unmanned halt from the same date, passengers collecting their tickets from the signalman. The goods yard points, eastern crossover road, and associated disc signals were removed on 20 November 1961, and the western crossover road, with its associated disc signalling, following suit on 16 September 1962. The signal box closed on 21 June 1965, with the halt closing to passenger services on 7 March 1966. Today, the 'up' platform survives although overgrown, with the edging stones removed, and the 'down' platform has been cut-back with the station buildings now forming two private residences.

Footplate comments

The climb from Sherborne is a severe one for eastbound trains with gradients of 1 in 100 and 80. When the overbridge and the Milborne Port 'up' distant signal came into view at the top of the bank most footplatemen would place the firing shovel on the shovelling plate, the injector would be singing away and the driver would ease the regulator and the reverser, as the line now dipped sharply through Milborne Port station and onwards to Templecombe. I, like many other footplatemen, have had my share of rough trips on the footplate. However, the following incident happened to a fireman at Yeovil Town. He was booked on one day with his driver to haul a large permanent way crane and associated vehicles from Yeovil Junction to Templecombe, their engine being one of the Maunsell U class 2-6-0s, usually a free-steaming class, but on this day they came to a stand on the Sherborne bank with the engine fighting shy of steam. So there they stood with the fireman poking the fire with the pricker to try to rally the engine around. But help was near at hand, the driver of the PW crane (which was in steam), seeing that the engine was in trouble offered to help by opening the regulator on the crane to give the engine a push. The offer was quickly accepted with the result that the engine, now with a bit of steam was assisted up the bank by the PW crane! This was probably the only time that a crane has pushed a locomotive up the Sherborne bank. Of course, this incident became the talk of the enginemen's cabin at Yeovil Town for a few days after!

Sherborne

The historic market town of Sherborne, famed for its 15th century abbey, public schools, two castles, and once the home of Sir Walter Raleigh, was a strong contender to be connected to the railway system. A public meeting was held in the town on 26 March 1846 when supporters of both rival gauges held a noisy and vociferous debate. Sherborne was the point where the companies' lines were planned to cross – at one time the GWR had proposals for a branch line to Sherborne from the WS&W line, and a line to connect Yeovil with Salisbury from a point on the Weymouth line north east of Yeovil to Wilton on the Salisbury line. Representatives of the Wilts, Somerset, & Weymouth Railway, the Bristol & Exeter, and the London & South

U class No. 31792 from Yeovil Town shed pulls onto the 'up' main line at Sherborne whilst shunting the yard on 9 June 1962.

C. L. Caddy

Western Railway were present. Local dignitaries supporting the broad gauge included Mr Robert Gordon of Leweston (former Secretary to the Treasury) and Earl Digby. The 'narrow gauge' had an equally powerful lobby in the owners of the silk factories in Sherborne and the glove factories at Milborne Port. The vote (I am pleased to state) at the end of a very noisy debate came down heavily on the side of the 'narrow gauge' 'Central' route.

On 7 May 1860 the line came into operation between Gillingham and Sherborne (to Yeovil on 1 June) and there was a day of celebration in the town, bells pealed out a welcome, bands played triumphal marches, cannon were fired, and 1,200 schoolchildren gathered on a slope overlooking the station sang the National Anthem as the

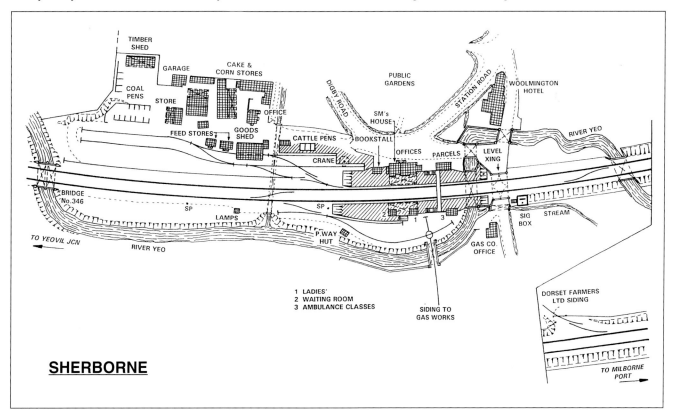

SHERBORNE

1 LADIES'
2 WAITING ROOM
3 AMBULANCE CLASSES

Sherborne looking west on 20 September 1968 with the goods shed and former 'up' goods yard to the right. Freight facilities were withdrawn on 18 April 1966. A line of condemned EMUs stands in the yard. Propelled by a diesel locomotive, they were used in the film *Goodbye Mr Chips* starring Peter O'Toole and released in 1969. Many of the outside locations were filmed in and around Sherborne.

C. L. Caddy

train arrived. Flags were well displayed, as were many banners proclaiming 'Where there's a will, there's a way'.

The station lies at the foot of the ascent to Milborne Port and in steam days some spectacular running was achieved by eastbound trains storming through to attack the bank in fine style – or swooping down the incline and hurtling over the level crossing with a warning blast from the whistle whilst heading west. The pleasing Tite main station buildings constructed in the mellow Ham stone are grouped on the 'up' platform with a waiting shelter provided on the 'down'. The level crossing is positioned at the end of the platforms on the Milborne Port side of the layout. The goods shed containing a 30 cwt crane, and goods yard with a 5 ton crane were situated west of the station, alongside the 'up' main line. A gas works (established in 1836 before the arrival of the railway) on the south side of the station was equipped with a railway siding in 1876. A wagon turntable of 14 ft 3 in diameter was positioned at the end of the siding to enable coal wagons to enter the gas premises and vast quantities of coal were imported by rail – 4,035 tons in 1915,

increasing to 7,000 tons in 1948. The gas company provided the bridge to carry the siding over the River Yeo. The gas-making process came to an end in 1957 with the completion of the main gas grid system from Poole.

The 18-lever signal box which stood alongside the 'down' main line on the Milborne Port side of the level crossing was closed on 18 December 1960 when replaced by a 30-lever, brick-built BR(S) Type 16 box situated alongside the 'up' main line opposite the site of the former box. Incidentally, the old box was in such a state towards the end of its life that it actually used to shake with some vigour with the passage of 'down' through trains! However, the new signal box of 1960 succumbed to closure itself on 4 January 1970. The building is still extant and was advertised by British Rail a few years ago as being suitable for an 'artists studio', etc. A siding situated east of the station and the River Yeo was opened in 1890 serving the Sherborne Coal & Timber Company (later the Dorset Farmers Ltd). In the Southern Railway Western Appendice of 1935 the following instructions applied to the siding . . . A competent shunter

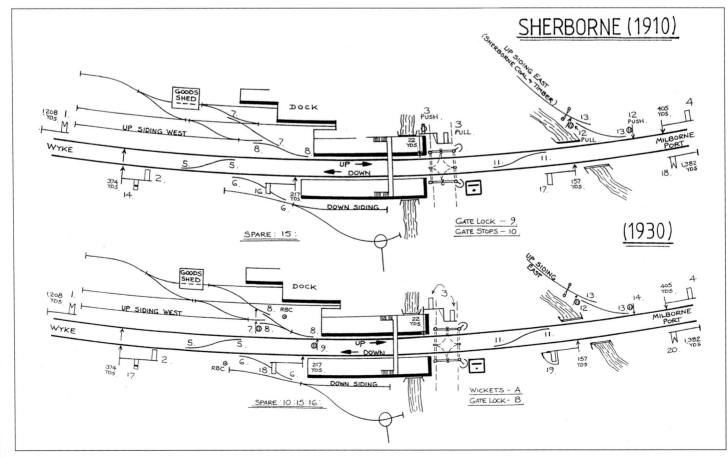

must always be provided to supervise shunting operations and a member of the Dorset Farmers' staff must always be in attendance during such operations. Engines are prohibited from passing beyond the gate, and a sufficient number of wagons should be attached to the engine to obviate any necessity for this . . . The siding was removed in 1965.

The nearby milk factory provided a good scource of revenue for the station with 38,182 gallons being forwarded in 1936. Passenger takings at Sherborne have always been good with 48,169 tickets being issued, and 63,268 received in 1928. The public schools always provided peaks in the traffic at the beginning and end of terms and at one time special trains were run to and from Waterloo for the benefit of the pupils. In my firing days I well remember working a Waterloo–Sherborne school special, (we relieved a Nine Elms crew at Salisbury) – the train consisting of twelve well-filled carriages with a rebuilt 'Merchant Navy' Pacific at the head. After an uneventful journey we arrived at the aforesaid station where our packed train of schoolgirls of all shapes and sizes detrained in a babbling mass, with the station staff taking some time to clear the luggage vans of countless trunks and cases, etc. We then departed, hauling the empty stock to Yeovil Town.

The 1910 *Bradshaw*, as well as showing the station well served by main line stopping trains on weekday services, also had two 'up' and two 'down' express services with catering facilities calling at Sherborne, namely:

6.10 am Waterloo–Plymouth (Breakfast car to Exeter) depart Sherborne at 9.4 am, this train running non-stop from Yeovil Junction and arriving at Exeter Queen Street at 10.12 am.

8.50 am Waterloo–Plymouth (Luncheon car to Exeter) depart Sherborne at 11.59 am, running non-stop from Yeovil Junction and arriving at Exeter Queen Street at 1.8 pm.

7.20 am Exeter–Waterloo (Breakfast car Exeter–London) depart Sherborne at 8.40 am, stopping at Templecombe and Salisbury only, and arriving at Waterloo at 11.3 am.

2.15 pm Plymouth–Waterloo (Dining car Exeter–London) depart Sherborne at 5.31 pm, arriving at Waterloo at 8.7 pm.

On Sundays the (April 1910) 'down' services calling at Sherborne included:

8.30 am Waterloo–Yeovil Town stopper,

12.30 pm Waterloo–Plymouth (Luncheon car to Exeter) depart Sherborne at 3.1 pm, running non-stop from Yeovil Junction and arriving at Exeter Queen Street at 4.10 pm.

2.29 pm Salisbury–Exeter Queen Street stopper.

5.49 pm Waterloo–Yeovil Town stopper.

The 'up' Sunday services:

6.10 am Yeovil Town–Waterloo

10.55 am Plymouth–Waterloo

2.40 pm Plymouth–Waterloo (Dining car Exeter–London) depart Sherborne at 5.47 pm, arrive Waterloo 8.30 pm.

The 1932 freight working timetable shows the following scheduled goods and milk trains calling at Sherborne:

Down

9.50 pm Waterloo–Yeovil Junction – *Empty churns.*

4.30 am Salisbury–Exmouth Junction Sidings – *to detach only.*

12.10 am Nine Elms–Exmouth Junction (MO).

9.20 am Templecombe–Yeovil Junction.

3.10 pm Salisbury–Yeovil Junction.

11.35 am Clapham Junction–Yeovil Junction – *Empty churns.*

Up

8.35 am Yeovil Junction–Salisbury.

9.55 am Yeovil Junction–Salisbury – *Milk and horseboxes.*

3.42 pm Yeovil Junction–Templecombe.

4.50 pm Sherborne–Victoria – *Milk train.*

6.05 pm Sherborne–Waterloo – *Milk train.*

4.43 pm Exeter–Waterloo – *Milk and Parcels.*

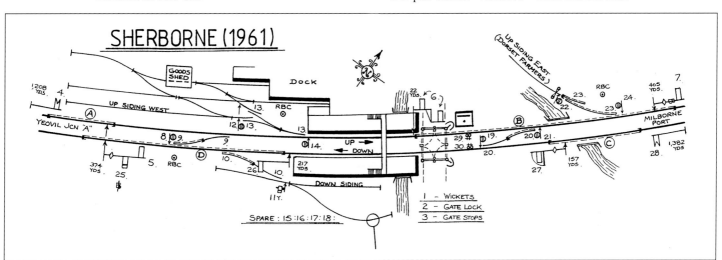

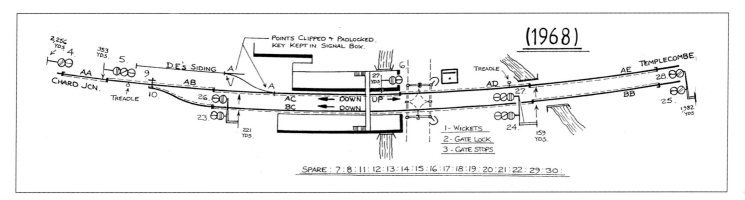

Sherborne looking east on 10 July 1991 towards the level crossing equipped with full barriers and the disused signal box. The barriers are lowered by a member of the station staff. The control box for operating the barriers can be seen to the left of the colour light signal at the end of the 'up' platform. The 'up' line to the left is bidirectional between Templecombe and Yeovil Junction.

John Scrace

Class 47/7 No. 47707 *Holyrood* rumbles into Sherborne with the 14.42 Exeter St Davids–Waterloo on 10 July 1991. Note the goods shed still standing in the distance. Part of the former 'up' yard has been turned into a car park.

John Scrace

Sherborne signal box stands out of use on 26 April 1970. As with most of the new boxes opened on the line this one had a short life, opening on 18 December 1960 and closing on 4 January 1970. The old L&SWR box which stood opposite lasted from 1875 until 1960. One of the full lifting barriers installed in 1970 can be seen to the left of the box.

C. L. Caddy

A W. H. Smith bookstall was positioned on the 'up' platform for many years, serving the passengers with newspapers and magazines. The 'down' waiting shelter was replaced in 1926 by a structure complete with awning using the original columns as support. Freight services were withdrawn on 18 April 1966. The goods shed still exists, and part of the former goods yard is now in use as a car park. The main line westwards from Sherborne to Chard Junction was singled on 7 May 1967 but this was such a disaster – causing excessive delays – that the double-track section between Sherborne and Yeovil Junction was reinstated on 1 October of the same year. From 4 January 1970 the level crossing gates were replaced by full-lifting barriers, and upon the sound of a warning bell giving notice of the approach of a train, a member of the staff operates the barriers from a control panel at the end of the 'up' platform. The barriers are raised by the passage of the trains themselves. The station still retains double track as it is on the section between Templecombe and Yeovil Junction with the 'up' line being signalled for bidirectional working. The station buildings have hardly altered over the years and are well worth a visit (by train of course). The pleasant town is just a few minutes walk away with a stroll around the shops in Cheap Street and with an enjoyable meal to be had at one of the many cafes, etc., being recommended, and followed by a visit to the famous abbey in this beautiful Dorset town – before catching the train home.

Footplate comments

It always paid the driver of a heavy Salisbury bound freight train heading towards Sherborne to go as fast as possible to have a good crack at the bank, and yet not too fast in case of adverse signals at Sherborne. Thundering along in the darkness with an S15 4-6-0 and a long train of freight

wagons of all shapes and sizes rumbling along behind us I would be laying the fire, with the vivid glare from the firebox reflecting against the night sky. I would hope that the distant signal would be clear, this low-lying stretch of line around Lenthay Crossing is very prone to mist and fog which made things more difficult whilst trying to spot the oil-lit semaphore, even though it was mounted on a tall post for ease of sighting. When the signal was observed as standing clear the regulator would be opened wide, and with sparks erupting from our exhaust, we would thunder through the station, over the level crossing and storm the climb to Milborne Port. In 1962 the Sherborne 'up' and 'down' distant signals were replaced by colour light signals, the 'up' colour light was positioned at 2,266 yards from the signal box, and with the introduction of the AWS system, was a tremendous boon to us footplatemen – shining out like a welcoming beacon in the dark on a wild winter's night.

Wyke Level Crossing

The L&SWR Type Five signal box with ground-level frame was opened circa 1892 at this sometimes busy farm-crossing and was located alongside the 'down' main line on the Sherborne side of the gates. The box was fitted with a closing switch and worked on the Preece 1-wire open block. A gateman's cottage was provided. Supplies of coal and stores, etc., here and at Lenthay Crossing were dropped off by the 9.20 am freight from Templecombe when required. The 'down' distant signal at 1,028 yards was replaced by a two-aspect colour light (at 1,540 yards) on 25 November 1962. Abolished as a block-post on 29 May 1960 the box remained until closure in December 1964, and is now preserved and operational on the narrow gauge Gartell Light Railway at Templecombe.

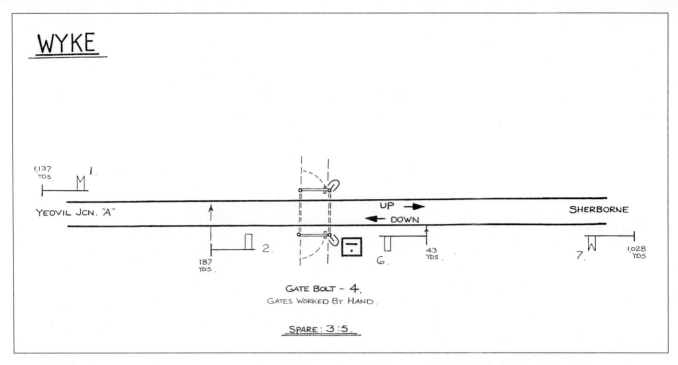

WYKE

YEOVIL JCN. "A"

UP →

← DOWN

SHERBORNE

1,137 YDS

187 YDS

43 YDS

1,028 YDS

2.

6.

7.

GATE BOLT – 4.

GATES WORKED BY HAND.

SPARE: 3:5.

Yeovil Junction

In its heyday one of the largest and most impressive stations in terms of track layout, etc., on the whole route between Salisbury and Exeter – complete with its four tracks between the platforms, the double-track branch line to Yeovil Town – an M7 tank in the branch line bay with a push-and-pull set working the Yeovil Town shuttle, express trains whistling through non-stop on the through tracks, two signalboxes, a turntable busy with light engine movements, and goods sidings packed with freight wagons. What a far-cry from the layout today – with empty sidings and all passenger services using the former 'up' island platform.

Using the Bradford Abbas cutting and crossing over the GWR Weymouth main line, the S&Y opened its services (worked by the L&SWR) on 1 June 1860 from Salisbury to Yeovil. (Opened to goods on 1 September.) This used the Bristol & Exeter station at Hendford on the western outskirts of Yeovil as a temporary terminus until the opening (a few

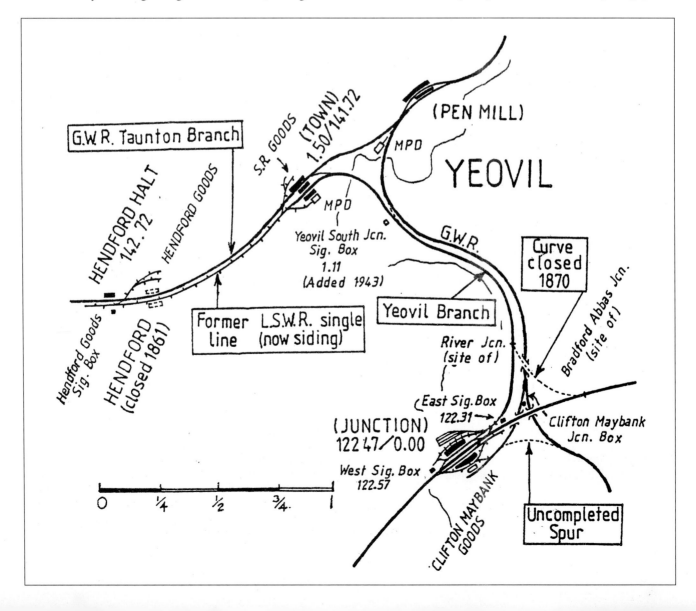

YEOVIL JUNCTION

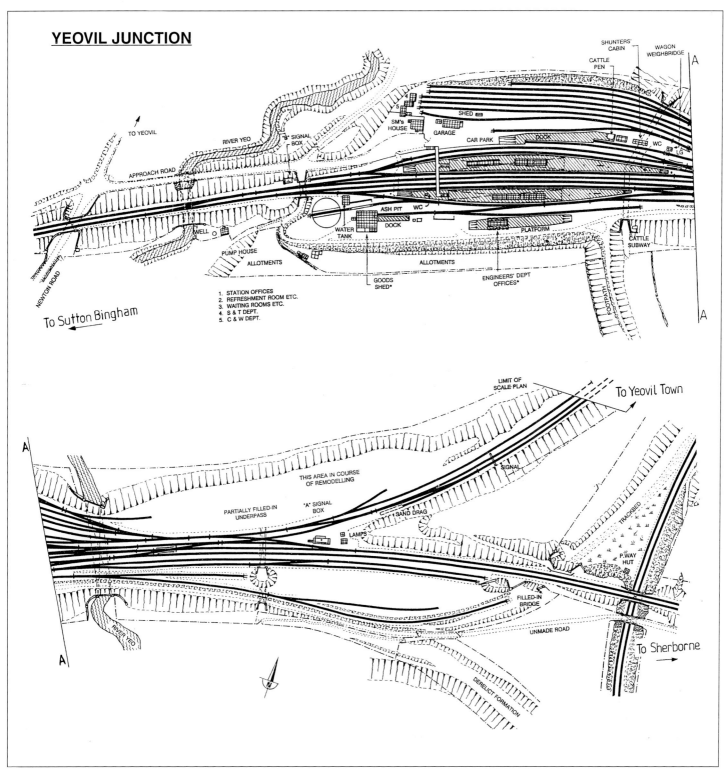

TO YEOVIL

RIVER YEO

APPROACH ROAD

'B' SIGNAL BOX

NEWTON ROAD

WELL

To Sutton Bingham

PUMP HOUSE

ALLOTMENTS

SM's HOUSE

GARAGE

SHED

CAR PARK

DOCK

WC

LG

WATER TANK

ASH PIT

DOCK

WC

ALLOTMENTS

PLATFORM

GOODS SHED*

ENGINEERS' DEPT OFFICES*

SHUNTERS' CABIN

CATTLE PEN

WAGON WEIGHBRIDGE

A

CATTLE SUBWAY

FOOTPATH

A

1. STATION OFFICES
2. REFRESHMENT ROOM ETC.
3. WAITING ROOMS ETC.
4. S & T DEPT.
5. C & W DEPT.

LIMIT OF SCALE PLAN

To Yeovil Town

THIS AREA IN COURSE OF REMODELLING

SIGNAL

A'

PARTIALLY FILLED-IN UNDERPASS

'A' SIGNAL BOX

SAND DRAG

TRACKBED

LAMPS

P.WAY HUT

RIVER YEO

FILLED-IN BRIDGE

A'

UNMADE ROAD

To Sherborne

N

DERELICT FORMATION

'King Arthur' class 4-6-0 No. 742 *Camelot* makes a superb sight whilst storming through Yeovil Junction with the 'down' 'Atlantic Coast Express' on 21 May 1935.
H. C. Casserley

With a scream on the whistle, No. 746 *Pendragon* races through Yeovil Junction with the 'up' 'Atlantic Coast Express' on 21 May 1935.

H. C. Casserley

Rebuilt 'Battle of Britain' class 4-6-2 No. 34090 *Sir Eustace Missenden Southern Railway* runs into Yeovil Junction with the 9 am Waterloo–Exeter Central on 16 August 1964.

C. L. Caddy Collection

With the Yeovil Junction–Yeovil Town branch in the background 'King Arthur' class 4-6-0 No. 30449 *Sir Torre* heads away from the Junction towards Sherborne with an 'up' local train formed of a three set and a van in 1955.

C. L. Caddy Collection

YEOVIL JUNCTION EAST (1910)

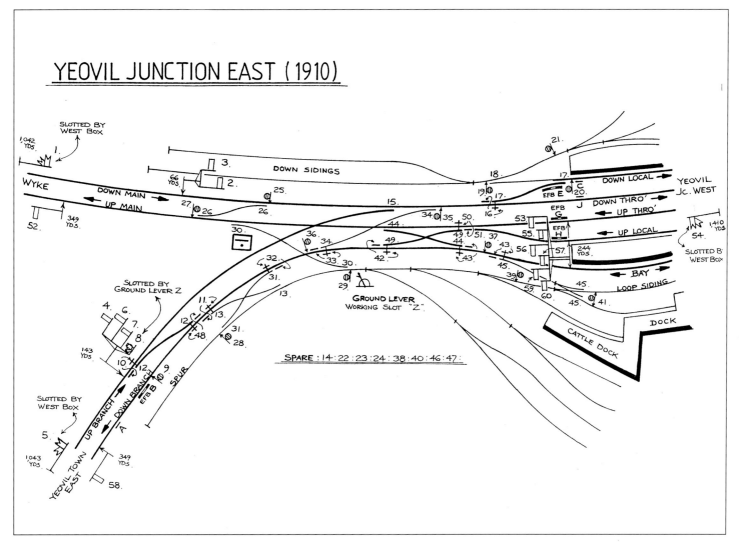

YEOVIL JUNCTION 'A' (1959)

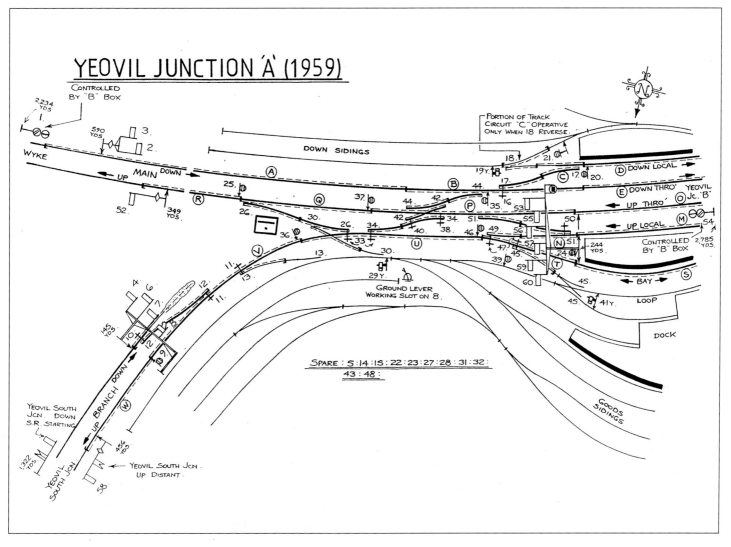

weeks later) of the L&SWR extension from Bradford Abbas Junction to Exeter. The B&E anticipating the arrival of the Salisbury & Yeovil, agreed to build a joint station (Yeovil Town) at the junction of the new line (S&Y) with the B&E branch from Hendford to the GWR station at Pen Mill. The Bristol & Exeter, whilst awaiting the completion of the new joint station laid an independent single ('narrow gauge') line from the site of the proposed station, for approximately one mile alongside the broad gauge branch (Hendford–Pen Mill). To accommodate the L&SWR at Hendford, the B&E also mixed the gauge in Hendford yard so that it could be used by the standard gauge South Western passenger and goods trains. The initial service at the outset was four trains from Salisbury, and five from Yeovil on weekdays, plus two each way on Sundays. The new joint station was opened a year later on 1 June, with both companies using the station from this date. Hendford was then relegated to goods traffic.

Just seven weeks after the arrival of the Salisbury & Yeovil Railway direct line to Yeovil (Hendford) the L&SWR extension westwards to Exeter from Yeovil Junction opened on 19 July as a single line. From the opening of the complete route the main line services (except for at least one service) now used Yeovil Junction instead of the temporary terminus at Hendford, running via the *easterly curve* at Bradford Abbas. The August 1860 *Bradshaw* discloses that a weekday service of four trains ran between Salisbury and Exeter (one on Sundays), with five eastbound services (two on Sundays), and at least one train each way ran via the original easterly curve and the Bradford Abbas cutting – Sherborne–Hendford–Yeovil Junction – and vice versa for eastbound trains. A connecting service ran between Yeovil Junction and Hendford until 1861 when they then ran to the new joint Town station. November 1860 shows a weekday service of

five 'down' trains – four of these starting from London, and one from Salisbury (5.55 am) and five 'up' services (one terminating at Salisbury). Sundays (November 1860) two services ran from Exeter to London – one 'down' train from London (9.15 am) and one service starting from Yeovil (Hendford) at 7.20 am stopping at all stations – arriving in Queen Street station at 9.30 am. A daily Yeovil to Torrington service started in 1872 and was worked by locomotives based at Yeovil Town shed. Locomotives used in 1872/3 included 'Volcano' class No. 84 *Styx* and 'Falcon' class No. 25 *Reindeer*, being joined by No. 91 *Spitfire* in 1875/6.

The whole route between Salisbury and Exeter was doubled by 1 July 1870 while the original Salisbury & Yeovil direct line through Bradford Abbas Junction had been closed on 1 January of the same year. Henceforth, trains from Salisbury to Yeovil Town and vice versa had to reverse at Yeovil Junction. The bridge which carried the original route over the GWR main line was not removed until 1937, and traces of the earthworks can still be identified today. In order to improve efficiency of exchanging goods between the L&SWR and the GWR at the congested goods depot at Hendford, the broad gauge, under the auspices of the GWR, arrived at Yeovil Junction with the opening on 13 June 1864 (under powers obtained on 25 May 1860) of a single-line goods branch known as the Clifton Maybank Siding. The goods only line branched off the GWR Weymouth main line at a junction situated between the bridge carrying the original Salisbury & Yeovil Railway direct line to Yeovil Town and Hendford, and the bridge carrying the L&SWR Salisbury–Exeter route over the GWR main line. The goods branch burrowed underneath the L&SWR main line curving and rising up a gradient of 1 in 85 before terminating in exchange sidings and a transhipment shed adjoining the L&SWR station at Yeovil Junction. A second spur, west of

'Merchant Navy' class 4-6-2 No. 35025 *Brocklebank Line* takes the through 'up' line to thunder past Yeovil Junction with the Eastbound 'Atlantic Coast Express' on 27 July 1964.

John Day

'Battle of Britain' class 4-6-2 No. 34070 *Manston* departs from Yeovil Junction and takes the Yeovil Town branch on 20 October 1963. The civil engineers' yard is to the right, and wagons of locomotive coal destined for Exmouth Junction stand on the 'down' sidings to the left.

Rodney Lissenden

Clifton Maybank Junction giving access from the Weymouth direction to the transfer sidings was authorised but the earthworks only were constructed. There was no physical connection between the two companies' tracks until the GWR gauge conversion in 1874. After the gauge conversion, transfer trips were worked by L&SWR and GWR locomotives. From 1900, prior to the First World War, a total of 1,500 freight wagons were exchanged monthly, the transfer taking place daily (except Sunday) at 10.30 am and 3.30 pm. The goods branch was closed on 7 June 1937 with the track being removed by December of the same year. After closure of the branch exchange traffic between the GWR and the SR reverted to travelling via Yeovil Town.

The initial cramped layout at Yeovil Junction, consisting of two island platforms under an overall roof, and the far from satisfactory buildings, with the main line services

using the outer faces and the Yeovil Town shuttle using a single line between the platforms, was drastically remodelled in 1908-9. An impressive layout was created at a cost to the L&SWR of £50,000 including the provision of two long island platforms. The 'up' platform, 600ft long by 37 ft wide, contained buildings in two blocks – the western end comprising stores, porters' room, station master's office, booking, telegraph and cloak room, booking hall, general waiting room, and bookstall. The eastern block contained, refreshment room, ladies' room, and gentlemen's lavatories. The 'down' platform, 520 ft long by 33 ft 9 in wide, had buildings consisting of a store room, guards' room, inspector's office, general waiting room, and gentlemen's lavatories. All of the new buildings were constructed in red brick with red-glazed tile abutements. Previously, all through trains were subjected to a 20 mph speed limit.

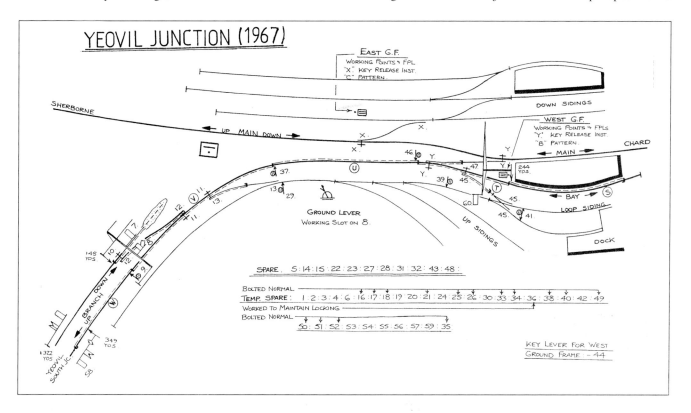

Steam drifts from the carriage steam heating pipes along the 'up' platform at Yeovil Junction on a murky 28 December 1963. 0-6-0 pannier tank No. 6435 stands on the left with the Yeovil Junction–Town station shuttle, to the right No. 35004 *Cunard White Star* takes water before departing with an 'up' working. Yours truly – fireman Derek Phillips – holds the pipe in the tender, whilst fireman Nigel Extance awaits my shout for him to turn off the water, meanwhile our respective drivers from Yeovil Town shed have a bit of a natter.

C. L. Caddy

Stopping trains now used the inner surfaces of the new platforms, whilst through traffic could use the centre tracks on the accelerated services to and from the West. The Yeovil Town shuttle trains used the outer face of the 'up' platform (No.1).

Several acres of land were purchased and added to the station yard on the 'up' side, with a large sandstone cliff being cut away, and new sidings laid. The old station buildings were swept away in the rebuilding. Other important alterations with regards to the signalling and pointwork were also implemented. Nearly two miles of sidings at Yeovil Junction were made up as follows: loading dock road, 134 yds; weighbridge and cattle loading road, 136 yds; goods shed road, 318 yds; No. 1 siding 353 yds; No. 2, 294 yds; No. 3, 326 yds; No. 4, 296 yds; No. 5, 259 yds and ballast train road, 182 yds. In the 'up' goods yard

there were cattle pens, loading dock, weighbridge, various workshops, and a small goods shed containing a 2 ton crane. On the 'down' side there were two sidings, 665 yds and 354 yds in length respectively. These were in addition to the GWR's three sidings, capable of holding 150 wagons and ran alongside the L&SWR 'down' yard. Staff at Yeovil Junction in 1909 consisted of Mr H. Barnes the station master, a booking clerk, seven goods guards, five brakesmen, two foremen, six signalmen, four shunters, and eleven other men. There were also two signal fitters, a gas fitter and three telegraph linemen. Two superb footbridges linking the two island platforms at their west and east ends were provided, the west end footbridge being covered. The refreshment room on the former 'up' platform is still in use today, and is in almost original condition, with tiled walls, and marble-topped counter. Here, a good pint of beer can

Drummond M7 0-4-4T No. 30129 heads the 11.43 am Yeovil Junction–Yeovil Town along the branch on 18 August 1962. The locomotive is approaching the Yeovil Junction 'up' branch advance starter which is coupled with the Yeovil South Junction 'up' branch 'distant' signal. The locomotive is on Yeovil Town Duty No. 517 worked by two sets of men – the first set on duty at 6.50am, with relief at 2.35 pm by the second set who booked on at 2.20 pm. The 'Branch' men made 22 return trips to the Junction between 7.22 am and 10 pm plus a couple of trips to the ex GWR station at Yeovil Pen Mill.

John Day

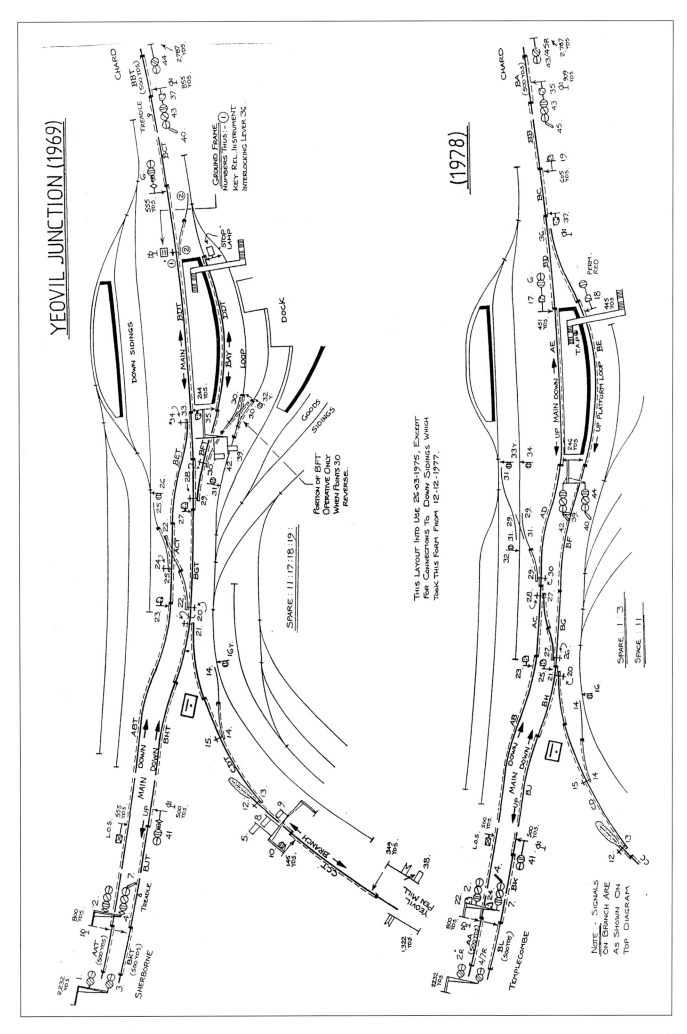

Yeovil Junction looking west on 6 March 1965 showing the 'down' platform to the left and the 'up' to the right, with the through tracks used by non stopping trains in the centre. 'B' signal box can be seen in the distance.

C. L. Caddy

quench the traveller's thirst just as much today as it could in the far-off days of its opening, and it is unique in the fact that it has been under private ownership since the beginning.

From 1875 two signal boxes controlled the station layout. The smaller West box was positioned alongside the 'up' main line west of the station with the larger, original East box, fronted by the 'down' sidings east of the platform. However, in the re-modelling of the station in 1908/9 the East box was abolished and replaced by an L&SWR Type 4A box in 1909. This was positioned approximately 300 yards from the station in the vee of the junction created by the main lines and the branch to Yeovil Town. The new box also received the suffix 'East'. From 18 December 1949 the East and West boxes received the suffix 'A' and 'B' respectively. 'B' signal box closed on 30 April 1967. The former 'A' box is still in use today and is the only working L&SWR signal box on the route although it has been somewhat 'Westernised' in recent years. GWR style

windows and a WR lever frame were fitted when refurbished in 1967 (see Signalling and Signal Boxes).

Incidentally, Yeovil Junction box now controls the only semaphores to be seen anywhere between London and Exeter, although they only apply to the Yeovil Pen Mill branch as all main line signals are colour lights. The neighbouring Pen Mill is even more traditional and retains a full set of lower quadrant semaphores.

The branch to Yeovil Town is synonimous with the Drummond M7 0-4-4 tank engines that plied to and fro on the shuttle from Yeovil Town, meeting the main line stopping trains at the Junction. The locomotive was always positioned at the Yeovil Town end of its two-coach auto-set. The turntable at the 'down' side of the layout is still in situ, and was in use by steam locomotives for the first time in many years when steam specials started using the route in 1986. During the steam era some main line services started and terminated at Yeovil Town, and the 1932 working

Push-and-pull set No. 351 approaches the branch platform at Yeovil Junction with the connecting service from Yeovil Town during the 1930s. Note the superb six-arm gantry seen here bearing L&SWR lower quadrants – the largest signal gantry between Salisbury and Exeter. The GWR Clifton Maybank goods line can be seen curving away to the far right – complete with a GWR lower quadrant signal.

Lens of Sutton

Yeovil Junction (former East) signal box pictured here on 14 May 1972, stands in the fork created by the Salisbury–Exeter main line and nowadays the branch to Pen Mill (formerly the branch to Yeovil Town). The box lost its suffix 'A' when the 'B' (former West) box closed in 1967.

C. L. Caddy

timetable shows the following weekday passenger trains to and from the joint station: 1.50 am passenger and mail from Eastleigh, 3.15 am news and mail from Salisbury, 6.25am to Ilfracombe, 6.45 am to Templecombe, 7 am to Waterloo, 7.37 am to Salisbury, 7.14 am from Templecombe, 7.46 am to Exeter, 12.52 pm from Salisbury, 1.28 pm from Exeter, 2.30 pm to Salisbury, 4.05 pm to Salisbury. 8.44 pm from Templecombe. Eastbound trains started tender first from Yeovil Town and ran around their trains at Yeovil Junction after arrival at platform one. Water columns were positioned on the 'up' and 'down' platforms and alongside the turntable road. The turntable itself was used quite extensively over a 24-hour period, with many light engine movements to and from the locomotive shed at Yeovil Town. Some locomotives, after detaching from their respective trains,

stayed at the Junction station after turning and taking water. A pit was provided for servicing and it was the responsibility of Yeovil Town shed to clear the clinker and smokebox ash from the turntable road. As well as an engine change-over point footplate crews were also exchanged here on the engines that were working through.

At times when the WR West of England main line was blocked, trains would be diverted from Yeovil Pen Mill to Yeovil Junction and Exeter using the wartime connection at Yeovil South Junction, and members of the 'Hall' class among others, would steam down the Southern main line with a pilotman aboard. Usually, Yeovil Town drivers were conscripted as pilotmen for trains heading west, and Exmouth Junction men vice versa. The WR drivers would gladly hand over the controls as soon as they left Pen Mill,

Standard Class 4MT 4-6-0 No. 75000 stands on to the turntable at Yeovil Junction in 1963. This was a 'foreign' engine easily distinguishable with its Western Region pattern lamp brackets. Nowadays when a locomotive from one of the steam specials that regularly use the route, trundles on to the turntable it is watched by a myriad of photographers. Yet I can remember using the turntable many times and not seeing a single photographer, although to be fair, most of the turning took place in the dead of night!

C. L. Caddy Collection

A unique sight at Yeovil Junction on 7 February 1965 as Class 1400 0-4-2Ts Nos 1442 and 1450 (now preserved) are turned together. The locomotives, en route from Yeovil Town to Exmouth Junction for service on the Seaton branch due to a diesel shortage, arrived from Yeovil Town bunker first and the chance was taken to turn them together before departure for Exmouth Junction.

C. L. Caddy Collection

'West Country' class No. 34023 *Blackmore Vale* lifts her safety valves impatiently whilst awaiting the 'right away' with an Exeter bound train at Yeovil Junction on 17 May 1964.

Barry Eagles

Class 50 No. 50048 *Dauntless* sets forth from Yeovil Junction with the 09.10 Waterloo–Exeter St Davids on 28 December 1986.

C. L. Caddy

With the 'up' bay to 'up' main starter raised, 'West Country' class 4-6-2 No. 34091 *Weymouth* (70E) sets forth from Yeovil Junction with the 11.50 am Yeovil Town–Salisbury on 20 October 1963.

Rodney Lissenden

or Exeter Central on the eastbound journey, as they had no idea where they were, which for them was uncharted territory! The connection at Yeovil South Junction still exists, albeit in a much simplified form, as a direct single line between the Junction and Pen Mill stations. It is used sparingly but still comes into its own when the West of England main line is closed – with High Speed Trains travelling over the old L&SWR route to and from Exeter. At other times, when the line is closed between Yeovil Junction and Salisbury, trains use the diversionary route – Yeovil Junction–Pen Mill–Castle Cary–Westbury–Salisbury.

As mentioned previously, the Drummond M7 0-4-4 tank locomotives were the prime motive power used on the push-and-pull shuttle services between the Town and Junction stations. This was Yeovil Town Duty No. 517, with the first crew booking on at 6.50 am. The engine was prepared for them, and they would pull out of the loco yard at 7.5 am, and then be coupled to the auto-set by the station shunter, and depart with the first trip of the day (7.22am) to the Junction to meet the 6.30 am Exeter–Waterloo. This was the first of many trips between the stations (including one to Pen Mill)

before being relieved by the late shift crew who booked on at 2.20 pm and relieved the early crew at 2.35 pm. The locomotive took water at Yeovil Junction at various times of the day, and would pop in to the loco at the Town station for a tub of coal between 12.54 and 1.40 pm. In my firing days the regular M7s included Nos 30129 and 30131 but other members of the class appeared on loan when the two regulars were away at Eastleigh for overhaul. O2 class 0-4-4 tanks were used now and again, but they were not as popular with the footplate crews as the M7s. The M7 tanks and their auto-sets were replaced by what, in my personal working experience were the dreadful and inferior, WR pannier tanks and Hawksworth push-and-pull trailers. The steam locomotive shuttle working between the Town and Junction stations came to an end on 4 January 1965 – when it was replaced by WR diesel rail-buses which had been made available by the closure of the Kemble–Cirencester branch in April 1964.

The branch service to Yeovil Town was withdrawn on 2 October 1966 and from that date the service ran between the former GWR station at Yeovil Pen Mill and Yeovil Junction

Yeovil Junction looking east on 3 March 1968, showing the track rationalization with the former 'down' lines to the right, now out of use as through tracks. The former 'up' through line has been lifted and the magnificent footbridge has yet to be cut back.

C. L. Caddy Collection

The evening shadows lengthen as 'West Country' class 4-6-2 No. 34092 *City of Wells* (now preserved) heads west between Yeovil Junction and Sutton Bingham with a 'down' freight train on 24 August 1962.

John Day

and was operated by a single unit 'Bubble-car'. It is interesting to note that this was the only *regular* booked service train to use the wartime Yeovil South Junction connection since its opening on 13 October 1943. The Pen Mill–Junction shuttle service survived until 4 May 1968.

A service was provided by the WR in the 1965 summer season – following the withdrawal in September 1964 of all services west of Exeter from Waterloo. A through Saturday service normally worked by a 'Hymek' diesel locomotive was provided from Paddington to Ilfracombe via Castle Cary, Yeovil Pen Mill, Yeovil Junction, Exeter Central and Exeter St. Davids – thus avoiding reversal at St. Davids. However, this working was not perpetuated by the Western Region after the 1965 season. The Yeovil Town branch (from Yeovil South Junction) was closed and taken out of use on 1 March 1967, and South Junction signal box was closed a year later on 26 May, the ex GWR Weymouth main line being singled at the same time. The connection to Yeovil Junction (from Pen Mill) was also singled from the same date. Today, trains between Pen Mill and Yeovil Junction are worked under the electric key token. Only the former 'up' platform at Yeovil Junction is now in use by passenger trains, with direct access from the westerly direction to Platform 1 via new pointwork being possible from 26 March 1975. Prior to that date, after the singling of the line, both 'up' and 'down' services used Platform 2. Nowadays all 'down' trains use the inside face of the island platform (No. 2). Both lines are signalled for reversible working. The former 'down' platform stands unused and shorn of its canopy, and the footbridge which once spanned the through and local tracks stands gaunt and truncated, serving the main platform only. A second footbridge, which spanned the tracks at the eastern end of the platforms, was removed in 1920 and reinstated at Overton station (Hants) and is still in use today. The former 'down' local and through tracks are now no more than sidings, used by the occasional engineers train – or the steam specials. Access is gained from points at the east end of the layout. The double-track section from Templecombe ends here, with single track onwards to Chard Junction. The whole station area has a melancholy air about

it today, as if it is waiting for a ghostly 'Atlantic Coast Express' to whistle through with a panting Bulleid at the head – the L&SWR buildings seeming at odds with the colour light signals and other modern items such as the dreadful, modern red-painted seating which now abounds at stations along the route.

Footplate comments

Of course, with my home shed at Yeovil Town – just down the line from the Junction station – I have many memories of this once important station. Trundling to and fro with light engines, changing over with other crews, etc., and heading east or west, shunting the two yards, or working on the shuttle train itself, was just part of the job. Much of our work at the shed I have previously mentioned in my book *Working Yeovil Steam*. I well remember one of my first trips on the main line as a young fireman after previously passing my firing test and exam with the Locomotive Inspector, Sam Smith. The job this day would be to book on at Yeovil Town, our engine which was one of the superb U class 2-6-0 Moguls (nicknamed 'Rivers' after the original tank engines, one of which was involved in the fatal accident near Sevenoaks in 1927) would be all ready and prepared for us.

After booking on and collecting my diddy box and tea can from my locker I enter the enginemen's cabin. This adjoins the shed office and, like all cabins in all steam sheds up and down the country, is the place where you meet your mates and have a chat or a mug of tea from the ever boiling kettle. There are other crews sitting at the tables, having either just booked on or off, or awaiting their next turn of duty. My driver, Arthur Hardwicke, comes in and this is the time to walk over to our engine. And there, standing on one of the shed roads, is one of the Yeovil-based 'Rivers'. Her coat of black paint is gleaming in the summer sunshine and the safety valves are lifting with the force of 200lbs per square inch as she waits impatiently to head for the main line. We climb aboard and stow our kit away in lockers. Although the engine has been prepared for us before leaving we have some checking to do. I check that the safety equipment is there, detonators, red and green flags, spare glass tubes for the boiler gauge glasses, and ensure there is a full complement of head lamps, complete with the movable red shades, bucket and small hand brush, firing shovel and the fire irons. Now a touch on the blower, open the firedoors and check they are working, turn on the lubricator and adjust the oil drips through the sight feeds, open the dampers and, armed with a spanner, check that the smokebox door is shut tight and the tail lamp is on the bufferbeam as we will be travelling tender first to the Junction, so now is a good time to give the coal a soaking with the pep pipe. Meanwhile, Arthur has been busy checking the vacuum brake, the valve gear and the sanding gear. Finally he checks his pocket watch and we are now ready.

The exit from the shed roads is controlled by a ringed lower quadrant signal which is normally at clear but returns to danger during movements in the station area, or when an engine returns to the shed. This signal is protected by catch points, and all signals are controlled by the Yeovil Town signal box at the end of the western platform. I release the tender handbrake, my mate opens the small and large ejectors and the twin arrows on the vacuum gauge rise to the regulation 21 inches and his hand lifts to the whistle cord to give a long blast. He spins the reverser into full forward gear, I check that no engines are moving near us, he opens the regulator and we move forward with steam roaring from the open cylinder cocks. The noise from the cylinders stops as the drain lever is closed. We rumble out of the shed yard, under the footbridge and stop just beyond the ground signals which control our exit through the station. The layout at the Town station is such that the signalman can send us on any one of the three tracks through the station to gain access to the Junction branch. This is especially useful during the station's busy periods.

The shed signal slams to danger with a 'bang' behind us. My mate spins the reverser into reverse gear, the points move behind us and the ground signal turns clear. In the distance the platform starter drops, the regulator is opened and we gather speed towards the station. Arthur notches up the reverser as we pass the branch tank which is busy getting up steam ready to follow us. We give a sharp blast on the whistle as we approach the barrow crossing and thunder under the road bridge. The engine lurches to the left as we run over the points. Just in front of us the Town advanced starter and the South Junction distant are showing clear, and we rumble over the bridge which carries us over the River Yeo. On the footplate the dust starts to fly about as the engine vibrates, the water bounces up and down in the gauge glasses and the firedoors rattle with the beat of the engine. Behind us our steamy exhaust trails into the distance as we approach Yeovil South Junction, the squat wartime signal box with its bomb-proof flat roof appearing on our right. This box is normally switched out, being brought into use on occasions to stop the equipment falling into disuse, and more importantly, when the Western Region West of England main line is closed through a blockage and WR trains are diverted to Exeter via Yeovil Junction. The ex GWR Weymouth main line runs alongside us here as we pass the many signals controlling the wartime connection. We are nearing Yeovil Junction, the signal box appears and we slow whilst approaching the gantry guarding our exit from the branch. The signal clearing us for entry into the branch bay is 'off' on the gantry and we rumble over the points and crossings and come to a halt at the branch platform. The second signal from the left, on the main line gantry, 'clears' and we pull onto the main line and stop alongside the signal box. After turning on the injector to keep the engine quiet and not annoy the signalman(!) I climb down and remove the tail-lamp from the front bufferbeam, the white disc codes are already in position for our main line trip

to Salisbury. Back on the footplate it is now time to give the fire a good stir up with the pricker. My mate gives some last minute attention to the trimmings in their brass boxes, I draw the pricker out of the firebox and place it on the tender and put a few rounds of coal on the fire. The 'Rivers' liked a low fire down the front and well packed under the door. I swill the footplate down with the pep pipe before turning off the injector.

There is a rumble, and the branch train appears off the Town branch propelled by its M7 Drummond tank engine, the Westinghouse pump panting away keeping the air pressure up for the driver's controls at the driving trailer end. Behind us the squat shape of a 'West Country' appears with its train of dark green coaches and stops at the platform, the fireman jumps down and uncouples, and the engine rumbles away down the Town branch towards the shed. The ground signal clears behind us and we reverse towards our waiting train. Timing on the Southern Region was very strict, and just as we buffer up to our coaches the starting signal clears on the gantry. I jump down and lift the coupling off its hook on the tender and swing it over the coach hook, screw it tight, and connect the vacuum pipes. As it was summer time, no steam heating was needed, (steam heating pipes were a devil to get off sometimes, and more than once a coal pick was needed to prise them apart). The U and N class engines were unique in that they were right-hand driven, unlike the rest of the Southern locomotives which were left-hand driven, so this means that all of the stations we arrive at (except Salisbury) will be on my side of the footplate. I climb back onto the engine and cross to my side of the footplate, the steam gauge is right on the mark – just below the red line. The shrill sound of the guard's whistle echoes along the platform, Arthur opens the regulator, the engine moves slowly forward and our pace quickens as the regulator is opened wider. The exhaust beat becomes softer as the reverser is notched back, we roll past the signal box and over the bridge carrying us over the ex GWR Weymouth main line. The 'up' advanced starter gives us a clear road. Time to put a few rounds of coal around the firebox and shut the firedoor as we pound over Wyke Crossing, our train of dark green coaches swaying along behind us. The engine is alive and vibrating with power, the pounding beat from the chimney, the heat on the footplate, and the gauges quivering in their brass cases; the sensation of power in its finest form.

Sutton Bingham

This small way-side station, although opened with the line, did not have the extravagant station buildings associated with other locations on the Exeter Extension. The small and pleasant station buildings, complete with canopy, occupied the 'up' platform. The platform-mounted signal box was sited on the 'down' side for siting purposes due to the curvature of the track from the West. A small shelter and canopy were also provided on this platform. Three small sidings were provided east of the station alongside the 'up' main line. In the 1950s a large reservoir was created near the station, and today this is a well-known beauty spot, popular with fishermen, boating enthusiasts and picnickers. A small and beautiful Norman church, complete with an early wall-painting, and half hidden in a wood awaits the visitor, is just a few minutes walk from the station site.

The 1910 *Bradshaw* shows a lavish weekday service of nine 'down' and seven 'up' passenger trains serving the station. By the final year of the station (1962) this had been reduced to six 'down' and five 'up' trains. All freight traffic for the station was circulated via Crewkerne – delivered and collected by 'up' goods services – and the 1932 working timetable discloses that the 4.4 am from Exeter Central, and

With the reservoir in the background – Sutton Bingham looking west on 16 July 1958 – viewed from the 'up' sidings looking across to the signal box and platform shelter on the 'down' platform. Note the superb upper quadrant semaphore with its tall lattice post for ease of sighting as 'up' trains approach on the curving main line. The station was closed to goods traffic on 4 April 1960.

H. C. Casserley

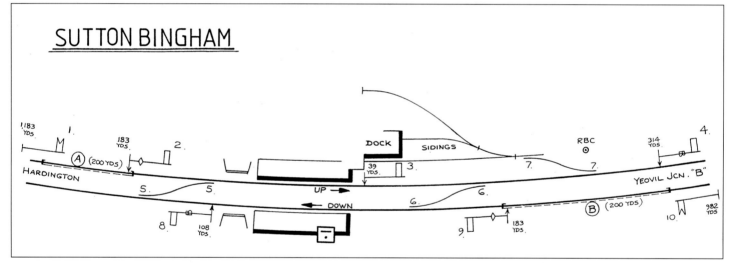

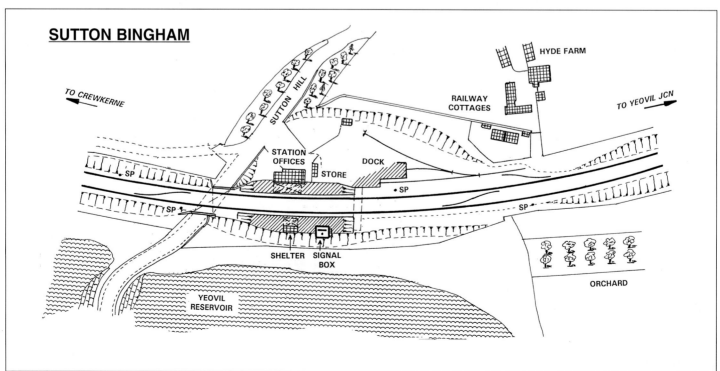

Sutton Bingham looking west in 1959. The 'down' platform isto the left with its typical L&SWR signal box and waiting shelter. The main station buildings are situated on the 'up' platform to the right. The station became an unstaffed halt on 1 August 1960, and closed to passenger traffic on 31 December 1962, the signal box lingering on until 14 February 1965.

C. L. Caddy

the 4.49 pm from Chard Junction were booked to pick up and set down wagons here. Crossover roads were positioned 146 yards from the box on the Yeovil Junction side, and a new crossover road came into operation on 6 January 1904 – 124 yards from the box on the Crewkerne side. However, retraction came in the 1950s when the east crossover was disconnected in 1955, followed by the disconnection of the west crossover the following year. Closure to goods traffic

came on 4 April 1960 and the station became an unstaffed halt from 1 August the same year. The pointwork into the sidings was abolished on 31 July 1961, with the station closing on 31 December 1962, but the signal box soldiered on until 1965 with the arms and lamps of the running signals being removed on 14 February. The box was abolished on 6 May of the same year. Only a few remnants of the former 'up' platform remain today.

The signal box at Sutton Bingham viewed here on 10 April 1965 closed on the previous 14 February.

C. L. Caddy

HARDINGTON (1900)

(1910)

SIDINGS ADDED 08-01-1909.

Footplate comments

Even in my firing days – during the 1950s – the name of Dugald Drummond, the autocratic Locomotive Superintendent of the L&SWR was still spoken with a kind of reverence amongst the older drivers. Many tales, which had been handed down over the years, were told over and over again in the locomotive cabins, but of course, these had become much embroidered with countless re-telling, but this is what is said to have happened one day in 1908 . . . On 10 June an 'up' West of England express headed by T9 No. 708 was running approximately 13 minutes late, and it so happened (unfortunately for the enginemen concerned) that Dugald Drummond was on the route that day, travelling westwards in his combined saloon/locomotive, known officially as 'Mr Drummond's Car', but known to the staff as *The Bug*. Drummond knew that the express was adrift timewise, and he was looking out of the saloon window to catch sight of the culprit. However, the express was seen approaching and not doing too well by all accounts, and not surprisingly – for as it approached the *Bug* near Sutton Bingham the smoke-box door was seen to be unclipped, opening and closing with the momentum of the locomotive. To say that Drummond was unhappy at that moment would be an understatement! He had his driver stop the *Bug* at Sutton Bingham, and after a discussion with the astonished signalman, he had the *Bug* crossed over to the 'up' line and set off back to Yeovil Junction in pursuit of the errant express. Apparently, No. 708 was in the process of being replaced by another locomotive at the moment Drummond arrived. One can imagine the horrified expressions of the locomotive men when Drummond appeared! To say that, at that moment, the erstwhile Locomotive Superintendent's fuse was lit, and shrieking skywards would be a very fair comment. Apparently, the bollocking that the footplatemen received on No. 708 was out of this world and became legendary amongst the locomotive shed's gossip. The upshot of it all being, that No. 708 was placed back upon its train, the smokebox door was securely clipped (as it should have been in the first place) and the train left for Waterloo with

Drummond, and the fireman of the *Bug* in charge of the T9. At a later hearing with Drummond the driver of the express was fined £6 and reduced to shunting turns, and the fireman fined £4 with a severe warning to boot. What a great pity we do not have a few Drummonds about today to shake a few people about!

Hardington Signal Box and Siding

Located 3 miles 150 yards West of Sutton Bingham, Hardington signal box was positioned alongside the 'up' main line. The box frame was extended in 1909 with three sidings (one serving a milk dock) being brought into use from 8 January of the same year. There being no crossover roads meant that all shunting was done by 'up' goods services with Crewkerne being the station in charge of working wagons to and from the sidings. Coal and stores for the box were delivered via the 10.15 pm freight from Plymouth Friary. Freight facilities were withdrawn from 7 February 1937. The box lingered on until closure in 1959 and nothing remains at this lonely location today, but traces of the railway land are still identifiable.

Crewkerne

The station which opened with the Exeter Extension line, is approximately one mile from the pleasant town of Crewkerne which has been a place of importance since before the Norman Conquest. Captain Hardy (Nelson's Flag Captain on HMS *Victory*) was a pupil at the famous grammar school founded in 1499. The good-sized Tite style buildings dominate the former 'up' platform to this day, a large brick-built shelter being provided on the 'down' platform in better days. A wooden 12-lever signal box which stood at the Yeovil end of the 'up' platform was superseded by a brick-built BR(S) Type 16 (24-lever) box on 6 November 1960. The new box was situated east of the 'up' platform. Considerable shunting was done here, with a locomotive stopping en route from Yeovil Junction to Chard Junction and return with a pick-up goods twice a day. The main shunting yard was on the 'up' side of the layout with

CREWKERNE

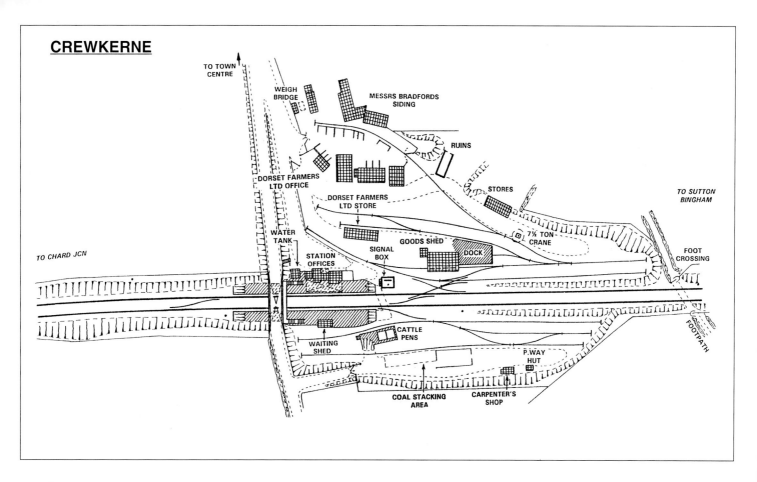

its goods shed complete with 40 cwt crane. Various traders' sidings and a 10 ton crane, and, at one time, a total of five 13 ft 2 in wagon turntables were provided in the 'up' yard. Horse power was also used here until the 1930s. Sidings were also provided on the 'down' side of the station, including one for the coal traders. Cattle vans were a common sight here, used to transport calves to Maude in Scotland, travelling north via Templecombe and the S&D.

Crewkerne looking east in 1930 with the 'down' platform and waiting shelter in the foreground. Advertisements for VIM and a Southern Railway poster extolling the virtues of Ramsgate adorn the end wall of the waiting shelter. The grand structure of the main station building can be seen to the left with its attendant L&SWR signal box on the 'up' platform. The goods shed stands in the background beside an L&SWR lower quadrant signal.

Brunel University: Mowat Collection

'Battle of Britain' class No. 34109 *Sir Trafford Leigh-Mallory* arrives at Crewkerne with the 3.20 pm Exeter–Templecombe on 6 September 1959. The train is conveying through coaches for Waterloo which will be attached to the 4.30 pm Exeter–Waterloo at Templecombe. The wooden 12-lever signal box on the platform was replaced by a new 24-lever box on 6 November 1960.

Derek Phillips Collection

Standard Class 4MT 2-6-0 No. 76009 shunts the 'up' yard at Crewkerne in 1958. This duty was worked by Yeovil Town (72C) crews and known as the 'Chard Shunter'. This was part of Salisbury Duty No. 478 worked by one Yeovil and two Salisbury crews. The early turn shunter (seen here) worked to Chard Junction from Yeovil Junction with a pick-up goods shunting there and at Crewkerne. The afternoon 'Chard Shunter', part of Salisbury Duty No. 479 would trundle a return pick-up goods from Yeovil Junction to Axminster, shunting at Crewkerne and Chard Junction en route. Shunting at Crewkerne was very heavy especially in the 'up' yard. It was not unusual for the fireman to have a go at driving so as to relieve the driver from the continual turning of the wheeled reverser fitted to this class of engine, which was not conducive for continous shunting.

John Day

A spectacular accident occurred on 24 April 1953 when No. 35020 *Bibby Line* broke a crank axle whilst speeding through with the 4.30 pm Exeter Central–Waterloo at over 70 mph. Fortunately no fatalities occurred in what could have been a very serious accident. One of the locomotive's brake blocks hit and demolished one of the cast-iron stanchions, bringing down part of the platform canopy, and another brake block hit one of the bridge abutments some ³⁄₄ mile of trackwork was damaged in the incident. Emergency single line working was set up between Chard Junction and Sutton Bingham, and the passengers from the stricken train were carried forward by the 4.35 pm stopper from Exeter which arrived at Crewkerne at 7.15 pm (due in at 6.10 pm). Normal double-line working was resumed at 9 am the following day. All 30 members of the 'Merchant Navy' class were temporarily withdrawn after the accident, and seven of the locomotives were found to have defective axles. This incident brought about an engine crisis for the Southern Region which was solved by the Western and London Midland Regions supplying 'Britannia' class 4-6-2s, and the North Eastern Region loaning six of Gresley's V2 class 2-6-2s until the Bulleid Pacifics were up and running again.

Freight facilities were withdrawn on 18 April 1966 and the signal box closed on 26 February the following year. Since the singling of the main line all trains have used the former 'up' platform which was lengthened in 1992 in readiness for the new South West Trains 'Turbo' units. Having had a spruce-up in recent years the Tite station buildings look quite grand – reflecting the elegant architecture of a by-gone age. The signal box, closed since 1967, is still standing. But, perhaps the greatest surprise of all, especially for students of railway history, is that apart from the removal of the rails, the goods shed, goods office, provender buildings, etc., in the former 'up' goods yard are still extant and in use under private ownership. The former 'down' platform is still in place and the 'down' yard is now used by a coal merchant. The replacement portion of the canopy on the former 'up' platform, brought down in the *Bibby Line* accident of 1953, is still recognisable today.

Footplate comments

Like many of my former comrades from Yeovil Town shed I have had my fair share of shunting at Crewkerne, especially in the sugar-beet season when wagon load after wagon load would be despatched. Many drivers would soon tire of the monotonous shunting in the 'up' yard and let the fireman have a go, whilst he (the driver) would sit on the fireman's seat, puff on a cigarette and read a newspaper (usually the fireman's!) and put a bit of coal around the firebox now and again. The problem was that the Standard Class 4MT 2-6-0s

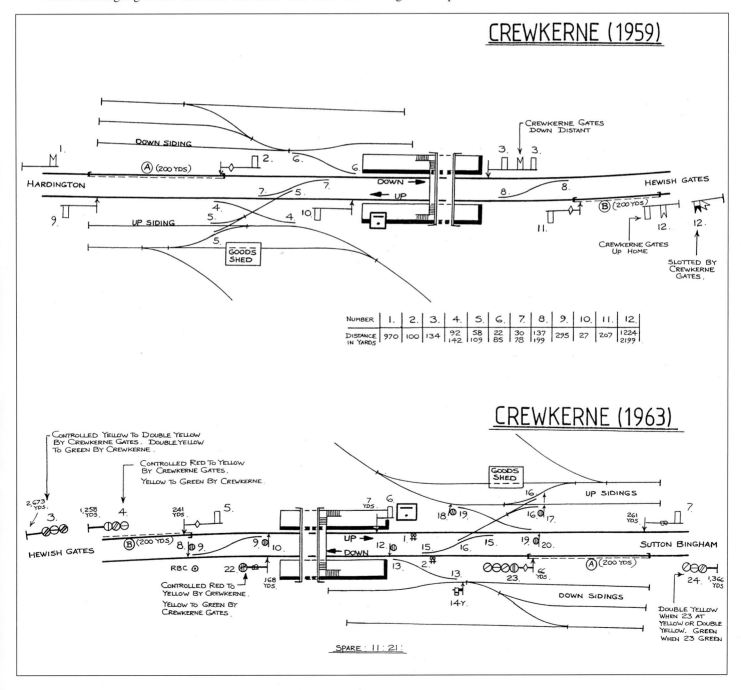

CREWKERNE (1959)

NUMBER	1.	2.	3.	4.	5.	6.	7.	8.	9.	10.	11.	12.
DISTANCE IN YARDS	970	100	134	92 142	58 109	22 85	30 78	137 199	295	27	207	1224 2199

CREWKERNE (1963)

SPARE : 11 : 21 :

Crewkerne 'up' goods yard looking towards the goods shed and station in 1958. Shunting was very heavy in this yard with the various traders, including Messrs Bradfords. A horse box can be seen to the left, a type of vehicle which was abundant at this location as they were used for transporting calves to Maud in Scotland via Templecombe and the Somerset & Dorset line. Sugar beet, when in season, was exported by rail from Crewkerne.

John Day

Crewkerne looking east on 3 April 1965 showing the new 24-lever signal box brought into use on 6 November 1960 replacing the wooden platform-mounted L&SWR box. The gradient can be seen descending away in the background towards Hardington. A multiple aspect colour light signal can be seen alongside the 'down' main line in the distance.

C. L. Caddy

used on the shunting had the 'mangle-wheel' type of reverser – quite useless and arm aching for continuous shunting. The knack at Crewkerne, especially in the 'up' yard, was to run up to the blocks with a raft of wagons then brake, thus compressing the buffers, allowing the shunter to cut out – then let the engine run back down the gradient whilst winding the reverser back – and keeping an eye on the shunter at the same time. Easy wasn't it? I don't think so – especially if it was pouring down with rain, with clouds of steam enveloping the engine from the steam brake fitted to this type of locomotive.

Crewkerne Gates
The level crossing located ½ mile west of Crewkerne station had its traditional wooden gates replaced by automatic half-barriers in November 1967. Coal and stores for the box when needed, were delivered via the 9.50 am freight from Yeovil Junction. An accident occurred to the gates on 5 June 1863 . . . "On Friday morning an accident which might have been serious, occurred at the level crossing between the tunnel and the Crewkerne Station. There is a steep descent between that interval and the engine whistle is always blown, in order to warn the gate-keeper. It seems, that on the morning in question the clock at the gate-house was seven minutes slow, and that the gate-keeper, thinking there were seven minutes to spare for the approach of the nine o'clock train, went to the bottom of the hill – a distance of about 100 yards – for water, leaving the gates shut across the line and the signal near the mouth of the tunnel set for "caution". To his horror, while engaged in filling his pitcher, the sound of the whistle fell upon his ears. He immediately endeavoured to reach the gate, but, being crippled, with a wooden leg his speed was not rapid, and before he had proceeded, the train came dashing by, taking the gate from its hinges and carrying it along – the wheels snapping and crunching it into fragments. The train was stopped after having thus proceeded some 200 or 300 yards, and fortunately no further hurt was done than the destruction of the gate . . ." *Nowlens Weekly Chronicle*, 6 June 1863.

Crewkerne Tunnel to Pinhoe

Crewkerne Tunnel

The 1 in 80 three-mile long climb for westbound trains culminates at the east end of the 206-yard long tunnel, located one mile west of Crewkerne station. The tunnel was a formidable challenge for locomotives and footplatemen in steam days.

Footplate comments

The 1 in 80 climb starts almost from Hardington (east of Crewkerne). Let me take you back over the years and put you, the reader, on the footplate of an S15 with a heavy Exeter bound freight train. Our train consists of coal, petrol, timber, covered vans, etc. The first half a dozen or so vans from the engine are coupled to the vacuum to give us a bit more breaking power. With some 45 to 50 wagons behind us, rumbling and swaying along, we have rattled past Sutton Bingham and down the bank to Hardington Marsh. My mate has the regulator cracked half way open as the weight of our train will do the pushing. Up ahead of us the track is as straight as an arrow, with the outline of the station in the far

With the Crewkerne Gates 'up' distant signal in the 'off' position H15 class 4-6-0 No. E332 (rebuilt Drummond F13 class) is about to enter the dark confines of Crewkerne Tunnel with an 'up' express from Exeter on 2 August 1928.

H. C. Casserley

Drummond L11 class 4-4-0 No. E154 plods out of Crewkerne Tunnel on 2 August 1928 with a 'down' goods train.

H. C. Casserley

distance and the track can also be seen rising as the incline begins. On the footplate the fire is stacked under the firedoor burning and dancing away, the boiler gauges show about three parts of a boiler full, with the water dancing up and down in the glass tubes. A shovelful of coal lies ready on the tender flap, my mate is leaning out of the cab, smoking his old pipe. He opens the regulator to its widest extent as our train starts to slow as we hit into the bank. The locomotive vibrates with the massive forces at work in her cylinders, steam erupts from our chimney and a quick glance into the firebox shows me where the coal has to go. Up with the shovel, turn, swing and into the right-hand back corner of the firebox, then a shovelful into the left corner, then a couple under the door. My mate has his hand on the firedoor handle, and as he senses me turning from the tender, he will open the door, and then immediately close it as I turn back towards the tender; don't forget he is looking out towards the front at all times. A loud ring on the AWS bell from the Crewkerne distant signal echoes around the cab, the reverser is moved forward even more, making our exhaust note deeper and heavier. Again and again the firebox is tended to. Steam and smoke beat down everywhere, the heat from the firebox is breathtaking, and I turn the injector on as the water is coming down the glass. There is time to spray the tender and footplate down with the pep pipe whilst the injector is on, then turn the injector off and put a few rounds of coal around the firebox. We are now approaching Crewkerne station, another ring on the AWS bell – this time it's the Crewkerne Gates distant – and as we plod through the station to the worst part of the bank our S15 is thumping away like a good 'un'. We beat around the curves and thunder over Crewkerne Gates level crossing, the steam pressure gauge should be showing ample steam requirements for our approach to the summit as we are now almost at a walking pace. Every part of our engine is alive and pulsating with power, and with the regulator and reverser wide open we are now cracking towards the tunnel and our exhaust beats muffle as the cutting encroaches upon us. The dark gaping mouth of the tunnel appears ahead of us, no more firing now as we have ample fire in the box, turn on the injector to keep the boiler topped up for the run down to Chard Junction and, with a loud blast on the whistle, we thump into the tunnel. The roof of the tunnel is lit up by the glare from our firebox and steam beats back down from the roof onto the footplate making breathing difficult. Sparks and cinders shower down, the noise is indescribable, made even worse by the scream of an 'up' train dashing past, with the glare from the carriage lights reflecting against our wagons. Our exhaust beat softens as we exit from the tunnel and climb the last few yards before running down the bank towards Chard Junction. The regulator and reverser are eased back. Time now for the fireman to light up a cigarette and cool off, but not for long as the next climb, which will be the worst, is from Axminster to Honiton.

Hewish Gates

Situated 2 miles 1,579 yards from Crewkerne, the signal box was sited alongside the 'up' main line on the Chard Junction side of the level crossing. A public siding off the 'down' main line operated by a ground-frame came into use in April 1900. The siding was shunted by westbound goods trains only – and the 1934 Southern Railway Western Appendices state – 'A competent man from Crewkerne accompanies train doing work at siding'.

During the Second World War a substantial 'down' loop was provided and was brought into use on 4 October 1942, the original (1900) siding was shortened for the new trackwork and altered so that the entrance of the siding, worked by a ground-frame ran from the new loop. The signal box lever frame was also extended for the new loop

A T9 in full cry – No. E284 runs down the bank at Hewish with a 'down' holiday relief on 2 August 1928.

H. C. Casserley

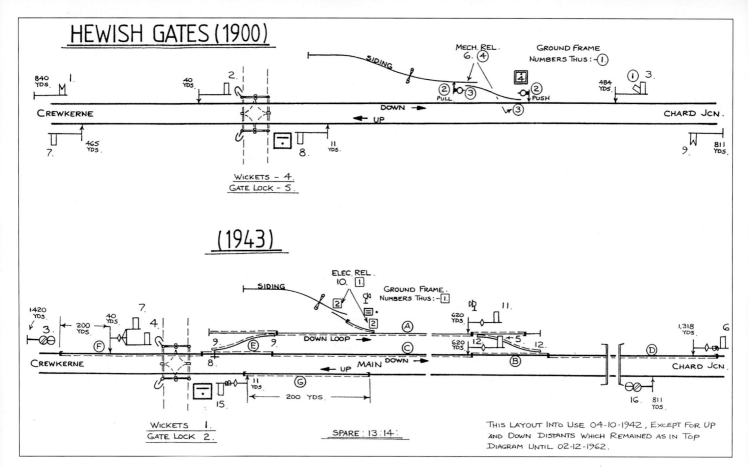

HEWISH GATES (1900)

GROUND FRAME
NUMBERS THUS :- ①

MECH. REL.
6. ④

SIDING

PULL
② ③

PUSH
② ③

④

40
YDS.

2.

840
YDS.
M
1.

DOWN

UP

484
YDS.

① 3.

CREWKERNE

CHARD JCN.

7.

465
YDS.

8.

11
YDS.

9.

811
YDS.

WICKETS - 4.
GATE LOCK - 5.

(1943)

ELEC. REL.
10. ①

SIDING

② ②

GROUND FRAME.
NUMBERS THUS :- 1.

11.

1420
YDS.

3.

200
YDS.

40
YDS.

7.

4.

9.

E

9.

8.

A

620
YDS.

12.

5.

12.

1,318
YDS.

6.

F

DOWN LOOP

C

B

620
YDS.

D

CREWKERNE

UP   MAIN   DOWN

CHARD JCN.

11
YDS.

G

200 YDS.

15.

16.

811
YDS.

WICKETS 1.
GATE LOCK 2.

SPARE : 13 : 14 :

This layout into use 04-10-1942, except for up
and Down Distants which remained as in top
Diagram until 02-12-1962.

---

pointwork and its associated signalling. Coal and stores were delivered to the crossing box via the 9.50 am 'down' freight from Yeovil Junction when required. The siding was closed on 2 September 1963 and abolished with its attendant ground-frame on 25 November of the same year. The signal box was reduced to a ground-frame (for the gates) on 30 April 1967, and closed on 30 August of the same year with the provision of AHBs.

An accident occurred here in 1916 . . . "Considerable derangement of the train service between Yeovil and Exeter on Tuesday and Wednesday resulted from a mishap which befell the Monday night goods train between Chard Junction

---

No. E330, a rebuilt Drummond 4-6-0, slams over the level crossing at Hewish Gates with a 'down' express on 2 August 1928.

H. C. Casserley

106

No. E456 *Sir Galahad* is about to thunder over the road crossing at Hewish Gates with an 'up' express on 2 August 1928.

H. C. Casserley

and Crewkerne. It is surmised that a bale of camp equipment became dislodged from one of the centre trucks, and in falling on to the line, derailed the truck from which it fell. The permanent way was damaged for some distance near Hewish siding, several thousand 'chairs' being smashed or displaced. The accident happening about midnight so the difficulties of the situation were accentuated. Coming to a standstill at Hewish the front part of the train was uncoupled and proceeded to Crewkerne, whilst a breakdown gang from Yeovil was telegraphed for and commenced operations at dawn. Throughout Tuesday and part of Wednesday all traffic was run on the down line, and the delays at Chard Junction to the up trains and expresses in having to be

shunted back to the down line were unavoidable. The railway officials did their utmost to minimise the inconvenience to the travelling public . . ." *Pullmans Weekly News*, 5 September 1916.

Footplate comments

The 'up' distant signal for Hewish Gates was always a welcome sight for enginemen, glowing faintly out of the darkness on a wet winter's night like a welcoming beacon, as we plodded up the bank towards Crewkerne Tunnel with a heavy freight on our tail. The locomotive would be shrouded in steam and straining for all its worth on the sharp incline. Only once in my footplate days was I signalled into

No. E754 *The Green Knight* heads a westbound express over the crossing at Hewish gates on 2 August 1928.

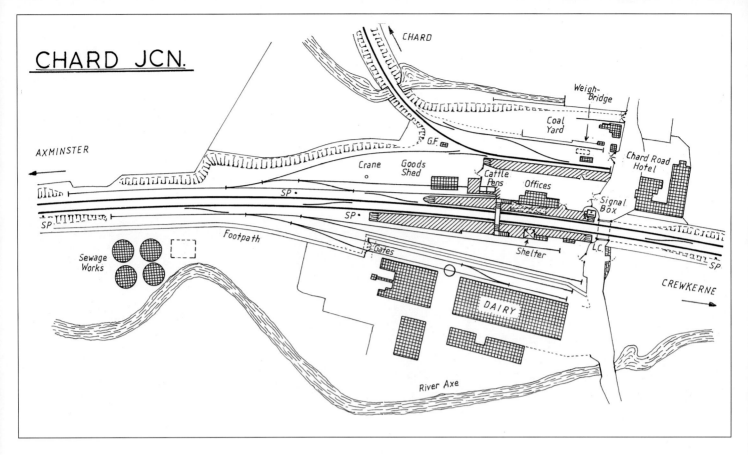

CHARD JCN.

the 'down' loop, whilst working a train of empty stock towards Exeter, having to clear the way for a following passenger train.

Chard Junction

Opened with the line as Chard Road, and later re-named Chard Junction in August 1872. The main station buildings, in their distinctive style, were grouped on the 'up' platform. The signal box was situated at the Crewkerne end of the 'up' platform standing adjacent to the level crossing. The 'down' platform, connected by a footbridge, was served by a brick-built waiting shelter. Sidings were located along both sides of the main line, with the goods shed and cattle pens being situated alongside the 'up' bay line. Between the 'down' platform and the River Axe stands the large United Dairies complex which had its own sidings for the vast amount of rail-borne milk traffic which was once handled here. The complex had its own diminutive diesel shunter for shuffling the tankers in and out of the dairy. The full milk tankers were then shunted over to the 'up' sidings by the BR

In the last month of its operation, the combined 10.40 am (SO) Exmouth/11.7 am Sidmouth through train for Cleethorpes, formed with ten LMR/ER coaches, speeds through Chard Junction behind N class 2-6-0 No. 31855. This train will be routed northwards via Templecombe and the Somerset & Dorset line. To the right of the photograph can be seen two coaches of a train standing at the branch platform awaiting departure to Chard Central.

Stephen Derek

Steam issues from the steam heating pipes of 4575 class 2-6-2T No. 5503 whilst standing in the branch platform at Chard Junction with a train for Taunton on 23 February 1952.

Derek Phillips Collection

engine engaged on the Chard shunting duty, in readiness for collection by an eastbound passenger train. With the displacement of churn traffic by rail bulk tanks from 1931 Chard Junction, Semley and Seaton Junction became the major distribution centres for rail-borne milk tanker traffic on the route until the mid 1960s. The nightly move of milk to London was quite a complex operation as long trains of rail-tankers had to fit in with the freight, ballast and other trains. This of course had to be balanced with equally long

trains of empty tanks returning to the West, and as cows do not stop producing milk at 5 pm on a Friday night, and the Capital demands an ever-increasing supply, the milk traffic would continue over the weekends. Nowadays this traffic is conveyed by vast juggernauts thundering along our over-choked road system. Far better it was still carried by rail.

In my firing days on the 'Chard shunter' we would often have to move empty and full tanks between the dairy complex and the main line. Chard Junction was something

Chard Junction looking east towards the level crossing on 2 March 1956 – the main station buildings are grouped on the 'up' platform to the left.

R. M. Casserley

CHARD JUNCTION BRANCH (1900)

(1936)

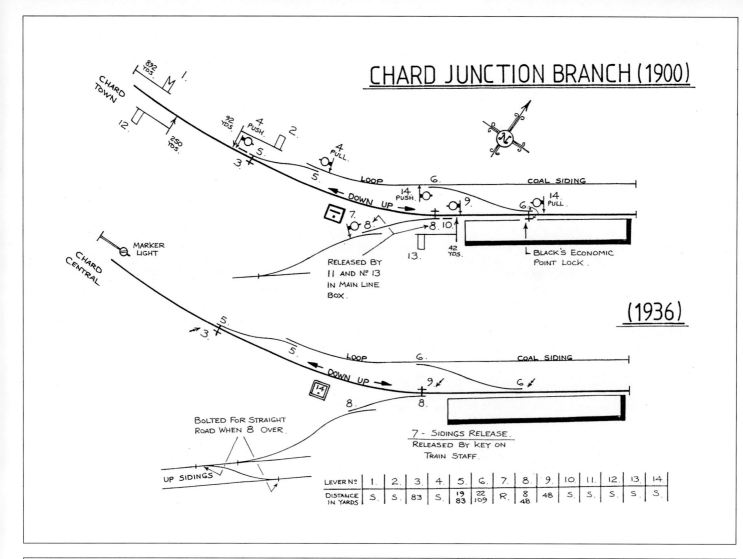

LEVER Nº	1.	2.	3.	4.	5.	6.	7.	8.	9.	10.	11.	12.	13.	14.
DISTANCE IN YARDS	S.	S.	83	S.	19 83	22 109	R.	8 48	48	S.	S.	S.	S.	S.

CHARD JUNCTION

1968

THIS LAYOUT FULLY INTO
USE 07-05-1967.

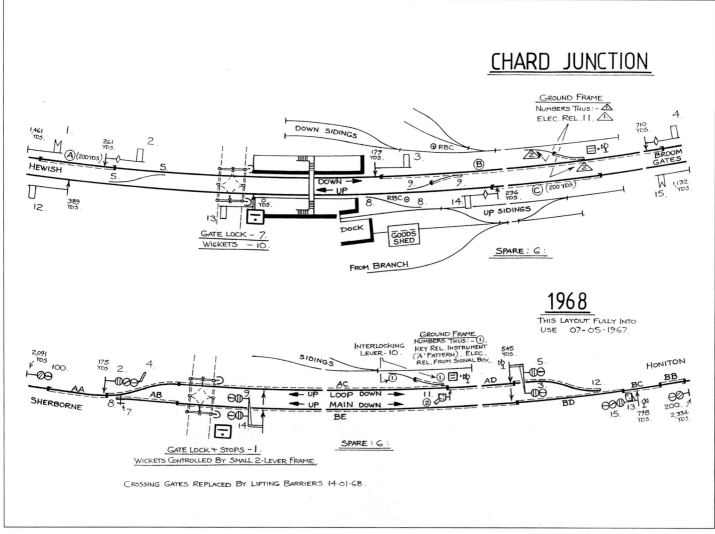

of a train spotters' paradise with the 'down' expresses hammering down the Chard bank and sweeping over the level crossing with whistles screaming, and the Salisbury bound trains tearing through, steaming equally hard (if the boards were off) and attacking the climb to Crewkerne Tunnel with the bit between their teeth. I well remember as a young fireman, having my work cut out on more than one occasion ascending the Chard bank on an S15 with a heavy freight hanging on our tail. The sure-footed 4-6-0s would tackle the gradient in fine style with a superb bark throwing smoke and steam high into the air. The 1963 timetable shows a weekday service of ten down and eight up passenger services, and a Sunday service of four down, and six up workings (including an excursion).

The short, single-track branch to Chard Town opened on 8 May 1863, the inaugural train hauled by a coke-burning 2-2-2 well tank, *Firefly*. This locomotive is believed to have been built especially for the branch between Chard Road and Chard Town. *Firefly* was re-constructed at Nine Elms in March 1863, using new parts, plus the frames, boiler and leading wheels from an earlier Rothwell single, No. 76 *Firefly*. Chard Town had a single platform and a small station building constructed of corrugated iron. A large brick-built goods shed, small signal box and an engine shed were also provided at the branch terminus. An initial weekday service of six return trips, plus three return services on Sundays, was provided from the start and worked by the L&SWR. All trains on the branch were worked by a single locomotive which was based in the shed at Chard Town. Other early locomotives known to have worked the branch include 2-2-2WTs Nos 31 *Orion* and 9 *Chaplin*. Up until the turn of the century 2-4-0 Beattie well tanks, Adams Radials and, as with the other branch lines on the route, the ubiquitous 0-6-0 'Ilfracombe Goods' would make the

occasional appearance. An O2 0-4-4 tank is reported as being allocated to Chard Town in March 1900. Yeovil Town was parent shed to Chard, supplying locomotives on a weekly basis.

The broad gauge Bristol & Exeter Railway – arch rival to the standard gauge London & South Western Railway – opened the (joint) station at Chard (from Taunton) on Tuesday, 11 September 1866. The L&SWR spur line connection to the new joint station (opened on 26 November 1866) ran from a point just short of its original terminus at Chard Town. Trains continued to use the old terminus, but had to back out again, before proceeding along the spur line to the joint station. However, some of the L&SWR services were redirected to terminate at the new station, rather than proceed to Chard Town. At the joint station each company had their own station master and staff, their own signal boxes, and booking offices. An unmanned platform with a shelter was provided on the new L&SWR link line (in 1871) adjacent to the Town station for passengers using trains that ran straight through to the joint station from Chard Road. Chard Town was closed to passenger traffic from 1 January 1917, and thereafter the GWR operated the train service between the joint and junction stations (except for Sunday summer workings in 1938 by the SR). The former L&SWR terminus was relegated to a goods depot, surviving until 18 April 1966. The branch closed to passenger working on 10 September 1962, and lifted between Creech Junction (on the WR main line) to Chard Central by 6 August 1964, the remainder of the branch surviving until 1966 for freight traffic, and being closed on 3 October of the same year.

The suffix 'Junction' in the station nameboard of the main line station at Chard Junction was something of an exaggeration. To the casual observer standing on the 'up' main line platform in the late 1950s there would be no

The L&SWR signal box standing off the end of the 'up' platform at Chard Junction, pictured here on 3 April 1965, remained in use until September 1982 when it was replaced by a modern box which is still in use controlling the passing loop.

C. L. Caddy

S15 4-6-0 No. 30845 hustles past the goods shed at Chard Junction with the 12.15 pm Exmouth Junction–Nine Elms freight on 19 March 1961. The gruelling climb up the Chard Bank to the summit at Crewkerne Tunnel lies ahead. When I was a young footplateman I could wish for no better class of engine than this to work heavy freight trains over the notorious gradients of the old 'South Western' main line between Salisbury and Exeter.

John Cornelius

physical evidence of a railway junction in the normal sense, either in the way of signalling or trackwork. To find this junction we had to walk through the booking hall and out on to the station forecourt, and there in front of us was a small single-bay platform devoid of any covering or shelter (at one time an attractive awning graced the platform). A loop line trailing through the head shunt to a coal-trader's siding was used by the locomotives to run-around their coaches before returning to Chard Central. At the end of the platform a set of points lead to the left, making a trailing connection into the main line goods yard. This was the actual junction, and it was an awkward one to operate as the connection lead into the head shunt from the goods shed. If an excursion train arrived from Taunton, bound for Lyme Regis or Seaton, the stock had to be split up, and it took some complicated shunting to get the coaches to and from the Southern main line. The small L&SWR 'knee' frame signal box (Chard Junction Branch), controlled the branch layout here, at one time the box had signalling under its control but, this was removed when the box was reduced to a ground-frame on 5 March 1935, and taken out of use on 28 July 1964, with points converted to hand operation.

Chard Junction closed to passenger services on 7 March 1966, and to freight on 18 April of the same year. Sidings are still retained into the milk factory but remain unused. A raft of rail milk tankers were based here at one time for transporting milk on an emergency basis to any part of the railway system. Today, the station buildings have long gone, the goods shed still survives, but the branch platform now forms part of a coal yard. The old style level crossing gates were removed on 7 January 1968 and replaced by full lifting barriers which came into use seven days later on 14 January. The L&SWR signal box, which opened in 1875, survived until September 1982 when replaced by a modern building. The layout today at Chard forms the important crossing loop on the long single-line section between Yeovil Junction and Honiton, and as with other passing places on the line, is signalled for bidirectional working. Of interest, the nearby Chard Road Hotel was the scene of a spectacular accident

when a brake van and a six-plank open wagon ran away (due to a shunting error) from Chard Town to Chard Junction, knocked down the stop-blocks, crossed the main road and ended up on the forecourt of the pub. Fortunately no one was injured, and the wheel marks of the run-away wagons can still be seen in the driveway of the hostelry to this day.

Mr J. S. Perry became station master at Chard Central in December 1960 and ultimately became the last person to hold that position there. This is his account of those days.

"I assumed charge of Chard Junction station in mid 1963 at a time of great upheaval. At the beginning of that year a major change took place in the geographical area of the railway Regions and a new management structure was implemented. In the West Country the principal change being that the whole of the Southern Region lines, west of Salisbury were transferred to the control of the Western Region. A new Divisional Management structure was created to replace the existing District Operating, Commercial, and Motive Power functions. At local level it was decided that station masters' posts were to be abolished and replaced by Area Managers in charge of groups of stations and depots. Although these arrangements were intended to apply to every region, the Southern Region successfully pleaded that, because of their special circumstances, the arrangements were not to be implemented and they were allowed to retain station masters. It was fully 20 years before that Region adopted an Area Management organisation. Early in 1963, arrived the Beeching report which proposed extensive line and station closures. The West Country would be particularly badly hit if the published proposals were to be implemented and there was considerable alarm amongst the staff at their effect. For ex-Southern Region staff employed at stations west of Salisbury, not only had the unthinkable happened and they had passed into the control of the Western Region, but they had visions of their line losing its prestigious named express trains, and at best being reduced to the status of a secondary line, if not totally closed.

It was against this background that I assumed control of

Chard Junction in addition to my other duties in charge of the (by then freight only) branch from Taunton to Chard. Staff at Chard Junction consisted of a booking clerk, two senior and two leading porters, three signalmen at Chard Junction, one at Broom level crossing, together with crossing keepers at Broom and Axe crossings. Passenger traffic from the nearby village of Tatworth was quite light, the principal earnings from the station were in respect of rail-tanks of milk from the United Dairies whose premises adjoined the station. Goods traffic was also light and mainly consisted of coal received for a local distributor, and some timber and fertiliser. The greatest challenge for myself in assuming these new responsibilities was in the administrative area. Although the railways had by then been nationalised for some 15 years and, in theory at least, all practices should have been standardised, this was not the case and the Southern Region, in particular, had successfully fought uniformity and standardisation in many areas. It was a case of learning a new system and then converting it to a new, uniform system.

Pay was a particularly sensitive issue. Whilst pay was paid on a common day (Thursdays) for both Regions, the period to which it referred to was not. Southern Region staff who worked on Sundays, for which enhanced rates applied were paid the following Thursday, just four days afterwards, whilst Western Region men had to wait for eleven days before they were paid. Strong objections would have been raised if Southern Region men had been required to be paid under the Western system and it was a case of 'leave alone for the time being'. Accounting for station revenue also differed between Regions. Although the balance sheets produced at the end of each calendar month were standard, how the figures were accounted for was not and different books of account were used. Many of the station masters employed on the line did not wish to work under Western Region control and, in any case, it was intended to abolish

their posts. Those who did not retire, opted to return to the Southern Region, where such posts would continue to exist, and over the succeeding 18 months or so, every man who did so was, in fact, transferred on promotion. Few of the ordinary station staff could afford to do this and several ingenious ruses were employed from time to time to demonstrate their Southern loyalties. I found it the best policy not to enquire too deeply into such matters!

The General Manager of the Western Region at that time was Mr (later Sir) Stanley Raymond. His robust style of management was something rarely encountered by railwaymen before, and on one occasion I was instructed to meet his Inspection Saloon at Chard Junction where it was to stop on its way from Yeovil to Exeter. The saloon arrived and he alighted, followed by the jovial, rotund figure of the newly appointed District Manager at Exeter, Mr J. J. Donovan. Mr Raymond said to me, "You did not expect to see me back quite so soon did you?" (a few weeks previously I had travelled with him in his saloon when he travelled from Taunton over the freight only branch to Chard Junction). Whilst we were speaking on the platform, he turned towards the sidings at the United Dairies and said, "I see they are still there then" pointing to a line of some 30 or so empty mineral wagons (green carded) awaiting repair. He quickly strode to the end of the platform pursued by a perspiring Mr Donovan and myself. Rapidly examining the labels he returned and said, "Just as I thought, some of those have been here more than three months, there is rust on the wheels and there are birds nesting in the axles! That's Exmouth Junction (the wagon repair works) storing up work against a rainy day. Get them shifted at once; if Exmouth Junction can't deal with them, send them elsewhere. No wonder we can't get empty coal wagons in South Wales, they should be earning money, not providing nesting for birds!" Action was swiftly taken, and when I arrived for work the following morning, there was not a wagon to be seen."

The 'down' platform at Chard Junction with its impressive wooden waiting shelter that was later replaced by a brick-built version. The rail-served United Dairies Creamery can be seen in the background. Freight facilities were withdrawn from Chard Junction on 18 April 1966 and rail milk tanker traffic ceased from April 1980.

Lens of Sutton

Chard Junction looking west with Class 4MT 2-6-0 No. 76066 standing in the yard to the left, a 'down' freight can be seen in the distance heading west hauled by an S15 4-6-0. Freight wagons abound in this view taken in June 1962.

R. C. Riley

By mid 1964 the goods stations at Ilminster and Thornfalcon (on the former GWR Chard branch) were closed and the line was lifted from Creech Junction to Chard Central. Freight traffic for Chard Town and the sidings at Chard Central was all re-routed via Chard Junction, and the line between Chard Junction and Chard Central was worked as a siding. Shortly after, the station master at Crewkerne returned to the Southern Region in respect of his option and I was asked to take over control of this station on a temporary basis pending the introduction of the local Area Management organisation which was some months away. The staff here consisted of a booking clerk, three porters, three signalmen, a goods porter and two lorry drivers, together with a crossing keeper at Crewkerne Gates. Although over a mile from the Town Centre, the station had a substantial ticket revenue, mainly long distance tickets to Salisbury, London and beyond, also local traffic to Exeter. Freight and parcels traffic was heavy – consisting of received coal, fertiliser and cattle foods, and manufactured textiles were despatched. It was while I was at Crewkerne one day that onto the platform came the 'pork pie' hat and familiar figure of Mr (later Sir) John Betjeman. Knowing of his interest in steam trains, and at this time steam traction was being phased out, I made a quick telephone call down the line to find out if the train he intended to catch (I believe it was the 10.10am Exeter Central–Waterloo) was steam hauled. He beamed with evident pleasure when I told him that his train would indeed be pulled by a steam engine!

At the beginning of October 1965, the new Area Management organisations were introduced between Yeovil and Exeter and the time had come for me to hang up my hat. I was then aged 36, had 20 years service, 14 of which had been spent as a station master in every grade from Class 5 to Class 1. I had now secured a post as chief clerk based in the Axminster Area, other Area Managers being located at Yeovil, Honiton, and Exeter. The Area Manager at Axminster

controlled that station and the branch to Lyme Regis, Seaton Junction and the Seaton branch, Chard Junction and the freight only branch to Chard Town and Central, a total of eight staffed passenger stations, three signal boxes, and three staffed level crossings. However, within a few weeks of the new organisations being created, news came that the Beeching proposals were being put into effect early in March 1966. From that date, Axminster station only would remain open for passenger traffic, all other stations would close, and a similar fate befell the Honiton area where only that station remained open. On the day that the branch line services ceased and it was reminiscent of the time, nearly four years previously when I had closed the Chard Branch to passenger traffic. The Area Manager and myself spent the day touring the area, and on one of the last trains from Lyme Regis to Axminster, there was a lady in her 90s who claimed that as a small child she had been taken on the train when the line opened all those years ago, and wanted to ride on the last day.

There was an interesting sequel to the closure of the Seaton branch in the summer of 1966. Situated at Seaton adjoining the station are two large holiday camps which used to receive substantial numbers of campers each summer by train. When the line to Seaton closed it was thought that such passengers who travelled by rail to the camp would detrain at Axminster station and catch the hourly service bus from Taunton to Seaton which stopped at the top of the Axminster station approach. Indeed, one of the conditions laid down was that before a train service was withdrawn, an adequate substitute bus service must be provided. On the first Saturday of the summer timetable, the campers duly arrived and alighted at Axminster, but in far greater numbers than expected. They were then faced with a walk of almost 100 yards up the approach, then to cross a road and wait at the bus-stop for the bus. When it arrived, many could not get on and luggage was a problem as only limited accommodation was provided. Those who did not get on were then faced with

BROOM GATES (1959)

ELECTRICALLY CONTROLLED BY AXE GATES.

AXE GATES DOWN INNER DISTANT.

200 YDS

1,672 YDS. 3

68 YDS.

4

CHARD JCN.

DOWN →

← UP

AXMINSTER

1 - GATE LOCK
2 - WICKETS.

5

6 YDS.

Ⓑ

200 YDS

AXE GATES UP HOME.

960 YDS.

6

GREEN WHEN LEVER 3 REVERSED, SIGNAL 3R AT 2 YELLOWS OR GREEN.

TWO YELLOWS WHEN LEVER 3 REVERSED, SIGNAL 4 AT YELLOW. GREEN WHEN 3 REVERSED, SIG. 4 AT GREEN.

GREEN WHEN LEVER 4 REVERSED (AXE GATES 7 REVERSED AND ARM 6 OFF)

(1963)

200 YDS

1,754 YDS. 3R

906 YDS. 3 7R

68 YDS. 4 7

Ⓐ

CHARD JCN.

DOWN →

← UP

AXMINSTER

1 - GATE LOCK
2. - WICKETS.

5

6 YDS.

Ⓑ

200 YDS

6

AXE GATES NUMBERS THUS :- 1.

6 5 980 YDS.

GREEN WHEN LEVER 6 REVERSED, ARM 5 OFF (AXE GATES 5 REVERSE)

---

an hour's wait unless they went by taxi at their own expense. Repercussions to this state of affairs were swift, the local press likened the sight as similar to Napoleon's retreat from Moscow! The Area Manager was hastily summoned to a meeting, and on the following Saturday, when ever greater numbers arrived, far better arrangements had been made. Special buses were chartered and waited in the station yard at Axminster. Passengers alighted from the train and placed their luggage on barrows before boarding the bus. Luggage was loaded into a railway lorry and this, together with the buses, travelled direct to the camps at Seaton. Similar arrangements applied in the reverse direction, buses being timed away from the camps to connect with the trains at Axminster with minimal delay. This service continued throughout the summer, adjusted as necessary to cope with varying numbers.

In the late summer of 1966, the Axminster Area Manager left on promotion to a post at Worcester, and Axminster came under the control of the Yeovil Area Manager. By the time that I left, a few weeks later on promotion to a post in West Wales, rumours were already circulating, remarkably correct as it turned out, of intended track and signalling alterations. These envisaged a single line between Salisbury and Exeter with crossing points only at Tisbury, Gillingham, Yeovil, Chard Junction, Honiton and Exeter. Several stations were to be reduced to one platform only to save bridge and platform costs, and many of the level crossings were to be converted to automatic half-barrier working. This all came to effect over the succeeding few years. Staff on the line tend to be long serving and Axminster, for instance is synonymous with the name of Derek Grayes. I believe that he was born in the Axminster Station House which forms part of the station buildings. Certainly his father was station master there for some years. He started as a lad clerk at Axminster in the early 1940s and apart from a few years away on National Service, spent the whole of his railway career there. He died, still working, only a few years ago, and it is fitting that his 45 years service, was commemorated by his colleagues who, at their own expense, erected a plaque recording this, over the booking office window where he had worked for over 25 years. When the station was recently re-constructed, the plaque was removed, but repositioned at its former site when the work was complete."

Broom Gates

Located almost two miles from Chard Junction, the ground level box was positioned alongside the 'up' main line on the Axminster side of the level crossing. The original frame was replaced circa 1925. The level crossing gates were worked by hand instead of the wheel arrangement used at the nearby Axe Gates. Colour light signals were installed on 17 September 1962. The instruments were removed on 11 June 1967 with the box being abolished on 20 August of the same year, the gates being replaced by automatic half-barriers.

Footplate comments

On the afternoon Chard shunting turn we would leave Axminster with a pick-up goods bound for Yeovil Junction, our locomotive would be one of the Standard Class 4MT 2-6-0 tender engines. Timed into the trip would be a booked stop at Broom Gates to drop off the cans of fresh water which were supplied daily for the crossing keeper as there was no mains supply. The gateman would be waiting for us as we came to a stand with a clanking of buffers from our short freight train. He would receive the cans of water down from the footplate and at the same time he would throw a couple of sacks aboard, which I would duly fill with coal for his fire, and in return we would receive a couple of bottles of home made cider, so green you could almost see the apple cores floating about. It was lovely stuff – guaranteed to clear any thirst!

Coaxden Siding

The sidings (also known as Broom Ballast Siding) were

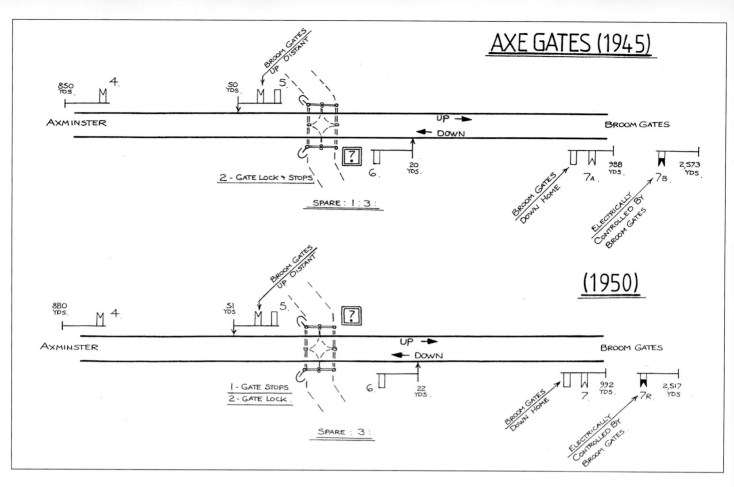

situated one mile south of Broom Crossing and gravel was removed in large quantities by rail. It is recorded that in 1894 a Roman coin was found at Exeter amongst ballast removed from the siding. Entry was gained to the sidings from the 'up' main line via a ground-frame – operated by an Annett's key obtained from Axminster box. Axminster station was in charge of working wagons to and from the sidings which were served by 'up' local goods trains including the 11.20 am Axminster–Chard Junction on weekdays, and the 11.25 am Axminster–Chard Junction on Saturdays.

Axe Gates

The original ground level box fitted with a wheel for working the gates stood alongside the 'down' main line and was abolished as a block post on 5 April 1913. The frame was moved to a new non-standard building positioned alongside the 'up' main line in August 1949. The box was abolished on 6 August 1967 when automatic half-barriers were provided.

Axminster

The station, long associated with the Adams 0415 class tank engines used on the Lyme Regis branch, opened with the main line in July 1860. The large and impressive main station buildings with their tall chimneys and highly pitched gables – the hallmark of Sir William Tite – dominate the former 'down' platform to this day. The substantial goods yard was located on the 'down' side of the station layout and included the usual goods shed, yard crane and weighbridge serving the local merchants, etc. A small engine shed, believed to have been constructed from corrugated iron and dating from the 1860s, was situated at the end of the goods yard. This housed a locomotive for banking trains up over the Honiton bank and stationed here in 1882 was a 2-4-0, No. 4 *Locke* previously in the engineers' dept.). A coal stage

N15 'King Arthur' class 4-6-0 No. 30452 *Sir Meliagrance* near Axe Gates on 27 June 1959 with the 10.37 am Exeter Central–Templecombe.

S. C. Nash

9F 2-10-0 No. 92220 *Evening Star* runs past Axe Gates level crossing with the 'Farewell to Steam' railtour on 20 September 1964.

B. L. Jackson

and accommodation for the footplate staff were also provided. The shed was demolished when the earthworks for the Lyme Regis branch were constructed but during the First World War two 460 class 4-4-0s, Nos 0460 and 0472 were based here for banking heavy goods trains to Honiton.

The station had become a junction in 1903 when the Axminster & Lyme Regis Light Railway, with an intermediate station at Combpyne, opened on Monday 24 August. This linked Axminster with the beautiful Dorset seaside resort of Lyme Regis, and although built by an

independent local company under powers granted on 15 June 1899, the 6¾ mile single-track line constructed under a Light Railway Order, was worked by the L&SWR from the start and absorbed by them in 1907. To refer to Axminster without mentioning the famous carpet of the same name would be akin to intimating cod without chips! Founded in 1775 by Thomas Whitty, the erstwhile company traded until 1835, succumbing to bankruptcy when the machinery was sold off to a Wilton weaver (where carpets became equally famous). However, fortunes changed and a factory,

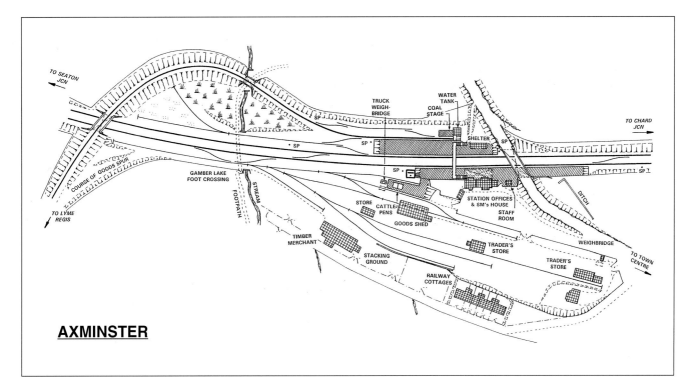

AXMINSTER

Axminster looking east on 23 February 1952. Adams 0415 class 4-4-2T No. 30584 stands to the left in the bay line used by the Lyme Regis trains. The driver takes time to top up the lubricator alongside the smokebox before running the engine around its train for the next trip to Lyme Regis. Nos 30823 and 31793 take water at the far end of the 'up' platform.

Derek Phillips Collection

D1 class 0-4-2T No. B359 (former LBSCR *Egmont*) stands in the bay at Axminster on 4 May 1930 with the 1.18 pm Sundays only to Lyme Regis. The Lyme Regis branch with its gradients and tight curves always provided problems to the Motive Power Department in providing suitable locomotives. A D1 class 0-4-2T No. B612 (former LBSCR No. 12 *Wallington*) arrived at Exmouth Junction in October 1928 for trials on the branch, the locomotive was successful, although it was too heavy. No. B612 and three other members of the same class – Nos B276 (former *Rudgwick*), B359, and B633 (former No. 33 *Mitcham*) had their water tanks reduced to 580 gallons, and the coal bunker cut down to 1 ton. This brought the weight of the locomotives down to 41¼ tons. The work was completed at Brighton Works in March-September 1929. However this work was to no avail as the branch proved to be a hard taskmaster and the locomotives were replaced by Nos 0125 and 0520, two of the 0415 class 4-4-2 tank locomotives that the D1s had been sent to replace.

H. C. Casserley

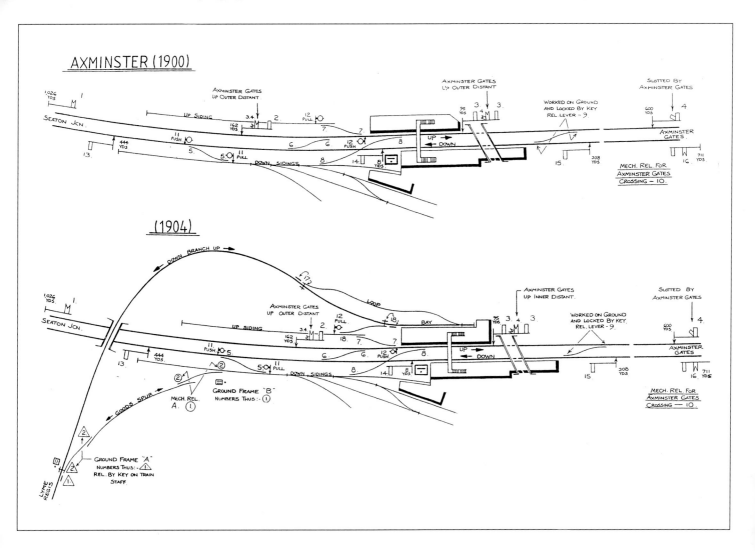

AXMINSTER (1900)

(1904)

adjacent to the goods yard, re-opened at Axminster in 1937, providing extra revenue for the railway company. The station layout remained almost unaltered from 1903 until the end of steam – a goods shed with an internal crane (40 cwt), an outside crane (5 ton) and a 15 ton weighbridge were situated in the goods yard to serve the local traders. The signal box was located at the Exeter end of the 'down' platform. A direct connection on a 1-in-40 gradient from the goods yard to the branch, worked by two ground-frames, existed until removal on 5 September 1915. This had seen little use and had been considered an inconvenient method of gaining access to the branch by freight trains.

The branch trains used the bay platform on the 'up' side of the layout, trains departing for the branch were faced with an ascent of 1-in-80, curving and rising over the South Western main line. A run-around loop, coaling stage and water column were provided for the branch locomotives. The water tank on its tall brick-built base, complete with tall brick chimney for the stationary steam engine which was used for pumping water from the River Axe, was a feature at this end of the station. Other water columns were provided at the ends of the 'up' and 'down' platforms. Providing suitable motive power for the branch, with its severe curves and undulating gradients, gave the operating department a pain in the backside from day one. Two LBSCR 'Terrier' 0-6-0 tanks Nos 734 and 735 (formerly Nos 46 *Newington* and 68 *Clapham*) were used from the opening of the line, although they had to run with water tanks half full to avoid exceeding the limited axle weight of 12 tons. The 'Terriers' were replaced by O2 class 0-4-4Ts in 1907 but the familiar story of strained frames, excessive flange wear and leaking tanks was to be repeated time and time again over the years. However, in 1913 Robert Urie (then CME of the L&SWR) modified two of the Adams 0415 class 4-4-2Ts for trial work

on the branch including reducing the water capacities of the locomotives to 800 gallons each. The trials were a success and the Adams Radial tanks were to become synonymous with the Lyme Regis branch, and this most handsome design of tank engine was eventually to become the most photographed and popular class of locomotive on the whole route between Salisbury and Exeter. The two original modified engines, Nos 0125 and 0419 on the L&SWR duplicate list, were later joined by No. 521 (modified in 1914) and, apart from the trials of other locomotives including ex LBSCR D1s in 1928/30, (popular at first, but eventually defeated by the old problem) the Adams tanks worked the branch well into BR days.

The deteriorating condition of the Radial tanks in their later years was a cause of concern to the motive power department and in November 1958 an ex GWR 14xx 0-4-2T, No. 1462, was trialled on the line, but was defeated by the curvature of the line – and suffered some steaming problems – and was about as much use as a chocolate fireguard! And so the Adams tanks still plied back and forth as they had done for many years. In 1959 certain sections of the track were renewed and some curves were slightly eased, thus allowing an Ivatt Class 2MT 2-6-2T, No. 41297, to be tested on the line on 18 September of the following year. The engine performed successfully, albeit the motive power dept. had their doubts due to the Ivatt's weight, but with the condition of the Adams tanks continuing to deteriorate the 2-6-2Ts were given authority to be used and appeared in 1961 replacing the Adams trio, by now numbered 30582/83/84. Nos 30582 and 30584 were scrapped in 1962 and 1961 respectively, but No. 30583 (No. 488 of 1885) is now preserved on the Bluebell Railway, being one of the most important locomotives to enter preservation. Two-car DMUs were introduced on the branch in November 1963,

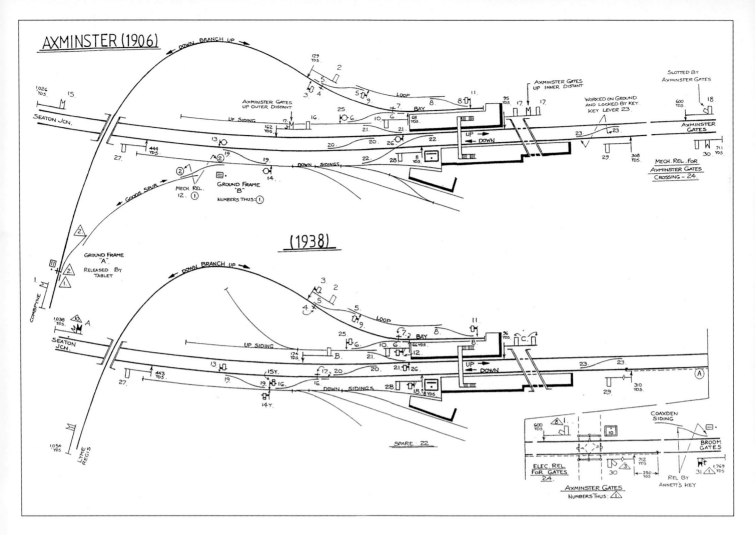

Adams 0415 class 4-4-2T No. 30584 (72A) takes water in the branch bay at Axminster on 23 February 1952. The fireman can be seen behind the cab roof as he keeps an eye on the 'bag'. This handsome and popular class of locomotive has always been associated with the Lyme Regis branch trains. This particular locomotive was built by Dübs & Co. in 1885, and with other members of the class, was put into service when new on the heavy London suburban traffic of the L&SWR, and carried the number 520.

Derek Phillips Collection

although steam returned briefly in February 1965 due to a DMU shortage, with 2-6-2T No. 41291 and a Hawksworth auto-trailer. However, the reign was brief as single-car diesel units appeared in March, and remained until closure of this popular branch line on 29 November of the same year.

When opened the branch offered six return trips on weekdays, this being (increased to eight by the L&SWR in 1907. In 1908 nine trains each weekday were scheduled: five passenger, two goods and two mixed. Summer Sunday services commenced in 1930, and at their peak in 1938, eleven return trips were provided. The winter Sunday service ceased in 1951, but the summer Sunday service continued with some eight to eleven return trips. In its later years a single mixed train was more than enough to cope with the shrinking freight service. Summer Saturdays in the 1950s gave railway enthusiasts the sight of not one, but two Adams Radial tanks in action on the branch – a sight not to be missed. The summer Saturday through traffic for the branch was heavy – far too heavy for a single locomotive. The change-over engine, fresh off wash-out from Exmouth Junction worked in tandem with its intended replacement, both locomotives hauling the two-car set from Axminster to Lyme Regis. They returned from Lyme Regis at 9 am with the branch set plus through Waterloo-bound coaches, then returned to Lyme Regis with the coaches off the 7.45 am (later 8.5 am) ex Waterloo plus the branch set. Both locomotives then returned to Axminster with the branch set, and the engine due for wash-out departed for Exmouth Junction.

From 1953 the 10.45 am ex Waterloo conveyed through coaches for Lyme Regis and Seaton, carrying a rear portion of four or five coaches bound for Lyme Regis. The Adams

tanks then made a further round trip, albeit without the branch set. The stock off the 10.45 am ex Waterloo then formed the 2.35 pm from Lyme Regis and then combined at Axminster with the 2.20 pm Seaton–Waterloo. The 2.35 pm ex Lyme Regis was altered later to 3.5 pm and the through coaches were then attached to the 12.45 pm Torrington–Waterloo. The through coach off the 1 pm ex Waterloo (detached at Templecombe) brought down by a Templecombe–Exeter stopper was left alongside the 'down' platform for the branch engine to collect and add to its train before departing for the Dorset resort. An 'up' through coach (ex Lyme Regis 11.37 am) was attached to the rear of the 8.55 am ex Ilfracombe at Axminster, and upon arrival at Salisbury (with the through Yeovil Town coach) was attached to the up 'ACE'. This was the first section on the days when the train was divided. As well as the through coaches to and from Waterloo, excursion trains were also run at peak periods, again a second locomotive had to be provided at weekends including Sundays to assist with the extra traffic. The intending traveller was well catered for at Axminster in steam days, with a selection of semi-fast and local stopping services, including the cross-country Brighton–Plymouth trains.

Weekday Passenger Services from Axminster 1963
Main Line – Down
  1.15 am ex Waterloo (Passenger and news)
  6.25 am Yeovil Town–Ilfracombe
  8.00 am Axminster–Exeter Central
  7.50 am Yeovil Town–Ilfracombe
  8.10 am Salisbury–Ilfracombe
  9.00 am Waterloo–Plymouth

'Battle of Britain' class 4-6-2 No. 34110 *66 Squadron* leaves Axminster and heads east with an 'up' stopping train in 1958. The 'down' platform in the foreground was particularly long as it stretched away past the bridge and reached as far as the signal box. The chimney pots of the main station building can be seen rising above the bridge parapet.

C. L. Caddy Collection

Axminster 25 February 1968. The former 'up' main line has been lifted and the signal box stands disused with signalling removed, although the water tank and columns still remained at this date. The main station buildings at Axminster were grouped on the 'down' platform.

C. L. Caddy

12.06 pm Yeovil Junction–Exeter Central
11.05 am Waterloo–Padstow (FX)
 1.50 pm Axminster–Exeter Central (SX)
 1.50 pm Axminster–Exeter Central (SO)
12.36 pm Salisbury–Exeter Central
11.30 am Brighton–Plymouth
 1.00 pm Waterloo–Plymouth
 3.19 pm Templecombe–Exeter Central
 1.05 pm Waterloo–Exeter (Q)
 3.05 pm Salisbury–Exeter Central
 3.00 pm Waterloo–Plymouth
 5.16 pm Templecombe–Exeter *not run when 3.05pm Waterloo runs.*
 3.05 pm Waterloo–Exeter
 6.00 pm Waterloo–Exeter
 5.00 pm Waterloo–Exeter – *shunts at Axminster 9.37–9.51 to allow 7.00pm ex Waterloo to pass.*
 7.00 pm Waterloo–Plymouth (SX)
 7.00 pm Waterloo–Plymouth (SO)

Main Line – Up

 6.30 am Exeter Central–Waterloo
 6.40 am Exeter Central–Waterloo
 6.50 am Exeter Central–Axminster
 7.30 am Exeter Central–Waterloo
 6.15 am Plymouth–Salisbury
10.17 am Exeter Central–Waterloo
 8.55 am Ilfracombe–Salisbury
11.12 am Exeter–Salisbury
12.30 pm Seaton Junction–Axminster – *empty coaching stock*
11.10 am Brighton–Plymouth
 1.10 pm Exeter Central–Salisbury
12.15 pm Ilfracombe–Waterloo
 3.20 pm Exeter Central–Templecombe
 4.35 pm Exeter Central–Salisbury
 6.15 pm Milk and Parcels Axminster–Clapham Junction (SX)

 4.00 pm Plymouth–Waterloo
 4.52 pm Plymouth–Eastleigh

Branch – Down Weekdays 22 June – 7 September 1963

8.45 am, 10.32 am (*runs as mixed if required*), 12.33 pm, 1.38p m (*commences 9 Sept*), 1.43 pm (*until 6 Sept inclusive*), 2.40 pm (*commences 9 Sept*), 2.48 pm (*until 6 Sept inclusive*), 4.21 pm, 5.40 pm, 6.47 pm, 8.59 pm.

Branch – Up

8.14 am (SX) *Mixed*, 8.14 am (SO), 9.48 am, 11.39 am, 2.9 pm (*commences 9 Sept*), 2.19 pm (*until 6 Sept inclusive*), 3.46 pm, 5.13 pm.

Freight services, which had been dwindling for many years, finished on the branch on 3 February 1964, with the complete closure taking place on 29 November the following year. Axminster lost its freight facilities on 18 April 1966, and the signal box was closed on 5 March 1967 with the main line being singled from the same year. Today all trains use the former 'down' platform, and the old 'up' platform is still in situ, although the footbridge, 'up' waiting shelter, and branch bay water tower have all been swept way. The station has had a spruce-up in recent years and looks most attractive. The abutments of the bridge which used to carry the Lyme Regis branch over the main line can still be seen and it is quite easy to stand on the station and gaze over to the disused platform and reflect upon happier days when the graceful Adams Radial tank engines stood steaming away in the bay platform.

Seaton Junction

Located just three miles west of Axminster, the station opened with the line and named at first 'Colyton for Seaton'. The main buildings were situated on the 'up' platform and included a hip-roofed waiting shelter and a canopy shelter. The signal box was on the 'down' platform.

'Battle of Britain' class 4-6-2 No. 34106 *Lydford* speeds through Seaton Junction on the 'down' through track with the 11.30 am Brighton–Plymouth on 18 August 1964. Note the superb L&SWR bracket with lower quadrant semaphore arms to the left.

Hugh Ballantyne

The Seaton & Beer Railway (authorised on 13 July 1863) opened on 16 March 1868, the station being re-named Colyton Junction from the same date. A change of name to Seaton Junction followed on 18 July 1869. The 4¼ mile long branch line with intermediate stations at Colyton and Colyford was leased to the L&SWR and worked by them from the start. The branch trains on arrival from Seaton had the disadvantage of having to reverse into the 'down' bay at the Junction. However, this was to end with the re-construction of the station in 1927/8. Two through tracks were provided with loops to the newly extended platforms (the original Tite main station buildings were retained), plus

After running down the Honiton bank at a fair old rate No. 34086 *219 Squadron* sprints through Seaton Junction on the 'up' through track on 18 August 1964 with the 11.10 am Plymouth–Brighton. A trio of six-wheeled 'Express Dairy' milk tanks stand on the right.

Hugh Ballantyne

Seaton Junction looking east on 24 September 1956. M7 0-4-4T No. 30045 and a two-car set stand in the branch platform to the right.

H. C. Casserley

Push-and-pull fitted M7 0-4-4T No. 30021 stands alongside the branch platform at Seaton Junction on 25 May 1958 during a lull between trips to Seaton. The M7s could really move when pushed, but like all Drummond loco-motives the injectors were apt to be slow, and they liked to run on about half a boiler full of water – or else they would prime. The Seaton branch opened on 16 March 1868 and closed on 7 March 1966.

Rodney Lissenden

No. 34052 *Lord Dowding* arrives with the 10.30 am 'up' train at Seaton Junction on 9 July 1949.

H. C. Casserley

SEATON JUNCTION

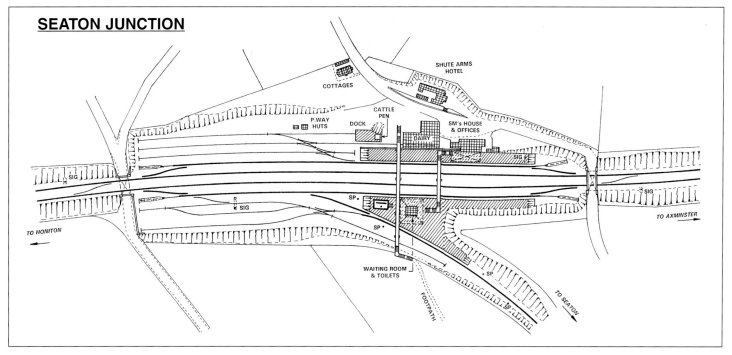

the provision of a new branch platform. The old signal box was removed, and a new 55-lever box positioned on the Honiton end of the re-constructed 'down' platform, coming into use on 3 April 1928. Considerable siding accommodation was to be found west of the station alongside both sides of the main line, although mostly lying alongside the 'up' line. Also on this side was the goods shed containing a 40 cwt crane, cattle pens, and a 5 ton crane in the yard. Considerable railborne milk traffic originated from the adjacent Express Dairy Depot, part of which adjoined the 'up' platform.

The branch to Seaton, which was successful from its opening, was worked at first by Beattie 2-2-2 well tanks, Nos 12 *Jupiter* and 33 *Phoenix* being involved from the start. An 'Ilfracombe Goods' 0-6-0 was recorded as having worked passenger services in the 1880s. O2 and T1 class 0-4-4 tanks replaced the Beattie engines in the 1890s and on occasions, an Adams 4-4-2T relieved the O2 tank on the branch. The timetables for 1909 (summer) show nine passenger trains each way on weekdays, with one goods and two mixed trains. There was flexibility in the working timetable for an extra early morning goods service, "if required". In June 1914, O2s Nos 201 and 214, fitted with cable and pulley motor train equipment, were sent to Exmouth Junction for work on the branch. Ex LBSCR D1 0-4-2Ts Nos B214 and B256 were transferred in 1930 from

the Central Section of the Southern Railway with Brighton two-coach auto-sets to work the branch. However, the D1s were replaced by O2, No. 183, which had been especially fitted with air-controlled auto-gear at Eastleigh. But it is the M7 0-4-4Ts that most people remember about the line. The engine on the auto-fitted trains always had the smokebox pointing towards Exeter with the Westinghouse air pump bolted on the side of the smokebox panting away. Excursion traffic brought a varied assortment of locomotives to the branch over the years: T9s, Q and Q1 0-6-0s, 2-6-0s of the U and N classes, and even Bulleid Pacifics on the odd occasion. Warners Holiday camp at Seaton was also responsible for generating rail-borne custom for many years. The branch engines would spend their time during quiet moments indulging in a bout of shunting milk-tanks at the Junction. However, on summer Saturdays the staff at Seaton Junction would brace themselves for the onslaught of the through traffic to Seaton.

On the branch two engines were rostered to handle the Saturday services, and in 1949 there were two sets of through Waterloo coaches, departing Seaton at 9 am and 10.10 am. The first working would consist of seven Waterloo-bound coaches, plus the two-coach branch set. The Adams 0415 tank (fresh off wash-out) would wind its way from Exmouth Junction to Axminster on Saturdays and was required to assist the M7 with the 9 am ex Seaton. The

Maunsell S15 4-6-0 No. 30824 arrives at Seaton Junction on 2 September 1959 with the 3.20 pm Exeter Central–Templecombe. The station was extensively rebuilt in 1927-28 giving the layout the through tracks thereby allowing non stopping trains to overtake their slower brethren, plus longer platforms and a new platform face for the Seaton branch trains which, in the previous layout, had to reverse into the 'down' bay. Note the superb L&SWR signal gantry with its lower quadrant 'up' starting semaphores for platform and through line, complete with repeating arms. The main station buildings are located on the 'up' platform.

Derek Phillips Collection

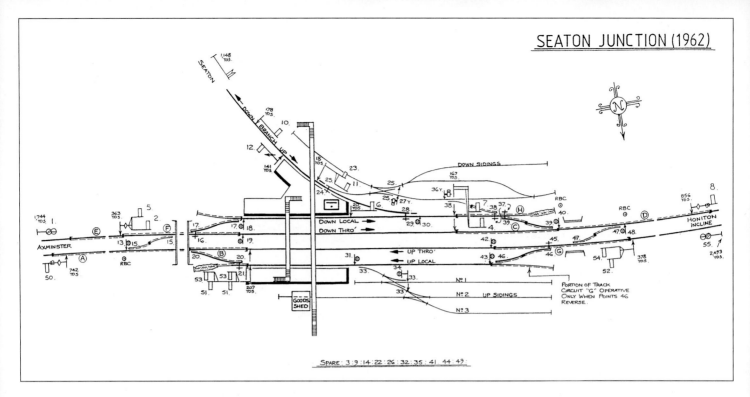

SPARE: 3 : 9 : 14 : 22 : 26 : 32 : 35 : 41 : 44 : 49

Adams tank then returned light engine to Seaton and worked the 10.10 am (on its own, being a lighter train) from Seaton to Seaton Junction before proceeding to Axminster. By 1951 both of the Adams tanks were required at Axminster to handle the through-working from Waterloo–Lyme Regis, and thus the Seaton branch required two M7s to handle the 9 am and 10.10 am departures. After working the latter, one of the M7s departed for Exmouth Junction. During certain Saturday afternoons the 0415 Adams tank en route from Axminster to Exmouth Junction was used for a return trip to Seaton. This was due to the timetable which provided two consecutive workings from Seaton Junction to Seaton without a balancing working. The Adams tank continued its journey to Exeter piloting the engine on the mid-day stopper from Salisbury.

By 1955 there was an extra afternoon train from Seaton to Waterloo, and the 8.22 am Waterloo–Ilfracombe had a Seaton portion. The 9 am Seaton *through* coaches by then consisted of two or three vehicles, combined at the Junction with the 8.30 am from Exeter Central and at Axminster with

With the lower quadrant advanced 'down' starter 'off' the long 8-mile slog mostly at 1 in 80 up to and including Honiton Tunnel lies ahead for S15 4-6-0 No. 30827 whilst leaving Seaton Junction on 2 September 1959 with the 3.34 pm Templecombe–Exeter Central. Milk tanks can be seen to the right on part of the extensive 'up' sidings.

Derek Phillips Collection

Rebuilt 'West Country' class 4-6-2 No. 34025 *Whimple* runs into the 'down' platform line at Seaton Junction with a pick-up goods on 22 August 1963.

C. L. Caddy Collection

the 9 am ex Lyme Regis. The 10.10 am from Seaton ran non-stop to Seaton Junction and was coupled to the 9.45 am Budleigh Salterton–Waterloo. Two 'down' trains appeared within short intervals of each other; the 8.5 am Waterloo–Exmouth detached two coaches which were then attached to the push-and-pull set. Then, the 8.22 am Waterloo–Ilfracombe appeared and dropped off two or three coaches for the branch. This brought both branch engines to the terminus at Seaton on successive trains, they then double-headed the 12.5 pm branch train back to the Junction, and then made a further round trip with as many as six coaches on the 10.45 am Waterloo and the 2.35 pm Seaton. The 2.35 pm was formed of the stock of both the 8.5 am and 8.22 am ex Waterloo plus the buffet-car off the 10.45 am from Waterloo. All this work went on, keeping both M7s busy until

the mid-afternoon and also with the main line stoppers arriving and departing, dropping off and picking-up passengers for the branch, plus the non-stopping trains whistling through – at this, one of the many busy junctions on the route. Busy summer Saturdays were to change with the abolishing of through-coach working in 1962. Some main-line passenger trains were shunted at the Junction in order to allow faster trains to overtake, one such service being the 1.45 pm Yeovil Junction–Exeter Central which had a booked wait of 52 minutes to allow the 11.45 am Waterloo–Ilfracombe free-passage. The 10.37 am (SO) stopper from Exeter Central was also booked to wait 13 minutes in order for the 9.10 am Torrington–Waterloo to pass. When the line was transferred to the Western Region in 1963 the long serving Drummond M7s and their auto-trailers

A gaggle of staff congregate at the top and bottom of the signal box steps while No. 34002 *Salisbury* with early British Railways lettering on the tender stands on the 'down' through.

H. C. Casserley

With the fireman attending to the firebox – for the climb ahead – No. 34072 *257 Squadron* starts the ascent from Seaton Junction to Honiton Tunnel with a 'down' train on 1 June 1963.

Rodney Lissenden

were replaced by WR 64xx 0-6-0 pannier tanks and their attendant Hawksworth push-pull trailers. DMUs were introduced on 4 November of the same year, but steam returned in February 1965 for a short revival due to a shortage of DMUs. A couple of 14xx 0-4-2Ts, Nos 1442 and 1450, were transferred to Exmouth Junction from Yeovil Town for use on the Seaton branch services, but this was only a temporary measure, with the diesels returning and subsequently working the line until closure on 7 March 1966. The last train over the branch carried only eleven passengers.

Not surprisingly for such a popular resort as Seaton, the figures for the branch were quite good in the 1950s and '60s when over 1,000 passengers used Seaton station on summer Saturdays. One of the WR pannier tanks used on the branch, No. 6412, can now be seen working on the West Somerset Railway. Seaton Junction was renowned as being one of the last outposts on the route with L&SWR lower quadrant

signals. The bracket signal on the London end of the 'up' platform with its lower quadrant arms and co-acting repeater for local and through lines was a fine example of L&SWR signalling at its best. Closure of the branch and station came on 7 March 1966, with general freight facilities being withdrawn on 18 April of the same year. Coal traffic continued until 8 May the following year, the signal box also closing in 1967 on 11 June, and milk traffic continuing for a short time after. The former 'up' loop was in use as a siding until the 1980s. Today, trains speed through the once busy Junction on the former 'up' through track, the main station buildings still remain and are occupied by small businesses. The former milk depot is also in use. The platforms remain until this day, although the former 'down' is covered in scrub and the two long footbridges, a feature of the station since its re-building are still in place, the longest being for a public footpath.

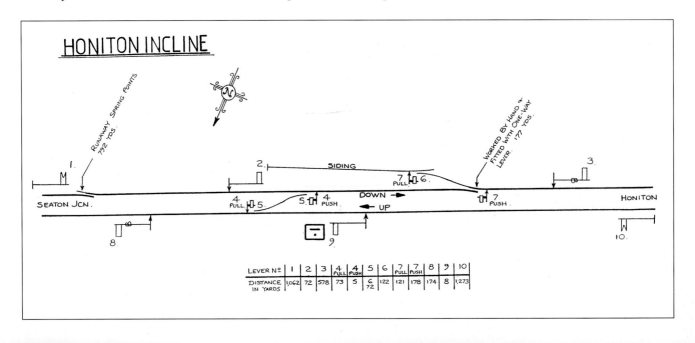

Honiton Incline signal box, pictured here in the background on 20 September 1964, was situated one mile east of the tunnel alongside the 'up' main line in the distance. The siding (controlled by spring points, permanently set for the siding, in order to catch runaway wagons from 'down' trains) leads off to the right. Note the sharp ascent of the main line compared with the siding which is standing on fairly level ground. The signal box was closed on 6 March 1966.

B. L. Jackson

Honiton Bank

Starting from Seaton Junction the nearly 8 mile-climb for 'down' trains between the valleys of the rivers Axe and Otter (mostly at a grade of 1-in-80) was a severe test of locomotives and footplatemen. And I, like many other fellow members of the footplate-brotherhood, have laboured up the bank in weather fair or foul, in daylight and darkness. Honiton Incline signal box was situated one mile east of the tunnel alongside the 'up' main line. The box controlled a crossover which was positioned 40 yards away (on the Seaton Junction side) and catch-points were also situated on

the 'down' line, 787 yards from the box, also on the Seaton Junction side.

The box was located on the steepest part of the bank and 'down' locomotives would be working flat-out at this spot. As a fireman I was always pleased to see the Incline box 'down' distant as it meant that we were nearing the summit and the end of the worst part of the climb from Seaton Junction. The Honiton Incline siding was operated by spring points which were always set to the siding to trap any runaway vehicles from a westbound train. The tunnel is 1,345 yards long and was the longest on the L&SWR. The

An 'up' express headed by No. 750 *Morgan le Fay* approaches the western portal of Honiton Tunnel on 4 August 1928.

H. C. Casserley

The 'up' 'Atlantic Coast Express' nears the west portal of Honiton Tunnel hauled by No. E746 *Pendragon* on 4 August 1928.

H. C. Casserley

S15 4-6-0 No. E827 bursts out of the west portal of Honiton Tunnel heading for Exeter Central on 4 August 1928.

H. C. Casserley

No. 34054 *Lord Beaverbrook* heads towards Honiton Tunnel with a westbound train on 1 June 1963.

Rodney Lissenden

The 'down' 'Atlantic Coast Express' hauled by No. 35020 *Bibby Line* heads westwards along the Honiton bank on 1 June 1963.

Rodney Lissenden

S15 4-6-0 No. 30841 rattles out of the eastern portal of Honiton Tunnel on 1 June 1963 with an Exeter–Salisbury local.

Rodney Lissenden

Rebuilt 'West Country' class 4-6-2 No. 34048 *Crediton* near Honiton with the 9.30 am Exeter Central–Waterloo on 5 September 1964.

S. C. Nash

Class 5MT 4-6-0 No. 73089 *Maid of Astolat* approaches Honiton Tunnel from the West with the 2.14 pm Exmouth–Waterloo on 28 August 1965.
S. C. Nash

With the east portal of the tunnel in the background, the fireman waves a gloved hand in passing as No. 34089 *602 Squadron* swoops down the Honiton bank heading the 11.15 am Exmouth–Waterloo on 28 August 1965.

S. C. Nash

Standard Class 5MT 4-6-0 No. 73162 approaches Honiton Tunnel with the 11.10 am Plymouth–Brighton on 5 September 1964.
S. C. Nash

Honiton station looking east on 7 September 1963 with the main station buildings situated on the 'down' platform and a waiting shelter for eastbound passengers on the 'up' platform.

C. L. Caddy

'down' distant signal was replaced by a colour light signal on the same site as the existing signal on 19 December 1962, with the box being closed on 6 March 1966.

Footplate comments

In my firing days the tunnel always seemed to have a 'screeching' wind blowing through it. We would blast into the tunnel, cinders and ash would be rebounding from the roof and the noise deafening, the fierce orange glow from the firebox reflecting against the roof and walls of the tunnel. Breathing would be difficult with steam and smoke billowing around – the west portal would slowly appear into view, and as we stormed out into the fresh air our exhaust beats would soften as the gradient eased, and the reverser was wound back for the run down through Honiton.

Honiton

The pleasant town of Honiton, long famous for its lace making and gloving industry – and notorious for its summer traffic jams until the opening of the by-pass in 1966 – entered the railway age upon the opening of the line in 1860. The station, situated approximately half a mile from the town centre had (until demolished) the standard William Tite buildings, comparable to Crewkerne and Axminster. These were positioned on the 'down' platform, complete with a large canopy, and a hipped roof waiting shelter was provided on the 'up' platform. The goods shed and sidings were located at the west end of the station on the 'down' side and a 5 ton crane, 20 ton weighbridge, and cattle pens were also provided in the goods yard. Sidings were also situated on the 'up' side west of the station. A private siding in the goods yard serving the timber merchants, George Blay Ltd, was brought into use in 1928. The signal box, located off the end of the 'down' platform was replaced by a 24-lever BR(S) Type 16 box on 16 June 1957, the new box being positioned west of the station on

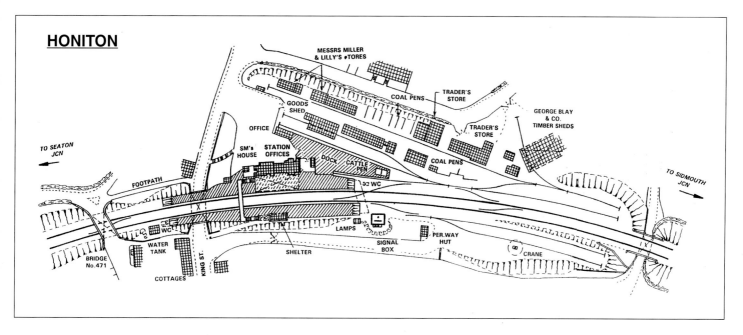

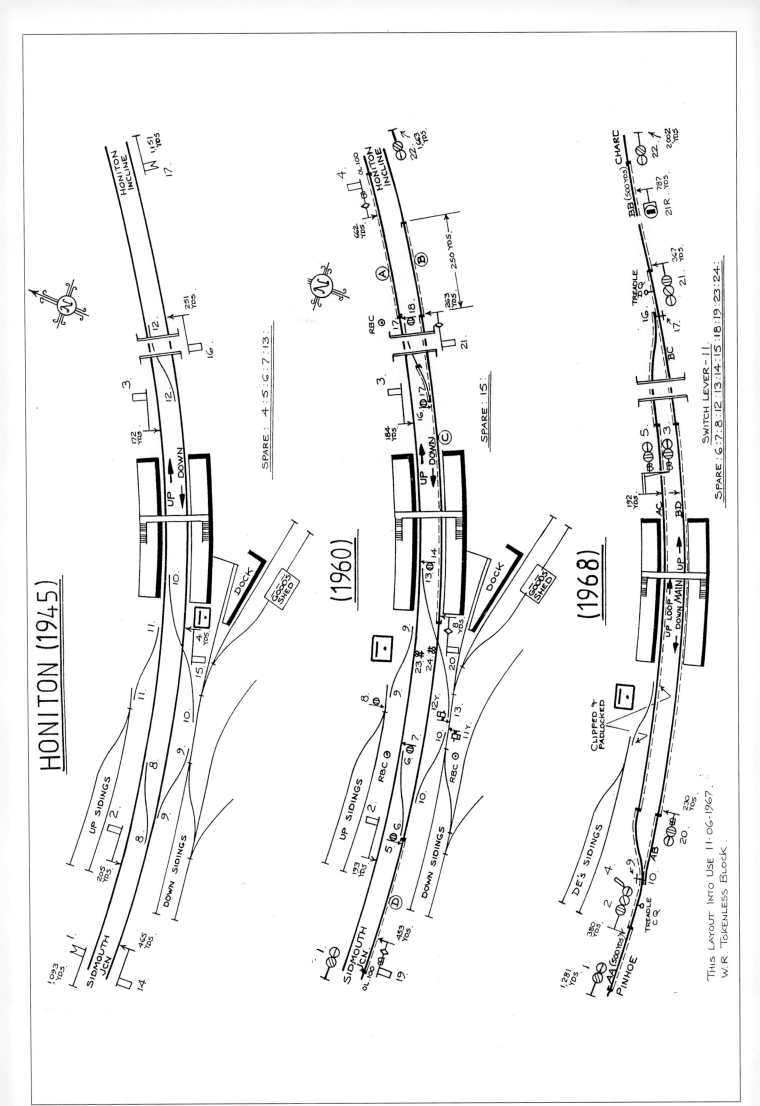

'West Country' class No. 34033 *Chard* stands at Honiton on 1 September 1958 with a 'down' stopping train for Exeter Central.

Adrian Vaughan Collection

Honiton looking east on 5 March 1988 showing the modern featureless buildings that have replaced the earlier structures.

C. L. Caddy

the 'up' side. As well as main line stopping trains, the station was also served by local trains worked to Honiton from Exeter hauled by tank engines in the morning and evening. The engine from the 8 am Exeter train was used to shunt the goods yard, and during school terms, a Sidmouth branch train was extended from Sidmouth Junction to Honiton for pupils attending Kings School, Ottery St Mary, the train returning as empty stock. For some reason the Tite main station buildings and waiting shelter were demolished (or destroyed for want of a better word), and replaced by an ugly and featureless CLASP system building. Freight facilities were withdrawn on 8 May 1967. The 1957 signal box is still in use controlling the passing-loop and the one remaining 'up' refuge siding. The 'down' loop is signalled for bidirectional working thus allowing Waterloo bound trains access to the 'down' platform for ease of passenger movements when no relevant westbound service is to be crossed. Here as at other stations west of Axminster, the commuter traffic to and from Exeter is considerable.

Sidmouth Junction

Opened to public traffic as Feniton on 19 July 1860 the station seemed to suffer from an identity crisis in its early years. Renamed Ottery Road on 1 July 1861, thence to Ottery St Mary (April 1868), and Sidmouth Junction when

the line to that erstwhile seaside resort opened on 6 July 1874. However, after closure on 6 March 1967, the wheel turned full circle on 3 May 1971 when the station re-opened as Feniton. The 8¼ mile branch to Sidmouth was worked by Beattie 2-4-0 well tanks at the outset, with 0-4-4Ts appearing from the 1890s. The section from Tipton St Johns (on the Sidmouth branch), to Budleigh Salterton was opened on 15 May 1897 – the last passenger branch to be opened in Devon before the end of the century. The L&SWR extended the line from Budleigh Salterton to Exmouth, which opened on 1 June 1907 to complete the 11¼ mile link from Tipton St Johns, by virtue of this new section. The L&SWR routed a number of Waterloo–Exmouth through trains via Sidmouth Junction and Tipton St Johns thereby avoiding Exeter Central. Not long after the opening of the new line, a number of trains used the 'circuit', travelling from Exeter Central to Exmouth via Sidmouth Junction, Tipton St Johns and Budleigh Salterton, then Exmouth to Exeter Central. These services lasted until the end of steam, and were not only a useful way to travel from Exeter to Exeter via Exmouth for the traveller and enthusiast, but also provided an additional stopping service for the main line stations between Exeter and Sidmouth Junction. G6 class 0-6-0Ts were used on branch freights until the 1930s while Ivatt 2-6-2Ts appeared in the 1950s and soon afterwards the Standard 2-6-2Ts and 2-6-4Ts were introduced, mainly displacing (but not

The 'up' 'Atlantic Coast Express' headed by No. 35026 *Lamport & Holt Line* bowls into Sidmouth Junction in 1957.

C. L. Caddy Collection

altogether) the Drummond M7s. Bulleid Pacifics have been known to have worked the branch on occasions, including a Plymouth–Sidmouth excursion in 1959.

Diesel multiple units appeared on the branch in 1963 working most of the passenger traffic, although 'Hymeks' and North British Type 2 diesel locomotives appeared on busy summer weekends. The main buildings at Sidmouth Junction in steam days were grouped on the 'down' platform, with a large brick-built waiting shelter provided on the 'up' platform. A level crossing was (and still is with the new Feniton) situated at the west end of the station. The crossing gates were worked from a small gate box equipped with five levers that was positioned on the Broad Clyst side of the crossing, alongside the 'down' main line. This box had

Sidmouth Junction looking west towards the level crossing on 12 September 1964. Passengers and their dog congregate on the 'down' platform.

C. L. Caddy

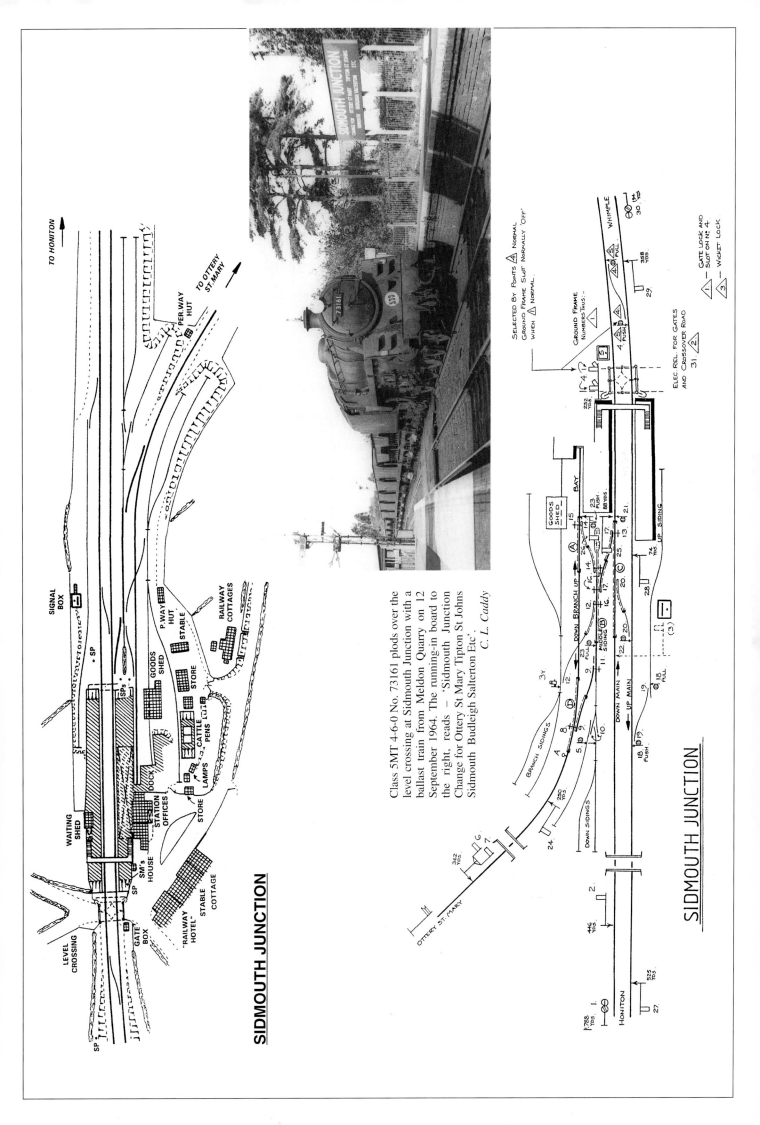

SIDMOUTH JUNCTION

Class 5MT 4-6-0 No. 73161 plods over the level crossing at Sidmouth Junction with a ballast train from Meldon Quarry on 12 September 1964. The running-in board to the right, reads – 'Sidmouth Junction Change for Ottery St Mary Tipton St Johns Sidmouth Budleigh Salterton Etc'.

C. L. Caddy

SIDMOUTH JUNCTION

Class 3MT 2-6-2Ts Nos 82011 and 82024 prepare to leave Sidmouth Junction with the coaches off the 11.45 am Waterloo–Exmouth on 6 September 1958. Trains for the Sidmouth branch and Exmouth via Tipton St Johns could be signalled from the 'down' platform as shown here, or from the bay to the left of the platform.

Derek Phillips Collection

Sidmouth Junction looking east on 2 September 1959. No. 34047 *Callington* approaches on the 'down main line. No. 82018 stands in the bay to the right. Signals read from left to right: 'up' platform starter, 'down' platform starter to 'up' main or branch, bay starter to branch with ground shunt signal on the post.

Derek Phillips Collection

The footplateman on board Class 3MT 2-6-2T No. 82023 sorts his kit out after arrival in the bay platform with the 2.55 pm from Sidmouth on 6 September 1958.

Derek Phillips Collection

previously stood alongside the 'up' main line. The gateman could not open the crossing gates until the locking was released by the signalman in the main signal box. This distinctive signal box, dating from 1875, was positioned east of the station alongside the 'up' siding and main line. Extensive siding accommodation was held here, and a turntable was positioned in the fork created by the branch and main lines. The goods shed, containing a 40 cwt crane, stood alongside the bay platform line and coaches were

often stabled on the shed road during busy weekends. A 5 ton crane was positioned in the 'down' goods yard which handled bricks, coal, stone, timber, lime, agricultural machinery, and outward bound traffic including milk, potatoes, sugar beet and cider apples.

Many coaches were detached from through trains and hauled to Tipton St Johns where the trains were split for the respective destinations of Sidmouth and Exmouth, and vice versa for the return workings. The station would become

With the distinctive signal box in the background – Class 3MT 2-6-2T No. 82024 arrives bunker-first at Sidmouth Junction with the 6.14 pm from Sidmouth on 24 August 1958. The train consists of two Maunsell brake thirds and an all-third coach.

Terry Gough

Whimple looking east from the 'down' platform on 12 September 1964 to the main station buildings located on the 'up' platform.

C. L. Caddy

very busy during the summer months, not only with the regular branch trains to Sidmouth and Exmouth, but also having to deal with the through trains as well. A staff of over 20 were based here including a station master, booking clerks, shunters, porters, crossing keepers and signalmen. Three platform faces were in use, the 'down' platform and branch-bay sharing a long canopy. W. H. Smith maintained a small bookstall here for many years, but surprisingly in view of the passenger traffic generated during the summer months, no refreshment facilities were accommodated at the station. The Railway Hotel (now the Nog Inn) stood adjacent, and therefore many a good pint of beer was to be quaffed at the hostelry by passengers awaiting their respective trains. Many main line trains stopped at Sidmouth Junction including the crack express trains of the day – the 'Devon Belle' and the 'Atlantic Coast Express'. Sidmouth Junction closed to goods traffic on 6 September 1965, and closed entirely from 6 March 1967 with the closure of passenger services to Sidmouth, and the section from Tipton St Johns to Exmouth. The signal box was also closed on 21 May of the same year after the final branch freight workings.

However, due to strong local support the station was re-opened on 3 May 1971 with its original name of Feniton, thus being the first station to re-open between Salisbury and Exeter, the first train to call, being the 07.18 from Exeter. All trains use the former 'down' platform which was reduced in length just before opening. Tickets were issued until 1974 from the Gate box, when an office and shelter were provided on the platform after the old buildings and goods shed were demolished. The level crossing gates were replaced by barriers in 1974, these being operated by a member of staff in the platform building, thus doing away with the old gate box. The station platform was re-constructed and lengthened in 1992 in readiness for the new 'Turbo' units and the station attracts a good deal of passenger traffic, especially commuter traffic to and from Exeter. A lot of new housing has sprung up in the area over recent years, and a new housing estate in a development known as the 'Signals' has

appeared on the old formation of the former goods yard. The former 'up' platform is still extant, but unused.

Whimple

Dating from the opening of the line, this was another of the stations that had its main buildings, complete with wooden valence, positioned on the 'up' platform. A waiting shelter and signal box were located on the 'down' platform. Crossover roads were sited 190 yards from the box on the Sidmouth Junction side, and (added August 1908), 181 yards from the box on the Broad Clyst side. A goods yard situated east of the station on the 'up' side was equipped with a 5 ton crane plus a 40 cwt version in the goods shed. Whimple is as synonymous with Whiteway's Cider, as strawberries are with Devon cream. The famous cider factory of Henry Whiteway & Co. had been established here in 1892. A great deal of traffic in coal, apples, bottles, wooden casks, cider and agricultural machinery was handled annually at the station and sidings over the years until 1989 when production at Whiteway's ceased and was switched to Whitchurch (near Bristol).

The 'up' and 'down' distant signals were renewed as two-aspect colour lights on 23 December 1962, but the signal box closed on 11 June 1967 and the public goods service ceased from 4 December of the same year, although the goods yard remained in use for Whiteway's traffic. The station became unstaffed on 5 October 1970, tickets being obtained in the mornings, from a hut on the 'down' platform situated near the footbridge steps. When the main line was singled in 1967; a half a mile of the 'up' road and the crossovers were retained with ground-frames to gain access to the goods yard. Passengers had to use the footbridge to gain access to the former 'down' platform which was then used by all trains. The sidings, crossovers and ground-frames were removed on 6 July 1990, and the goods shed demolished in 1991. The former 'down' platform and footbridge are now demolished, and a £117,000 improvement scheme involving new lighting, provision of a new passenger shelter, reconstruction of the 'up' platform, and slewing the single line alongside the

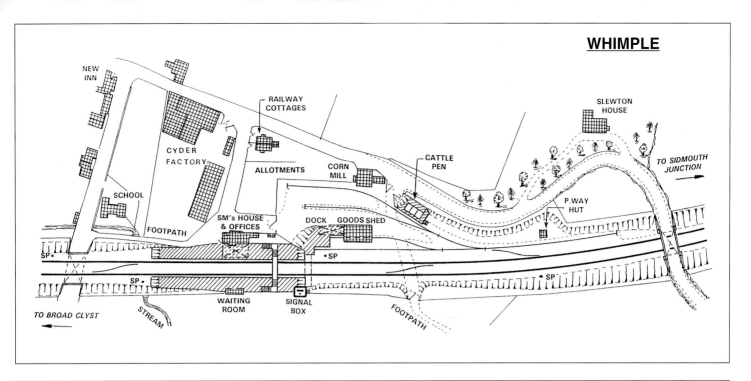

WHIMPLE

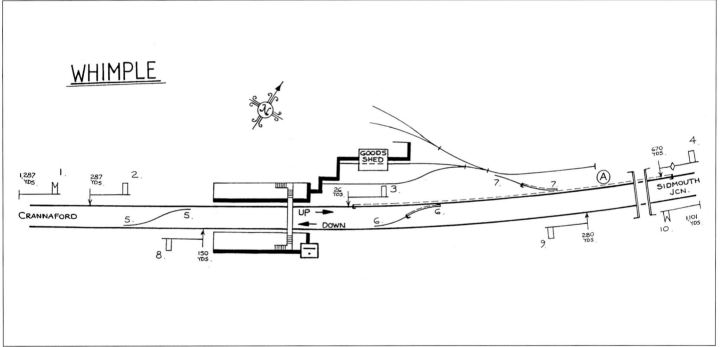

WHIMPLE

Whimple looking west on 1 September 1958. S15 4-6-0 No. 30823 (70E) arrives with the 3.20 pm Exeter Central–Templecombe.

Derek Phillips Collection

CRANNAFORD GATES

ABOLISHED AS BLOCK POST 15-09-1925

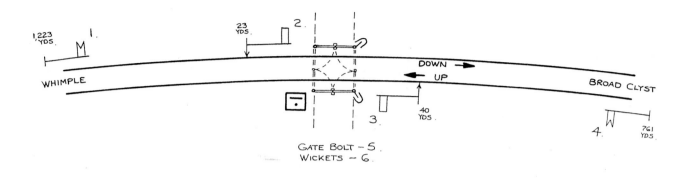

WHIMPLE

1,223 YDS.

1.

23 YDS.

2.

DOWN →

← UP

3.

40 YDS.

BROAD CLYST

4.

761 YDS.

GATE BOLT – 5.
WICKETS – 6.

former 'up' platform from the 'down' has been completed. The re-constructed platform was rededicated in a small ceremony on 19 February 1993; when a party of invited guests, councillors and railway officials was conveyed on a special return trip between Exeter and Honiton by three-car unit No. 159004.

Crannaford Gates

The lever frame was contained in an L&SWR lean-to ground level box positioned alongside the 'up' main-line on the Whimple side of the gates. Coal and stores, when

needed, were delivered to the box via the 9.2 am 'up' freight from Exmouth Junction Sidings. The box was abolished as a block post on 15 September 1925 and the 'down' and 'up' distant signals were renewed as two-aspect colour lights at 1,823 and 4,1061 yards respectively. The crossing box was closed on 22 October 1967 when the gates were replaced by automatic half-barriers.

Broad Clyst

The station was located approximately one mile from the village of the same name. The standard station buildings

Broad Clyst looking west in this view taken from the signal box steps on 12 September 1964. The main buildings are grouped on the 'down' platform. The three-wheeled invalid car seen to the left was of a type manufactured locally and loaded onto LOWFIT wagons at the station from an end dock – part of which can be seen to the left.

C. L. Caddy

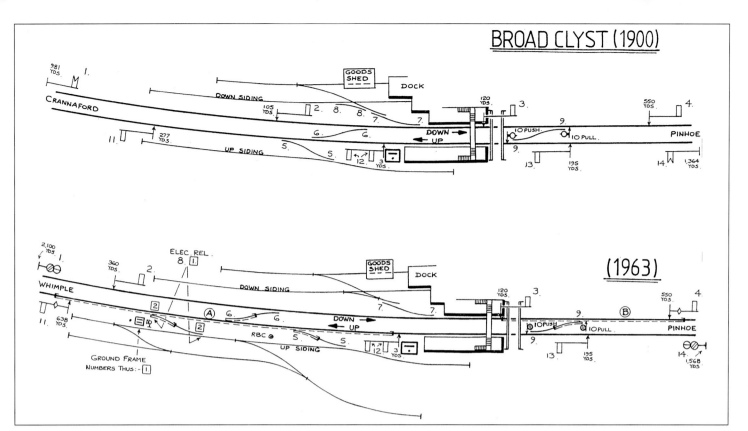

BROAD CLYST (1900)

CRANNAFORD
981 YDS. I.
GOODS SHED
DOCK
DOWN SIDING
105 YDS.
120 YDS.
3
550 YDS. 4
2. 8. 8. 7
7
9
10 PUSH
10 PULL
PINHOE
11
277 YDS.
UP SIDING
6 6
DOWN
UP
9
5 5
12
3 YDS.
9
13
195 YDS.
14
1,364 YDS.

(1963)

WHIMPLE
2,100 YDS. I.
ELEC. REL.
8 I
360 YDS.
2
GOODS SHED
DOCK
120 YDS.
3
550 YDS. 4
2
A 6 6
7
7
9
B
PINHOE
11
638 YDS.
2
RBC
5 5
DOWN
UP
12
3 YDS.
9
10 PUSH
10 PULL
9
13
195 YDS.
14
1,568 YDS.
GROUND FRAME
NUMBERS THUS :- I

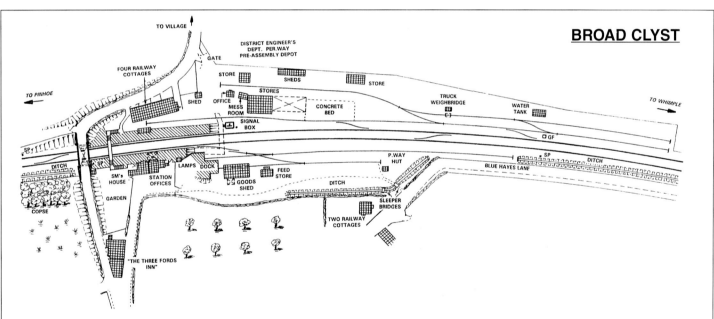

BROAD CLYST

TO VILLAGE
DISTRICT ENGINEER'S DEPT. PER.WAY PRE-ASSEMBLY DEPOT
GATE
FOUR RAILWAY COTTAGES
STORE
SHEDS
STORE
TO PINHOE
STORES
TRUCK WEIGHBRIDGE
WATER TANK
TO WHIMPLE
SHED
OFFICE
MESS ROOM
CONCRETE BED
GF
SIGNAL BOX
P.WAY HUT
SP
DITCH
DITCH
LAMPS DOCK
BLUE HAYES LANE
SM's HOUSE
STATION OFFICES
GOODS SHED
FEED STORE
DITCH
SLEEPER BRIDGES
GARDEN
COPSE
TWO RAILWAY COTTAGES
"THE THREE FORDS INN"

Standard Class 3MT 2-6-2T No. 82017 arrives bunker-first at Broad Clyst with the 10.20 am Sidmouth–Exeter Central on 2 September 1959. The signal box stands at the end of the 'up' platform, and part of the massive civil engineers yard can be seen to the left behind the platform. The goods shed stands in the 'down' yard to the right.

Adrian Vaughan Collection

143

The 14-lever signal box at Broad Clyst viewed here on 7 July 1962 was in use until 12 December the following year. The buildings behind the box form part of the permanent way yard in use by the civil engineers department. The depot which expanded in 1926 from an earlier version (1896), closed in 1964.

H. C. Casserley

Steam and smoke drift into the atmosphere as No. 34015 *Exmouth* prepares to leave Broad Clyst with the 10.37am Exeter Central–Salisbury on 12 September 1964.

C. L. Caddy

No. 34100 *Appledore* trundles past the signal box at Broad Clyst with an 'up' freight on 12 September 1962. A batch of locally made invalid cars has been loaded and await transportation from the dock siding to the left.

C. L. Caddy

were grouped on the 'down' platform, and a brick-built waiting shelter positioned on the 'up' platform. The 14-lever signal box was situated on the 'up' (Whimple) side of the layout, and crossover-roads were located 42 yards from the box on the Whimple side (moved further east on 21 June 1948), and 165 yards from the box on the Pinhoe side. The 'up' sidings to the east of the station had been occupied by the civil engineers since 1896, but were vastly expanded in 1929, and until closure of the permanent way depot in 1964 held stocks of rails, sleepers and other construction materials. A small 0-4-0 diesel locomotive (No. DS1169 from 1959 to 1964) was kept here to shunt the bogie-bolsters and other engineers' vehicles. A 30 ton rail weighbridge was also to be found in the yard. Entry to the civil engineers' yard was gained by a ground-frame which was electrically

released from the signal box (lever No. 8). A goods shed and small yard for the local traders was also established to the east of the station, but this was located on the 'down' side. Closure to goods was effective from 6 September 1965 and to passengers on 7 March the following year. The signal box closed on 12 December 1965 although in the final year it was only open on a 'when required' basis. The former main station building and goods shed still survive and are in use as commercial premises. Only remnants of the 'up' platform survive, with the 'down' completely demolished. Industrial units now occupy the site between the goods shed and station building.

Pinhoe

The station was brought into use on 30 October 1871 –

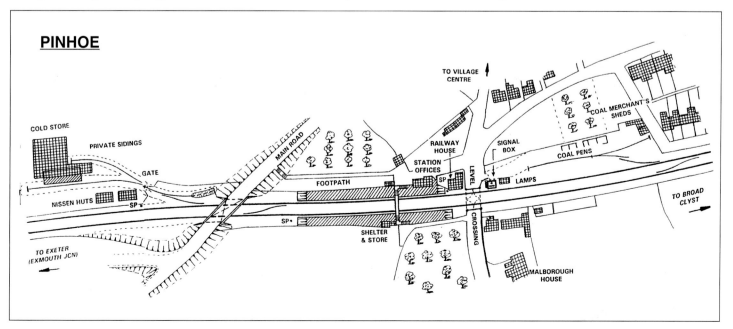

Pinhoe looking eastwards from the 'down' platform towards the signal box and level crossing on 12 September 1964. The station opened on 30 October 1871 and closed on 7 March 1966. However, fate has been kind – the station re-opened on 16 May 1983 and is well patronised with commuter traffic to and from Exeter.

C. L. Caddy

Pinhoe looking westwards over the level crossing on 8 July 1959 – the small single-storey brick-built building containing booking office/waiting room etc. can be seen on the 'up' platform to the right.

H. C. Casserley

Pinhoe 'up' platform showing the non-standard main station building containing the booking office etc. on 8 July 1959. This building was later demolished, but the station master's house survives.

H. C. Casserley

more than ten years after the opening of the line and therefore was one of the few stations along the route to have non-standard buildings, rather than the distinctive structures to the design of William Tite. A brick-built single-storey building stood on the 'up' platform containing the booking office, etc., and a small waiting shelter on the 'down'. The two-storey station master's house was situated

between the end of the 'up' platform and the level crossing at the eastern end of the station. The signal box, equipped with an 11-lever frame (extended to 17 in 1943) was located on the 'up' (Broad Clyst) side of the level crossing. A crossover-road was positioned 249 yards from the box on the Broad Clyst side of the layout. A solitary goods siding was opened on 3 April 1882, sited on the eastern side of

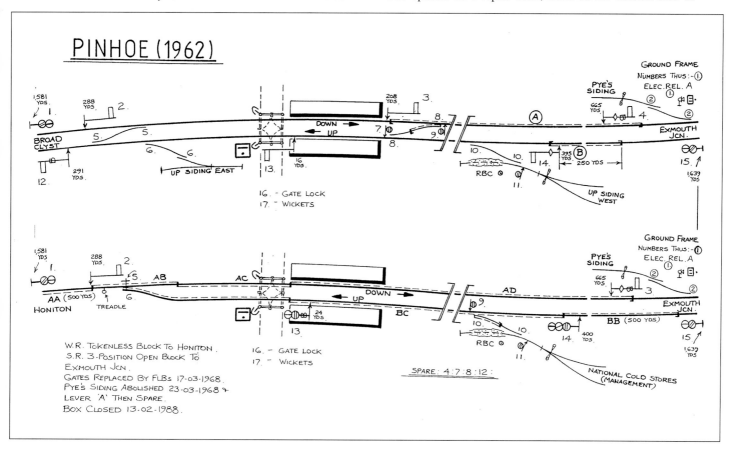

Standard Class 5MT 4-6-0 No. 73044 rattles over the level crossing at Pinhoe heading for Exeter Central with a 'down' relief service in 1962.

C. L. Caddy

The 8.30 am 'up' Padstow with No. 35004 *Cunard White Star* in charge, thunders through Pinhoe on 6 September 1958. The footbridge was removed and the station buildings (except for the station master's house) demolished after the station closed in 1966.

Adrian Vaughan Collection

the level crossing, alongside the 'up' main line. Sidings accessed from the 'up' main-line serving a Government cold-store sited west of the station were brought into use in 1943. These sidings remained until 1969, then reopened for a private cold-store company, finally closing in 1979. A siding for Pye Storage Ltd, opened west of the station alongside the 'down' main line, was worked by a ground-frame brought into use in September 1953 and was abolished on 23 March 1968. Poltimore Siding, situated between Pinhoe and Exmouth Junction on the 'up' side, was worked by a ground-frame released electrically by Exmouth Junction signal box. This siding was in use until September 1965.

Despite being positioned in the suburbs of Exeter and therefore an ideal candidate for commuter traffic, the station was closed to passenger traffic on 7 March 1966. The footbridge was removed and the station buildings demolished, except for the former station master's house which still survives. Closure to goods came on 10 June the following year. The level crossing gates were replaced by full lifting barriers on 17 March 1968. The signal box, dating from 1875, soldiered on until closure on 13 February 1988 – thus outliving the closure of 1966, and witnessing the re-opening of the station on 16 May 1983 – the second station to re-open on the route (after Feniton). The station has seen considerable success with commuter traffic since re-opening with a service of four 'down' and three 'up' trains in the Summer 1991 timetable. Pinhoe is nowadays the limit of double-track from Exeter and is the start of the single-line section to Honiton.

Exmouth Junction to Exeter Queen Street and Central

Exmouth Junction Shed

With the locomotive premises at Queen Street station becoming more and more congested, the decision was taken by the L&SWR to construct a locomotive depot on a large piece of ground north of Queen Street station, near the junction of the Exmouth branch with the main line to Salisbury. The shed was constructed in corrugated iron supported on a metal framework with four gables spanning eleven roads and was opened on 3 November 1887. Doors were provided at either end of the shed and there was a 55 ft turntable positioned at the rear of the building. A large wooden coaling stage with attendant ash pits, and sidings for storing coal, a washing-out shed, stores, offices, messrooms, wagon repair shop, and a lifting road equipped with shear-

legs for engine repairs, also complemented the shed. An enginemens' dormitory was positioned at the far west of the shed yard, standing adjacent to the water tank.

The shed layout was a great improvement on its congested neighbour at Queen Street. Adams 380 class 'Steamroller' 4-4-0s Nos 386 and 391 appeared in the late 1890s with Nos 0381/83/84 arriving in 1905 and in use until 1925. Also, ten of the Adams 395 class 0-6-0 goods engines were allocated in 1890, Drummond 700 class 0-6-0 'Black Motors' appeared here in 1898, Nos 690-692 and 694 being the numbers allocated. In 1957 Exmouth Junction Duty No. 532 was still rostered to a 'Black Motor'. T9 4-4-0s in 1903 comprised Nos 304/5, 706/7/9/15 and 460 class 4-4-0s Nos 0460-62 appeared in 1912 swelling the ranks of other classes

The driver and fireman of rebuilt Drummond 4-6-0 No. 333 pose for the camera at Exmouth Junction on 18 July 1925. Scaffolding behind the locomotive marks the construction of the new shed.

H. C. Casserley

Below: Exmouth Junction shed on 18 July 1925 showing the decrepit state of the old building with most of the corrugated sheeting missing. Adams O2 0-4-4T No. 228, and Adams Radial 4-4-2T No. 59 reflect the pride taken in keeping the locomotives clean, for which no less than 72 engine cleaners were employed.

H. C. Casserley

A panoramic view of Exmouth Junction taken from the 'up' 'Atlantic Coast Express' on 2 September 1959 headed by No. 35026 *Lamport & Holt Line*. M7 No. 30323 is reversing coal trucks onto the lifting gear, which takes one truck at a time to feed the voracious appetite of the hopper.

Derek Phillips Collection

including T3, X6, A12, K10, L11 and S11. At this time 90 locomotives were allocated with S11s, L12s and T9s being in the top link. M7s and O2 tanks appeared in great numbers after the First World War, taking over most of the branch lines services. By 1900 the elements had taken their toll of the building with the result that sheets of rusty corrugated iron flapped and banged with the force of the wind and rain. In a strong wind pieces of sheeting would be blown away from their fixings and many of the windows had parted company with their frames. Staff preparing locomotives

No. 35024 *East Asiatic Company* complete with 'ACE' headboard stands in company with a quartet of Bulleid Pacifics on the coaling line at Exmouth Junction on 8 July 1949.

H. C. Casserley

inside the shed would have been no worse off outside in the shed yard as rain poured in through the many holes in the roof and walls. The whole building would shake violently in the event of a storm and even on a day with the gentlest of summer zephyrs there would be a piece of sheeting flapping away somewhere. In my firing days many years later, one old driver told me, "You couldn't fart in that place, without something falling off the wall." Swelling engine allocations also demanded more space, especially with almost 40 of the new N class 2-6-0 Moguls being based here in 1925. These were mostly for working west of Exeter, in particular when the principal through trains ran from Exeter to Ilfracombe (instead of Torrington) with the introduction of the new timetable on 12 June 1925.

A new building was constructed in ferro-concrete to the rear of, and to the south of the previous building and lying nearer to the main line. With tenders for the main building being solicited in December 1923, Messrs A. Jackman & Sons of Slough gained the contract, the work starting in the summer of 1924. The new shed had to be built with the engines continuing to use the old premises at the same time, which was no easy task. An electrically operated 65 ft turntable supplied by Messrs Stothert & Pitt of Bath for the total sum of £1,419, was of necessity, being the first part of the remodelling and was installed near the main line to the south of the new shed. When completed, the massive new locomotive shed measuring 270 ft long by 235 ft wide, was supplied with 13 roads, each of which was 270 ft long with pits running the whole length of the building. This was equipped with electric light and the final bay to the north (No. 13) had its roof especially raised to incorporate an overhead travelling crane with a lifting capacity of 63 tons. Inside the northern wall of the building were situated the offices, stores, mess rooms, fitters' shop, machine shop and smiths' shop. A large mechanical coaling-plant, also constructed in concrete, was erected to the south west corner of the shed near the main line and held some 300 tons of coal. The hopper was notorious in my firing days for smashing up the coal, so that a tender of mostly dust would be the order of the day!

As parts of the new shed became usable so old portions of the former premises were demolished, the wooden coal-stage went with the opening of the new coal hopper, and the old wagon repair shop was rebuilt opposite the shed near the concrete works. It is reported that seven roads of the modern building were in use by May 1926, also the coppersmiths and blacksmiths workshops were in use at the same time. The new shed was mostly operational by 1927 although alterations were still being done to the repair shops in October 1929. All vestiges of the former premises were swept away, for the new order with Exmouth Junction was now the largest Southern Railway locomotive depot outside of the London area. Staff totalled over 400 including 120 pairs of drivers and firemen. In 1933 over 109 locomotives were allocated here, this number being swelled by engines from 'foreign' sheds visiting daily. The turntable was replaced by a 70 ft version in 1947 this being in use from 30 March. As with all sheds large and small, drivers and firemen were booked on Preparation & Disposal Duties and Exmouth Junction had twelve duties alone on this task involving the many locomotives arriving and departing at all hours:

No. 1 on duty 12.35 am	No. 2 on duty 6.30 am.
Dispose No. 620 MX	Prepare No. 586
Prepare No. 595	Dispose No. 508
Prepare No. 524	Prepare No. 611
Dispose No. 524 MO, 528 MX.	Dispose No. 546
Dispose No. 544 MX	

No. 3 on duty 10.20 am.	No. 4 on duty 12.32 pm Central
Perform Requirements No. 581	Relieve No. 595 at 12.52 pm,
Prepare No. 583	work, relieved 3.50 pm in
Dispose No. 6	Depot
Dispose No. 569	Dispose No. 568
	Dispose No. 4

No. 5 on duty 3 pm	No. 6 on duty 3.20 pm
Requirements No. 607	Dispose No. 586
Prepare No. 575 FX, No. 602 FO.	Dispose No. 553 FX
Prepare No. 586	Dispose No. 557
Dispose No. 505 MX	

Clinker and smokebox ash line the two disposal pit roads at Exmouth Junction on 30 August 1964.

Barry Eagles

A member of the 'Merchant Navy' class stands out of use inside Exmouth Junction shed in 1963 – the smokebox door is open suggesting that the locomotive is probably in for boiler wash-out. Two of the fitters, complete with hammers, are eyeing up a job up on the Pacific whilst a shedman cleans out the pit in the foreground.

Adrian Vaughan Collection

No. 7 on duty 4.20 pm.	No 8 on duty 4.30 pm	No. 9 on duty 10.10 pm.	No. 10 on duty 10.40 pm.
Dispose No. 549	Perform Requirements No.461	Dispose No. 525	Dispose No. 526
Relieve No. 578 at Ex Central-	Dispose No.614	Dispose No. 524	Dispose No. 588
at 7.23 pm and dispose.	Dispose No 609	Dispose No. 527	Dispose No. 611
Prepare No. 610	Dispose No.523	Prepare No. 589 Sat.	Dispose No. 546 FX, No.71 FO.
Dispose No. 550		Prepare No. 617 Sat.	

The tender of No. 34006 *Bude* is being topped up from the adjacent water column whilst she is being prepared for the road at Exmouth Junction on 2 April 1966.

S. C. Nash

No. 34077 *603 Squadron* is all prepared and ready to go – the disc headcode is already in place for the tender-first trip to Central station to work the 4.30 pm Exeter–Waterloo (2.20 pm ex Ilfracombe) on 30 August 1964 – the last full working year of steam to be seen on the line.

Barry Eagles

No. 11 on duty 10.50 pm.
Dispose No. 621
Prepare No. 557
Prepare No. 556
Part dispose No. 571
Prepare No. 585
Prepare No. 551 Sat.
Prepare No. 557 Sat.

No. 12 on duty 9 pm.
Dispose No. 589
Dispose No. 591
Dispose No. 594
Dispose No. 561
Prepare No. 573 MSX
Prepare No. 571 Sat.
Prepare No.524 Sat.

After being absorbed by the Western Region in 1963 the shed closed to steam on 1 June 1965 and in 1966 the remaining staff had moved to the WR shed at Exeter St Davids, or back to the Southern (if they were fortunate enough to escape the 'Western'). The turntable was removed, but the shed lingered on in an advanced state of decay with a few diesels abiding until closing completely on 6 March 1967. Nowadays a supermarket and its attendant car-park utilise the site.

Allocations 1934

4-6-0	448/9, 740/3/4/6/7/68/9, 823-7.
4-4-0	117/59/61/5, 283, 384/92, 401/2/3/6, 703/9/10/5/7/9/23/32/3.
0-6-0	3029/83,3433/6.
2-6-0	1406-9,1826/7/8/30/1/2/4-8/40/1/3-6/8/9/52-5/7-60.
0-4-2	644
4-4-2T	3125,3520.
0-8-0T	954
0-6-2T	2096,2135,2695.
0-4-4T	24,35/7/41/2/4/5, 123/33/83/7/98/9, 207/14/28/32/6/47/53, 320/56/74/5, 668/71.
0-6-0T	237/59/67/78.
0-4-2T	2359,2633.

Allocations 1945

4-6-0	738/53/87/9/90/1/2, 823-7/47.

4-6-2	21C1-5, 21C101-16.
4-4-0	135/7/8/56, 282/3, 301/29/96, 402/3/4/8/9/11/3/4/36/9, 722-5/30/3.
0-6-0	3029.
2-6-0	1406/9, 1635/8, 1795, 1828/30-38/40/1/2/5/7/51/3-6/69/71.
4-4-2T	3125,3520.
0-8-0T	954.
0-6-2T	2124/35, 2695/7.
0-4-4T	24,30/4/7/7/9, 46/9,55,105/24/33/92/3/9, 207/24/34/2/45/52/3/5/6, 320/3/56/74-7, 668/9/71.

Allocations 1950

4-6-0	30455, 30457, 30823-25, 30841-47.
4-6-2	34001-10, 34014-20, 34024-31, 34044-48, 35001-04, 35021-24.
4-4-0	30283, 30408/9, 30702/3, 30706/7, 30715-17, 30723.
0-6-0	30564, 30581.
2-6-0	31407/8, 31829-31835, 31837-41, 31845/47/53/55/56/69/74/75.
4-4-2T	30582-84.
0-8-0T	30954.
0-4-4T	30024/25/30/34/39/46/49/55, 30105/24/33, 30192/93/99/224/230/232, 30245/52/53/55/56/, 30320/23/74/76/77, 30668/69/71.

The 1950 list (123 engines) shows the usual combination of T9s, 2-6-0 Moguls, S15s, Radial tanks – although the 'King Arthur' contingent had dwindled to a total of two by this time, with the M7 and O2 tanks holding their own. The shed was a stronghold of the Bulleid Pacifics and in this list an impressive total of 30 light Pacifics – plus eight members of the 'Merchant Navy' class were now allocated to the depot. Sub-sheds of Exmouth Junction included Bude, Callington, Exmouth, Launceston, Lyme Regis, Okehampton and Seaton.

Class N 2-6-0 No. 31845 stands adjacent to the breakdown vans at Exmouth Junction on 30 August 1964.

Barry Eagles

Allocations 1965
4-6-0   75008/22/25.
2-6-4T   80037/41/64.
2-6-2T   41206/16/23/49/91, 41307/17/21, 82030/39/40/
           42/44.
0-6-0PT   4655/66/94/97.

The once impressive total of locomotives had shrunk to a motley selection of 23 in 1965 – the year that the depot closed to steam – and upon closure the engines went to Templecombe (83G), Gloucester (85B), Worcester (85A),

and Bristol Barrow Road (82E). Exmouth Junction locomotives carried the shed plate 72A from 1950 until 1963, the depot became part of the Western Region in December 1962 but the new shed-code, 83D, was not given official status until 9 September of the following year.

Footplate comments
We would approach Exmouth Junction with a lengthy freight train destined for Exmouth Junction Sidings from the east and from Pinhoe we would have been signalled under the 'yellow'. Normally the locomotive would be one of the

The crew of No. 34033 *Chard* await the call to travel tender-first to Central station on 30 August 1964. The headcode for light engines between Exmouth Junction and Exeter Central as shown here was rigidly adhered to. Engines would trundle down to the station from the shed in groups of four or more coupled together.

Barry Eagles

Class N 2-6-0 No. 31853 seen here at Exmouth Junction on 30 August 1964 shows the tired and neglected state of many locomotives towards the end of steam.

Barry Eagles

favourite S15s or an 'Arthur'. No matter, either one of these classes would have been sufficient. As the engine was coming off here and going to shed, the fire would have been run down ready for the P&D men who would have to square her up. The footplate would have been brushed clean and hosed down with the pep pipe as we clanked slowly past the outer home and came to a stand in front of the bracket signal. There would be a loud hiss from the vacuum ejector as my mate applied the brake and a loud banging and clattering from our train of wagons as the buffers compressed. The engine, which had been thumping away on the banks of Crewkerne and Honiton on the way down, just stood there nice and quiet with the injector singing away, and a slight hum from the firebox as the steam blower was turned on a fraction to stop the fumes from entering the cab now that the regulator was closed.

Away to our right the shed yard was busy with rows of smoking and hissing engines, engines lined up on the coaling roads awaiting their turn under the hopper, piles of clinker and smokebox ash lined the disposal pits, the turntable would also be busy as engines were turned in readiness for their next duty. Ahead of the shed stood the goods yard packed full of freight wagons with the shunting engine shuffling up and down. The concrete works was also busy. The 'down' sidings to our left also had plenty of freight traffic standing in them, and ahead of us on the main line was the signal box standing in the vee created by the main line and the Exmouth branch. We were awaiting the passage of an 'up' train, climbing up the bank through the tunnel, she would approach, and with a roar and a rattle would be gone on her way to Salisbury with a cloud of smoke and steam trailing behind the train. Up ahead of us the crossover-road was changing in our favour. The right-hand arm on the bracket signal was pulled 'off', my mate blew up the vacuum and opened and shut the regulator to take the weight of the train and avoid snatching the couplings. We trundled over the crossover and the 'up' main line clanging over the points and pulled into the west yard with the shunters waving us in, our long train of wagons of all shapes and sizes would follow us in like a flock of sheep until we would

come to a stand at the end of the yard. We would be cut off from the train, which would be dragged back by the shunting engine, and when the road was clear we would reverse back onto the ash pit, screw the handbrake down, pick up our kit and make our way to the enginemen's cabin in the shed itself. The shed was full of engines, some in steam, and some not as they awaited a boiler washout or attention from the fitters. T9s, 'Black Motors', M7s, O2s, Bulleid Pacifics, N class Moguls and S15s, would be everywhere as we walked through the shed. The enginemen's cabin, like all shed cabins large and small, would be a 'House of Parliament' all to itself as men awaited the next part of their respective duties. Everybody had their different point of view, and would put the world to rights on any subject under the sun, ranging from the best onions in their allotment, football teams, anything you can think of, had an 'expert' of some kind. The air would be thick with the aroma of pipe and cigarette smoke as the crews nattered on. As distinct from Salisbury shed where the cabin (also full of some kind of debate or other) was full of men with Cockney, Hampshire and Wiltshire accents as well as men from the ex GWR sheds with Bristol and Welsh accents, the Exmouth Junction cabin would resound to the 'burr' of Devon and Cornwall as men from their respective sheds made their point. But one thing that all the crews at 72A would agree on (myself included) would be their dislike of the engines and anything else to do with 'them down the road', 'them' being the Western Region down the bank at St Davids.

Exmouth Junction Sidings

The double-track junction with the lines to Exmouth opened 1 May 1861 – the line to Topsham being doubled 31 May 1908. This was always a very busy location with 30 freight trains departing and 27 arriving each weekday. Trains were marshalled and re-sorted in the busy marshalling yard adjacent, this being the main freight distribution yard to and from the South West and London for the SR. Exmouth Jcn Duty No. 619 was responsible for shunting the yard – the engine would be allocated to the marshalling yard from 3.45 am until 3.45 am the next morning (MX) when a fresh

S15 4-6-0 No. 30826 departs from Exmouth Junction and heads out on the long haul towards Salisbury with a heavy freight train on 17 July 1962.

C. L. Caddy

engine would be rostered off the shed. Exmouth Jcn Duty No. 622 shunted the Carriage & Wagon Works and the civil engineers siding. Freight trains arriving and departing from the yard on weekdays as seen in the 1932 working timetable include:

Down

dep 12.38 am to Launceston (MO).
arr 2.15 am, dep 3.15 am – 9.32 pm Nine Elms–Plymouth (NMM).
dep 3.26 am to Bude.
dep 3.48 am to Plymouth (MO).
arr 4.01 am, dep 5.01 am – 1.20 am Templecombe–Plymouth (MO)*. * (will not run when 1.40 am Q runs)
arr 4.16 am, dep 5.01 am – 1.40 am Templecombe–Plymouth (MOQ).
arr 4.11 am, dep 5.01 am – 1.50 am Templecombe–Plymouth (NM).
arr 4.33 am, dep 5.30 am – 10.10 pm Nine Elms–Torrington (NS).
arr 8.31 am – 10.47 pm Nine Elms–Exmouth Jcn Sidings (NS)
dep 5.58 am to Exeter Central.
dep 6.10 am to Exmouth.
dep 6.18 am to Barnstaple Junction.
dep 8.53 am to Eggesford.
arr 9.12 am – 4.30 am Salisbury–Exmouth Jcn Sidings (NM).
dep 9.18 am to Exmouth.
arr 9.55 am – 11.53 pm Feltham–Exmouth Jcn Sidings (NMM).
dep 11.27 am to Exeter Central.
arr 11.49 am – 12.10 am Nine Elms–Exmouth Jcn Sidings (MO).
dep 11.50 pm to Exeter Central Yard (NS).
dep 12.08 pm to Exeter St Davids Yard.
dep 3.35 pm to Exeter Central.
arr 4.27 pm – 3.12 am Feltham–Exmouth Jcn Sidings (MO).
arr 7.12 pm – 5.15 pm Sidmouth Junction–Exmouth Jcn Sidings.
arr 8.45 pm, dep 8.50 pm – 3.35 pm Templecombe–Plymouth (NS).

arr 10.30 pm – 4.30 pm Yeovil Junction–Exmouth Jcn Sidings.
dep 6.58 pm to Yeoford.
dep 11.59 pm to Launceston (NS).
arr 12.13 am – 6.25 pm Yeovil Junction–Exmouth Jcn Sidings.
arr 1.43 am – 5.00 pm Basingstoke–Exmouth Jcn Sidings.

Up

arr 12.30 am, dep 1.00 am – 5.00 pm Wadebridge–Salisbury (NM)
arr 2.40 am, dep 3.45 am – 10.15 pm Plymouth–Yeovil Junction.
arr 3.52 am – 12.50 am Plymouth News.
dep 4.04 am to Yeovil Junction.
arr 5.10 am – 4.50 am Exeter St Davids–Exmouth Jcn Sdgs. (MO).
arr 6.50 am – 1.58 am Plymouth–Exmouth Jcn Sidings (NM).
arr 7.10 am – 7.05 am Exeter Central Yard–Exmouth Jcn Sidings.
dep 7.37 am to Sidmouth Junction.
arr 9.00 am – 8.55 am Exeter Central–Exmouth Jcn Sidings.
dep 9.02 am to Whimple.
arr 10.19 am – 4.25 am Barnstaple Jcn–Exmouth Jcn Sidings (FO)
arr 11.00 am – 10.55 am Exeter Central–Exmouth Jcn Sidings
arr 12.10 pm – 4.25 am Barnstaple Jcn–Exmouth Jcn Sidings (NF)
dep 2.38 pm to Yeovil Junction.
arr 2.50 pm – 2.45 pm Exeter Goods Yard–Exmouth Jcn Sidings.
arr 3.15 pm – 2.40 pm Exeter St Davids–Exmouth Jcn Sidings.
arr 5.33 pm – 6.15 am Plymouth–Exmouth Jcn Sidings.
arr 7.10 pm – 8.12 am Plymouth–Exmouth Jcn Sidings.
arr 7.45 pm – 7.40 pm Exeter Central–Exmouth Jcn Sidings.

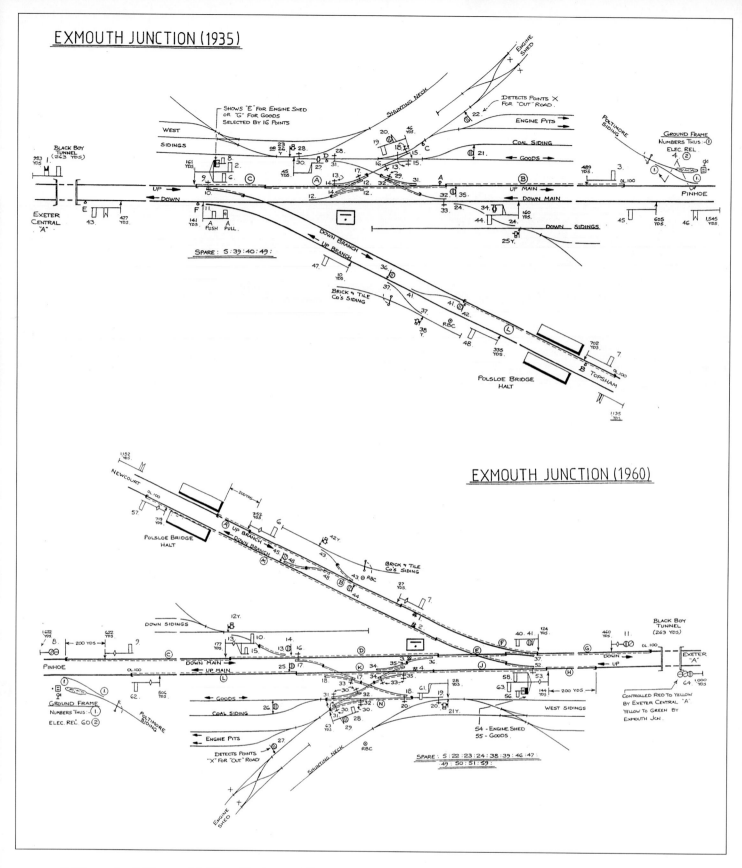

EXMOUTH JUNCTION (1935)

EXMOUTH JUNCTION (1960)

arr 7.58 pm, dep 8.37 pm – 12.45 pm Torrington–Nine Elms (NS)

arr 7.58 pm, dep 8.30 pm – 12.45 pm Torrington–Nine Elms (SO)

arr 8.17 pm, dep 9.35 pm – 5.18 pm Plymouth–Nine Elms.

arr 8.22 pm – 4.30 pm Padstow Fish–Exmouth Jcn Sidings (Q).

arr 9.00 pm – 2.07 pm Bude–Exmouth Jcn Sidings.

arr 10.03 pm, dep 10.54 pm – 12.45 pm Torrington–Salisbury

arr 11.40 pm – 11.35 pm Exeter Central–Exmouth Jcn Sidings (NS)

A glance at the above tables shows a service of 55 freight trains arriving and departing from the yard over a 24-hour period, and this carried on mostly to the end of steam. This was a superb location with freight trains being shunted back and forth, main line passenger trains rushing past as well as the intensive passenger services shuttling to and from Exmouth, light engine movements between Exeter Central and the locomotive shed with steam, smoke and noise drifting around the shed yard. Writing as a (then) young fireman this was a location that I always looked forward to when arriving from Yeovil, either with a goods or passenger train. Today, freight is no longer shunted day and night with the sound of clanking

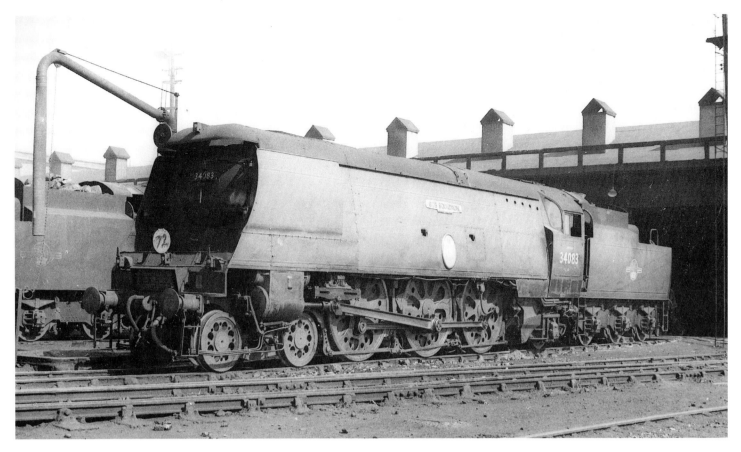

'Battle of Britain' class 4-6-2 No. 34083 *605 Squadron* awaits the next turn of duty at Exmouth Junction on 15 September 1963.

C. L. Caddy

buffers resounding around the area. The former concrete works site is now occupied by the coal concentration depot of Messrs Western Fuels, and the civil engineers department still use the repair shops here for their track machines.

An L&SWR Type One signal box formally controlled the junction, the frame of which was enlarged in 1927 in connection with the new locomotive depot. The L&SWR box was replaced on 15 November 1959 by a brick-built 64-lever box. The lever frame was removed on 30 January 1988 and a panel installed and brought into use on 15 February. Mount Pleasant Road Halt, standing adjacent to the main line near the east portal of Blackboy Tunnel, was opened on 26 January 1906 and served by railmotors (first and third class only) working on local services between Exeter Queen Street and Honiton, and the Exmouth branch trains. The

1910 *Bradshaw* marked the services as 'Motor Cars' in the timetable. Not being a success the halt closed on 2 January 1928. The line now dips sharply at 1 in 100 through the 263 yard long Blackboy Tunnel and situated in the cutting between the tunnel and Exeter Central is St James Park Halt – a two-platformed affair equipped with a basic shelter on the 'up' platform. The halt was originally named Lions Holt Halt and opened on 26 January 1906 – the name being changed on 7 October 1946. Well known as the 'station' for Exeter City Football Club, whose ground stands to the rear of the 'down' platform, it was served at first by the short-lived railmotor services when introduced in 1906 on the Queen Street–Exmouth services, and a varied selection of local main line trains. The halt is now served by trains using the Exmouth branch.

S15 4-6-0 No. 30827 rattles through St James Halt on the final lap of its journey to Exeter Central with a 'down' stopper.

Stephen Derek

Exeter Queen Street looking west c1910 – T9 4-4-0 No. 727 on the 'down' siding, and Adams T3 4-4-0 No. 576 on the 'up' through lines respectively – await 'up' trains. Part of 'B' signal box (demolished in 1927) can be seen in the left foreground. Queen Street goods yard to the extreme right.

Lens of Sutton

Exeter Queen Street

At 3 pm on 18 July 1860 the massive 20-coach train hauled by *Montrose, Vulcan,* and *Britannia* containing the directors of the company and other worthies, arrived at Queen Street station after a seven-hour journey from London. Those present at the opening ceremony included the Hon. Ralph Dutton, William Tite MP, George Braginton, Chairman of the Exeter & Crediton, North Devon, and Bideford Extension Companies. The well-known figure of Thomas Brassey Esq – the then lessee of the two latter companies – also attended. The station opened to public traffic on the following day together with the extension from Yeovil Junction which enabled the citizens of the City to benefit from the services of the mighty London & South Western

Railway to the Capital, as opposed to the Bristol & Exeter and Great Western Railway route to Paddington via Bristol from Exeter St Davids which had opened in 1844. The inaugural train (on the 19th) left London at 9 am, arriving in Exeter at 2.10 pm. The L&SWR timetable for November 1860 shows the following down weekday trains; 5.55 am from Salisbury, 6 am from London, 9 am from London, 10.15 am from London, 3 pm from London, the fastest of these being the 9 am arriving at 2.7 pm. 'Up' services consisted of; 7.30 am, 10.30 am, 1.15 pm, 2.45 pm to London, and the 6 pm to Salisbury. The fastest 'up' train to London (the 1.15 pm) stopped only at Honiton, Axminster, Crewkerne, Yeovil, Sherborne, Gillingham, Salisbury, Andover and Basingstoke with a booked arrival in London

Adams O2 0-4-4 tank No. 178 approaches the 'down' bay at Queen Street on 4 August 1928.

H. C. Casserley

Queen Street yard looking east c1910 showing an abundance of freight traffic to the left, and passenger stock in the umber and salmon of the L&SWR to the right on what was once the Queen Street locomotive shed. Set No. 208, as used on the Exmouth branch, stands in the right foreground.

Lens of Sutton

at 6.25 pm. Sunday services (1860) consisted of two trains each way: 7.30 am from Salisbury, 9.15 am from London, and the 7.30 am, and 1.35 pm trains to London.

The L&SWR station at Queen Street was described as having poor facilities, as well as being dark and gloomy under the overall roof. Constant criticism of the station was voiced in the late 19th century, but many years had to pass before improvements were made – unlike the company 'down the road' who completely rebuilt St Davids station from 1862-4. On 1 May 1861, less than one year after the opening of the main line from Yeovil, the 10½-mile long branch to Exmouth was opened. This was one of the most

Queen Street yard looking west c1910 – showing passenger stock standing on the site of the old locomotive depot to the left.

Lens of Sutton

Exeter Queen Street looking east from the St Davids end in 1911 – with the 'up' platform to the left in the dark and gloomy interior. Part of the 1875 'C' signal box can be seen to the right. This box was removed in 1925 allowing the provision of a 'down' through line. The new 'C' box was installed at the west end of the 'up' platform.

Lens of Sutton

successful lines that the L&SWR ever constructed and was worked by the Beattie 2-2-2 well tanks from the start, No. 36 *Comet* hauling the eleven-coach train at the opening.

Although Queen Street was at first in use as a terminus (albeit temporary) the L&SWR had their sights firmly set on expansion towards the West. The contract for the double-track standard gauge line between Queen Street and St Davids stations was let to James Taylor (contractor for the Yeovil & Exeter) for £19,550. The line, on a gradient of 1 in 37, passed through the curving St Davids Tunnel and then ran on a high embankment to its junction with the Bristol & Exeter. It was inspected and passed on 27 January 1862. The L&SWR secured the lease of the broad gauge Crediton branch from 1 February 1862 and a third rail was laid for mixed gauge operation. The Bristol & Exeter was then compelled to lay mixed gauge track from St Davids station to Cowley Bridge Junction in order to allow L&SWR trains access to the Crediton branch. As L&SWR lines west of Exeter are beyond the remit of this book and have been well documented elsewhere, we now return to Queen Street.

A three-road locomotive shed was constructed at the eastern end of the station occupying a cramped site lying on the 'down' side situated between the New North Road and Howell Road overbridges. The shed building was constructed in brick and designed as a 'through' shed with roads 170 ft long. The depot was also equipped with a 42 ft turntable and a coal stage. However, Exeter as well as being the major changing point for locomotives, was also the hub of expansion in the West by the L&SWR. The key link was the Exeter & Crediton Railway and therefore locomotive habitation was at a premium with the shed building being extended by 64 ft in 1872. In the late 1870s the shed was responsible for supplying and maintaining locomotives to

the out-sheds at Sidmouth, Seaton, Axminster, Holsworthy, Torrington and Exmouth. New works at the shed completed in 1877 consisted of a new coal-stage, engine pit traverser sidings and an improved water supply. The depot, however, became more and more congested with locomotives having to be stabled in the goods yard. Eventually, the new shed at Exmouth Junction was opened on 3 November 1887 and the Queen Street depot was then used as a turning, stabling area, and servicing point for many years. The old 42 ft turntable was replaced with a 50 ft version in 1888, the old table then being moved to Exmouth.

Queen Street shed housed many representatives of the Beattie and Adams classes. The Beattie 2-4-0WTs replaced the 2-2-2WTs on the Exmouth branch from the mid-1870s, and the Beattie 2-4-0 tender locomotives were used on the Waterloo–Exeter expresses in the 1860s. A 2-4-0 Well Tank of the 'Nelson' class, No.144 *Howe*, became derailed at Cowley Bridge Junction whilst hauling the 4.20 pm passenger train from Queen Street to Crediton on 17 May 1862. This was the first recorded L&SWR locomotive running west of Exeter (L&SWR services to Crediton had commenced three months previously). Cowley Bridge Junction was the scene of two more incidents involving the L&SWR. On 19 October 1865, the 9.10 pm 'up' L&SWR passenger train from Crediton ran into the rear of the slowly moving Bristol & Exeter Railway 7.43 pm 'up' goods from Crediton. Three passengers were slightly injured and the guard of the goods train was seriously hurt. Less than a year later, on 17 February 1866, a Beattie 2-4-0 of the 'Falcon' class, No. 79 *Harpy*, was derailed whilst working the 4.50 pm passenger train from Bideford to Exeter.

Beattie 2-4-0 tender locomotives of the 'Eagle' class, No. 30 *Vulture*, and 'Volcano' class, No. 89 *Saturn*, were based at Torrington in 1872 working to Exeter and back, with No. 61 *Snake* working the service from the Exeter end. Queen Street shed rostered all three members of the 'Eagle' class, Nos 27 *Eagle*, 28 *Hawk* and 30 *Vulture*, to work on the North Devon line, members of the 0-6-0 'Lion' class, Nos 3 *Transit* and 54 *Medea*, reported as being on the line in 1877/8. Adams Radial 4-4-2 tanks Nos 169-171, 480/85 and 491/93 were at work in the area in April 1886. The ubiquitous Beattie 'Ilfracombe Goods' 0-6-0s appeared in 1874 with Nos 300/93/94 going to Barnstaple shed and other members of the class working on various branches. For the opening of the line to Plymouth in 1876 William Beattie purchased six 4-4-0 tank locomotives from Beyer, Peacock & Co. of the 'Metropolitan' type. Numbered 318-323 they were all based at Exeter. However, due to their rough riding, they were soon replaced by earlier Beattie 2-4-0s on the Plymouth route.

After a series of trials with mechanical, Westinghouse air, simple vacuum and automatic vacuum systems to find a continuous system of braking now that trains were becoming faster with more powerful locomotives, the L&SWR decided to fit automatic vacuum braking to its locomotives and stock. Priority was given to the suburban services but by 1 September 1882 the following Waterloo–Exeter services were operated with continuous braked stock: 2.30 and 5 pm 'down' and 2.15 and 4.30 pm 'up'. The following 'fitted' locomotives were now used on the route: 2-4-0s Nos 18 *Albert*, 32 *Eclipse*, 64 *Acheron*, 95 *Centaur*, 98 *Plutus* and 99 *Phlegon*, and 4-4-0s Nos 348/52/4/7/67. There were 42 vacuum-fitted carriages. By 30 June 1887 436 locomotives and 1,542 carriages of the L&SWR had been equipped with the automatic vacuum brake – leaving one main-line locomotive and a motley collection of elderly four-wheeled excursion and branch line stock awaiting conversion.

Originally there had been two 'up' and two 'down' roads through the station, (local and through in each case) but 'C' signal box had been installed in 1875 at the west end of the station which blocked the 'down' through line and effectively turned it into a siding. All 'down' trains now used the platform line. 'A' and 'B' boxes governed the eastern approaches to the station. All of the boxes had the prefix 'Queen Street' in front of their respective letter. The main goods yard and goods shed were positioned on the 'up' side behind the platform. With Exeter having an important livestock market on Friday mornings the 4.25 am freight from Barnstaple conveying cattle, pigs and sheep was booked to arrive at Queen Street at 9.45 am (FO). The animals were unloaded in the goods yard and herded through the streets to the market – much to the amusement of small boys – and to the dismay of their mothers! A return (Friday) market working, left Queen Street at 3.42 pm for Lapford on the North Devon line in 1906. This service was extended to Eggesford in 1909.

Steam railmotors appeared in 1906 with two being allocated for working between Queen Street and Topsham on the Exmouth branch. The 1910 *Bradshaw* shows a service of nine trains each way on weekdays and five on Sundays for the railmotors, this fitting in with the already intensive service to Exmouth which was already heavily used as a commuter line into the City. The railmotors were transferred to the London area, the first in 1912 and the second in 1915. Passenger stock in the early days was mostly formed of four and six-wheeled coaches in the L&SWR dark brown livery. Bogie carriages appeared from the 1890s, however, to improve the already accelerating main line services. An order was placed with Eastleigh Carriage Works for 26 bogie corridor carriages to be used on the Waterloo–Exeter route, the order comprising four composites, eight third class, four second class, four first class, two dining cars, and four guards vans. Due to the fitting of steam heating equipment, the completion of the new carriages was delayed until mid-December of the same year. Ten T9 4-4-0s, Nos 113/9/20/1 of Nine Elms, Nos 280/2/4/5 of Salisbury and Nos 304/5 of Exmouth Junction,

Passengers flock aboard an 'up' express headed by No. E740 *Merlin* at Queen Street on 8 August 1928. The lengthening of the 'up' platform as seen in this view meant that two trains could use the platform simultaneously – hence the splitting signal.

H. C. Casserley

The driver of 'Paddlebox' Drummond T14 4-6-0 No. 461 puts a drop of oil around the straps and glands – while the fireman looks on nonchalantly – at Queen Street on 7 April 1919. These, the most successful of Dugald Drummond's 4-6-0s, were noted for their fast and free running.

Ken Nunn Collection LCGB

The driver of No. E749 *Iseult* chats to his counterpart (whose fireman is leaning against the lamp post to the right) on the platform at Queen Street before working an 'up' express on 3 August 1928.

H. C. Casserley

One of Robert Urie's handsome 736 series 'King Arthur' class 4-6-0s, No. 751 in original condition, stands at Queen Street station on the now lengthened 'up' platform with the 4.05 pm Plymouth–Waterloo on 6 August 1928.

Ken Nunn Collection LCGB

were fitted with steam heating equipment in connection with the new stock which was painted in the beautiful umber and salmon livery of the L&SWR – arguably one of the finest liveries ever introduced. (I admit to being biased!) The new steam-heated coaches, complete with their equally fitted locomotives, were used on trial runs to Exeter on 21 and 23 December 1900 and proved successful. The stock was brought into regular use in the New Year on the following trains: 10.50 am and 3 pm 'down' and the 12.10 pm and 4.15 pm 'up' expresses. All L&SWR coaches were equipped with steam heating by 31 December 1906. The 11 am from Waterloo to Exeter and Plymouth had been running since the late 1890s, and in 1925 the Southern Railway initiated a competition amongst the staff to find a suitable title for the express. A guard from Woking, Mr Frank Rowlands, won the competition with his suggestion of the 'Atlantic Coast Express' for which he received the sum of three guineas. The inaugural run with the new name took place on 19 July 1926. The Southern Railway had also proposed to name the 10 am Waterloo to Bude as the 'North Cornwall Express' and the 12 pm Waterloo to Seaton, Sidmouth and Exmouth, the 'East Devon Express' but these proposals were abandoned. Frank Rowlands transferred to Torrington (becoming a town councillor), but unfortunately he died from injuries received in a shunting accident at Marland in 1932. However his memory is perpetuated for all time in the grand title of the 'Atlantic Coast Express', a name that will always be associated with the Waterloo to Exeter line.

The first improvements to the cramped layout at Queen Street began in 1925 with the 1875 'C' box being removed

from the west end of the station and replaced by a new 35-lever 'C' box. This new box, positioned off the St Davids' end of the 'up' platform, opened on 13 September. The removal of the old 'C' box paved the way to reinstate the 'down' through line which had been closed upon the erection of the box. The 'up' platform was also extended to 1,210 ft in 1925, thus enabling it to accommodate two trains simultaneously on the main line face and creating an 'up' bay on the opposite face. The trackwork into the goods yard on the north side of the station was rearranged. Signalling was also altered, the Queen Street 'A' and 'B' signal boxes were abolished and replaced by a new Type 4A box east of

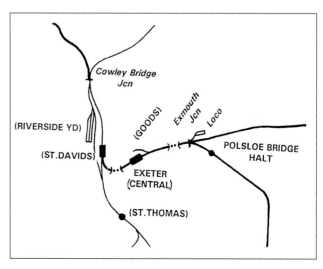

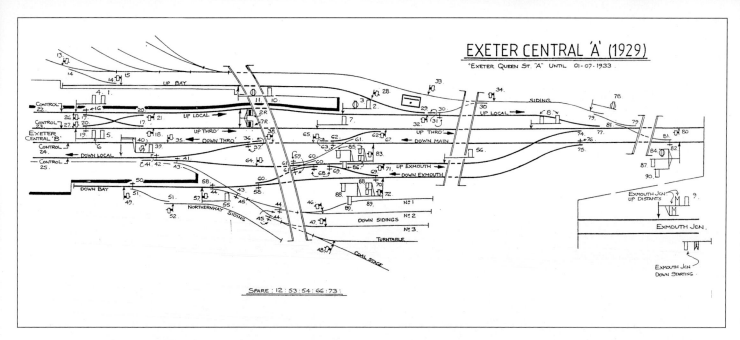

SPARE : 12 : 53 : 54 : 66 : 73 :

the 'up' platform. The new box received the suffix 'A' and opened on 15 November 1927, the 'C' box of 1925 was then renamed Exeter Queen Street 'B'. As well as controlling traffic movements at the west end of the station, the 'B' box also controlled the sidings at the top of the incline on the 'up' side. Wagon turntables (15ft 4in) from the No. 2 siding gave access to the sidings of East Devon Agricultural Co-Operative Society, R. W. & F. C. Sharp, Heywood & Sons, the Devon Trading Company and Bowden Bros.

Major improvements were still badly needed. Passenger traffic was very high with a total of 940,953 tickets being issued and collected at Queen Street in 1930. A large carriage cleaning shed came into use at the eastern end of the station on the 'down' side in 1930. In the second stage of reconstruction a total rebuild of the station came into operation, effectively sweeping away the old L&SWR building. Massive track alterations, including a double-scissor crossover, new slip crossings at the east end, and 'down' and 'up' bays for arriving and departing trains were installed. The old L&SWR entrance buildings were demolished and a brand new station frontage was built in Queen Street. Shops were provided on the ground floor, and Divisional offices were established on the upper floors. The two signal boxes were renamed Exeter Central 'A' and 'B' respectively.

Exeter Central

The superb new station was formally opened and renamed on 1 July 1933 – the canopy fronting the taxi rank in Queen Street proclaiming to all and sundry – 'Expresses to Salisbury, London, Portsmouth, Brighton, Plymouth, North Devon & North Cornwall'. It was no coincidence, that, 'the Company below' also made a series of improvements to their station during 1938-40. The new track layout at Exeter Central although in parts, not too different to the former layout, was a great improvement, making movements at this

Class 3MT 2-6-2T No. 82018 runs past the carriage cleaning shed at Exeter Central, heading the 3.36 pm from Exmouth on 12 August 1960.
Terry Gough

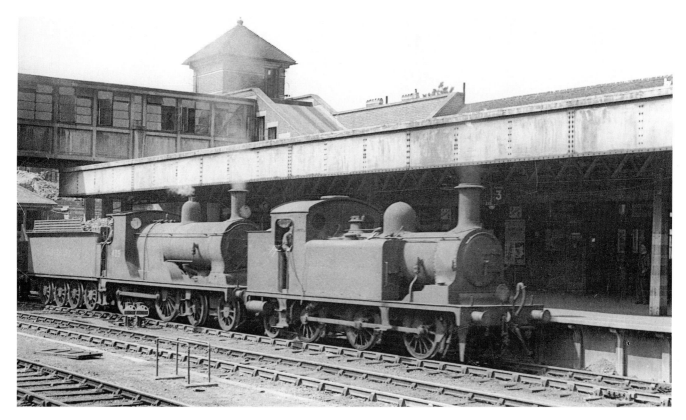

Above: An E1/R 0-6-2T in a grimy condition pilots an equally grubby 4-4-0, No. 435, along the 'up' platform line at Exeter Central on 28 August 1945.

H. C. Casserley

Exeter Central looking east – No. 34022 *Exmoor* on a 'down' train at the platform – and another Bulleid Pacific stands on the 'up' through line with a milk train from Ilfracombe.

David Lawrence

With safety valves lifting No. 791 *Sir Uwaine* stands at the east end of the 'up' platform, having arrived light engine from Exmouth Junction, and now waits, in order to work a Salisbury bound passenger train on 28 August 1945.

H. C. Casserley

EXETER CENTRAL 'A' (1950)

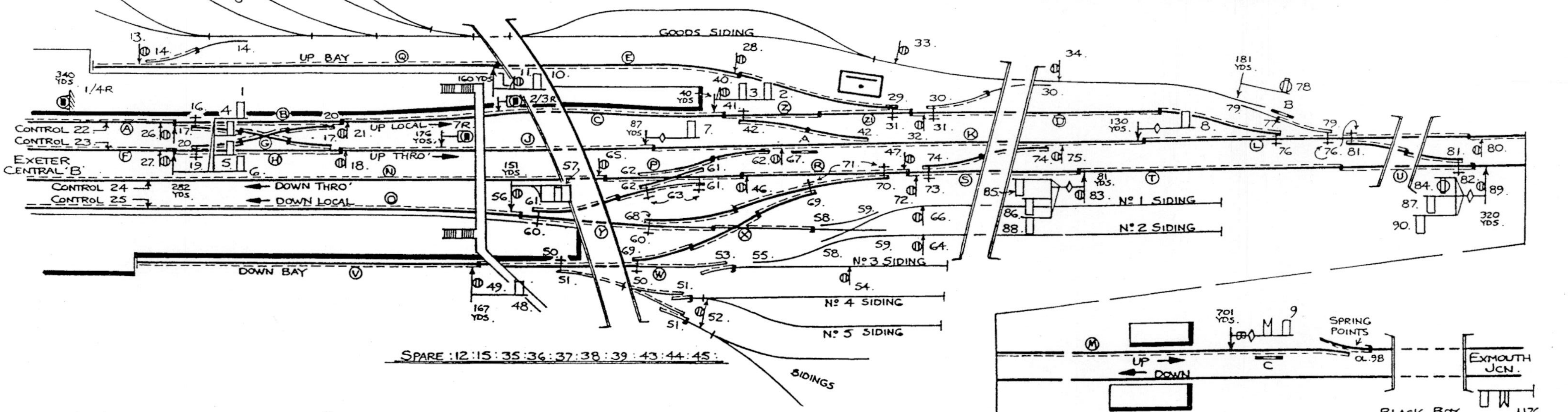

(1971)

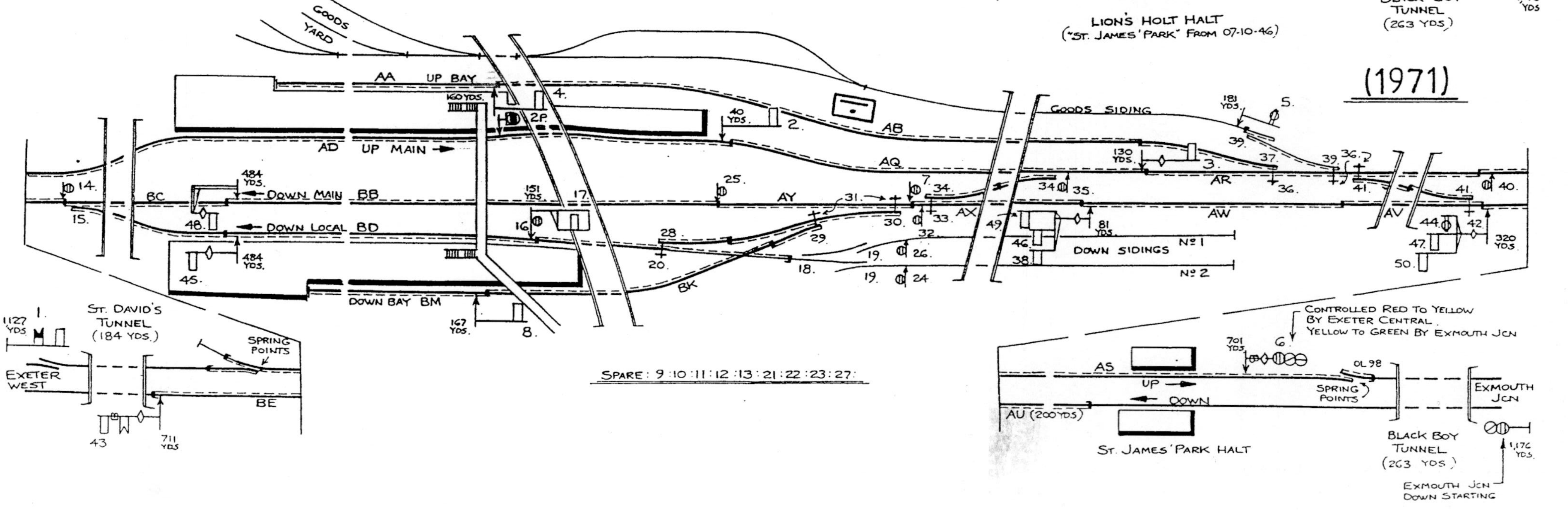

SPARE: 12:15:35:36:37:38:39:43:44:45.

SPARE: 9:10:11:12:13:21:22:23:27.

An elderly Adams 0-6-0, No. 3029, trundles towards the incline at the west end of Exeter Central on 28 August 1945.

H. C. Casserley

very busy location more versatile for the marshalling and remarshalling of West Country expresses. Two long platforms, each with an outer bay facing east (platforms Nos 1 and 4) were for the Exmouth branch service and local trains. No. 2 was the 'down' platform used by all main line trains arriving from the East, and No. 3 was used by all 'up' passenger trains and was equipped with a scissors crossing situated midway along the platform. This crossover was a godsend enabling various 'up' trains to be joined with the minimum of fuss.

The newly redesigned platforms, now out in the open air, with pleasant waiting areas and a superb refreshment room was a much-needed advance compared with the former L&SWR premises with its gloomy and spartan interior. The whole range (apart from a few exceptions) of Southern main line locomotives could be viewed at the station over the years until the end of steam – T9s, 'Black Motors', 'King Arthurs', S15s, U and N class Moguls, Bulleid Pacifics, M7s and Standard tanks scuttling about on the Exmouth branch trains, and M7s and O2s steaming up and down fussily shunting carriages or bumping wagons in the goods yard

with its Fyffes banana depot. Standing at the end of the platforms you could watch the spectacle of 'up' trains struggling up the incline with the banker pushing away at the rear, E1Rs, Z class 0-8-0s, and the massive Maunsell W class were all utilised at various times on banking trains from St Davids. Refreshment cars standing in the centre roads waiting to be attached to 'up' trains from Plymouth, Ilfracombe, or Padstow, the attendants laying out the knives and forks on the tables for the expected passengers. A gleaming Bulleid Pacific with the 'Atlantic Coast Express' headboard adorning the smokebox would await its fast run to London. Trains arriving from the East would come clanking along the 'down' platform and come to a halt, engines would be changed, ranks of coaches would be split into various portions for the West, the delightful former L&SWR lower quadrant would lower, and with a blast on the whistle, the train would rumble down the bank and enter the tunnel towards St Davids station.

The carriage sidings at the top of the incline would be packed with the green coaches of the Southern with shunting engines gliding in or out with a rake of Maunsell or Bulleid

The 'up' Padstow 'Atlantic Coast Express' rolls into Exeter Central on 25 June 1949 headed by No. 34007 *Wadebridge*.

S. C. Nash

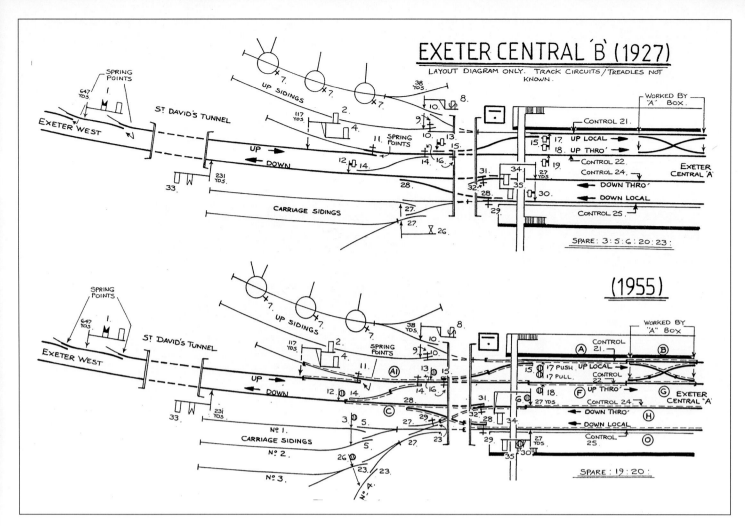

EXETER CENTRAL 'B' (1927)
LAYOUT DIAGRAM ONLY. TRACK CIRCUITS / TREADLES NOT KNOWN.

(1955)

carriages in tow. Carriages were also stored at the eastern end of the layout where the carriage cleaning shed was situated. Here again, rakes of coaches were marshalled in and out to be cleaned and tidied up for their next duty. Siding accommodation at the Central station was so vast that the sidings to the east of the station almost reached St James Park Halt. 'Up' trains from Meldon Quarry with a U class and three assisting engines would come storming up the bank dragging the heavy hoppers laden with ballast. The Winter timetable of 1959 shows the following 'down' main line services from Waterloo: first train down would be the 9 am conveying coaches for Plymouth, Ilfracombe and

With headboard in position, No. 35023 *Holland-Afrika Line* waits on the 'up' through line at Exeter Central in readiness to work the 'up' 'ACE' on 25 June 1949.

S. C. Nash

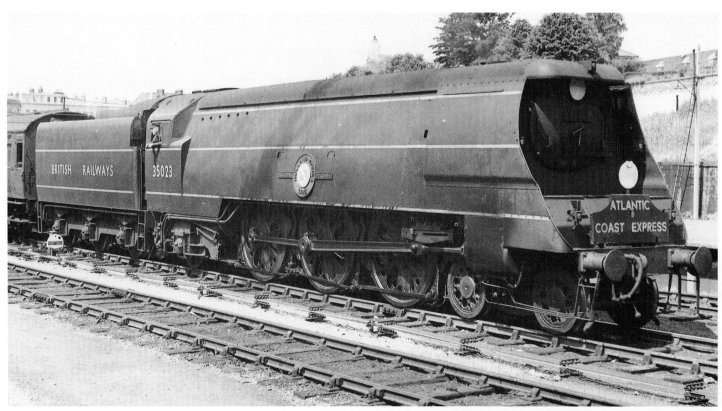

The driver of Z class 0-8-0T No. 30957 waits for the shunter to couple the leading wagon to the locomotive, whilst standing in the goods yard at Exeter Central on 17 July 1962.

C. L. Caddy

With the tail lamp on the front buffer-beam, the crew of No. 34069 *Hawkinge* await the road before proceeding to Exmouth Junction shed on 12 August 1958. Note the restaurant car alongside the 'up' platform waiting to be shunted on to an 'up' service.

Rodney Lissenden

To save track occupancy the banking engines would return to St Davids station coupled to a 'down' service as seen here – with E1/R 0-6-2T No. 2697 coupled to N class 2-6-0 No. 1406 in September 1939.

Brunel University: Mowat Collection

Torrington on winter Saturdays with a buffet car to Exeter Central, here the train was divided with the Plymouth section departing at 1.14 pm, and the Ilfracombe portion leaving at 1.26 pm. The 'Atlantic Coast Express', the most prestigious train on the line with full restaurant car facilities, left the Capital at 11 am stopping at Salisbury for water and crew change, and powered throughout by a Nine Elms 'Merchant Navy', took 3 hours 5 minutes to travel the 171¾ miles to Exeter. The 'ACE' conveyed portions for Plymouth, Ilfracombe and Torrington, with the restaurant car being detached at Exeter. The next train from Waterloo was the 1 pm – again with a restaurant car (detached at Exeter) and portions for Plymouth, Ilfracombe and Torrington, the train being divided at Central. The 3 pm from Waterloo was similar in respects to the 1 pm – but with the addition of a buffet car, the 5 pm from Waterloo ran as a stopping train from Salisbury to Exeter (shunting at Yeovil Junction and Axminster to allow the 6 pm and 7 pm 'down' trains to pass) arriving at Exeter at 10.40 pm. The 6 pm from London, also with a full restaurant car service, ran as a semi-fast with the train terminating at Exeter at 9.59 pm. The final evening train down was the 7 pm from Waterloo, stopping at Salisbury, Yeovil Junction and Axminster, this train also having a full restaurant car service, and again the 'pudding car' was detached, with the train now used as a stopper from Exeter to Plymouth arriving at 12.19 (SX).

Summer Saturday trains to the West from Waterloo on the main line in the post-war years became very hectic indeed, and Exeter Central as it had been for many years, was the vital operating hub to and from the network of Southern Region lines west of the station to Plymouth, North Devon and North Cornwall. Passenger figures were still high with 530,000 tickets being collected at Exeter Central in 1957, and 486,000 at Exmouth for the same year. From 1948 until the 1960s the Summer timetable from Waterloo remained virtually unaltered except for a few variations. Here is a taste of main line peak summer Saturday trains heading for the West from Waterloo or the South Coast in 1953.

Down

7.33 am Waterloo–Padstow.
7.40 am Waterloo–Ilfracombe.
8.05 am Waterloo–Exmouth.
8.22 am Waterloo–Ilfracombe.
8.35 am Waterloo–Ilfracombe.
9.03 am Portsmouth & Southsea–Plymouth.
8.54 am Waterloo–Ilfracombe–Plymouth. (divided at Exeter)
9.00 am Waterloo–Sidmouth.
10.15 am Waterloo–Ilfracombe.
10.35 am Waterloo–Padstow. 'Atlantic Coast Express'
10.45 am Waterloo–Seaton.
11.00 am Waterloo–Ilfracombe. 'Atlantic Coast Express'
11.15 am Waterloo–Plymouth.
11.45 am Waterloo–Exmouth.
12.00 pm Waterloo–Ilfracombe. The 'Devon Belle'
12.15 pm Portsmouth & Southsea–Ilfracombe.
11.30 am Brighton–Plymouth.
1.00 pm Waterloo–Plymouth–Ilfracombe. (divided at Exeter)
1.05 pm Waterloo–Exeter Central.
3.00 pm Waterloo–Plymouth–Ilfracombe. (divided at Exeter)
3.05 pm Waterloo–Exeter Central.
3.54 pm Clapham Junction–Exeter *milk empties*.
5.00 pm Waterloo–Exeter Central.
6.00 pm Waterloo–Plymouth.

Up

6.30 am Exeter Central–Waterloo.
7.30 am Exeter Central–Waterloo.
9.00 am Exeter Central–Waterloo.
9.00 am Seaton–Waterloo.
9.25 am Sidmouth–Waterloo.
9.08 am Exmouth–Waterloo.
8.10 am Torrington–Waterloo.
8.10 am Ilfracombe–Waterloo.

8.15 am Plymouth–Waterloo.
9.20 am Torrington–Waterloo.
8.05 am Wadebridge–Waterloo.
10.00 am Mortehoe–Waterloo.
8.30 am Padstow–Waterloo.
9.50 am Plymouth–Portsmouth & Southsea.
10.30 am Ilfracombe–Waterloo. 'Atlantic Coast Express'
10.48 am Torrington–Waterloo. 'Atlantic Coast Express'
11.00 am Plymouth–Brighton.
11.30 am Ilfracombe–Waterloo.
12.00 pm Ilfracombe–Waterloo. The 'Devon Belle'
11.45 am Bude–Waterloo. 'Atlantic Coast Express'
10.45 am Padstow–Waterloo. 'Atlantic Coast Express'
2.35 pm Seaton–Waterloo.
11.35 am Plymouth–Waterloo.
12.35 pm Ilfracombe–Waterloo.
1.45 pm Ilfracombe–Waterloo.
2.10 pm Ilfracombe–Waterloo. *
2.25 pm Plymouth–Waterloo. *
      *both trains combined at Exeter Central.
2.55 pm Ilfracombe–Waterloo.**
3.00 pm Plymouth–Waterloo.**
      **both trains combined at Exeter Central.
4.40 pm Plymouth–Eastleigh.

The above tables show a staggering total of fast and semi fast passenger trains heading to or departing from the West. The trains would pull into Exeter from either direction absolutely packed with passengers – with standing room only being the norm rather than the exception. On summer Saturdays the 9 am from Waterloo had coaches for Seaton, Sidmouth & Exmouth only. The 'down' 'ACE' ran in two parts, at 10.35 am and 11 am respectively, and the 10.45 am had through coaches for Lyme Regis and Seaton. The 8.54 am, 1 pm and 3 pm 'down' trains were divided at Exeter Central. The crack 'Devon Belle' (12 pm ex Waterloo) was also running at this time. Of interest is the cross-country service from Portsmouth & Southsea to Ilfracombe. As well as the Brighton–Plymouth service the 3 pm 'down' ran in two parts, the 3.5 pm running only to Exeter. Four portions of the 'up' 'Atlantic Coast Express' were running as well as the return 'Devon Belle' (12 pm ex Ilfracombe), the 2.10 pm ex Ilfracombe and 2.25 pm ex Plymouth were combined into one train upon arrival at Exeter. This also happened to the 2.55 pm ex Ilfracombe and 3.50 pm ex Plymouth. The busiest period at the station occurred shortly before 11.30 am with 13 long distance departures in 3½ hours – six of these trains running 'non-stop' to Salisbury.

To compound the operating problems the normal stopping and local trains to and from Exeter also ran, fitting in with the gambit of extra trains, added to this, the Exmouth branch trains were also running their intensive services in and out of the station. The whole operation had to run like clockwork as trains running late (which happened at times) would put the whole schedule astray. The station staff, shunters, signalmen and footplate staff would take on the well-polished air of having done it many times before, as carriages were shunted, restaurant cars attached or detached, trains split and rejoined, light engines trundling back and forth to Exmouth Junction, E1R tanks banking trains up from St Davids, hard-pressed signalmen pulling levers setting the road for the next movement, passengers crowding the platforms and joining the already packed trains, the refreshment room doing a booming trade. To stand and look at the station today with its through tracks and sidings removed and disused signal boxes, it seems hard to imagine that it all happened – but it did.

The goods yard, including the Fyffes banana depot, closed to general traffic on 4 December 1967, but was used by Blue Circle as a cement terminal until 1990. Cement trains to Exeter used the route Westbury–Yeovil Pen

Drummond M7 0-4-4T No. 30669 with just a wisp of steam from the safety valves – departs from Platform 4 at Exeter Central with the 8.50 am to Exmouth.

H. C. Casserley

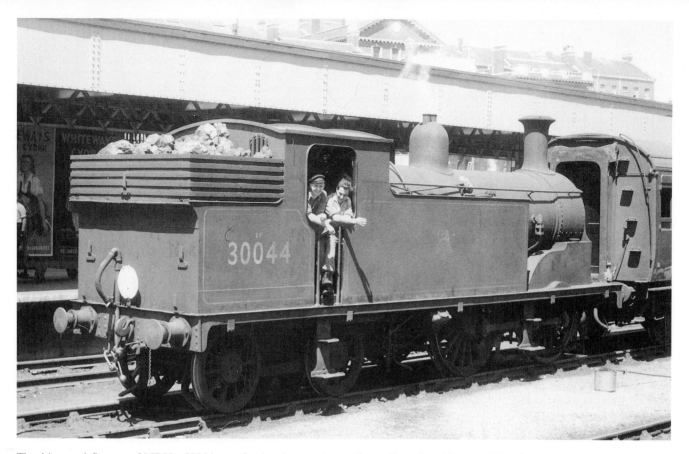

The driver and fireman of M7 No. 30044 pose for the photographer at Exeter Central on 29 June 1959. The engine is coupled to a coach which in turn will be attached to an 'up' service.

Rodney Lissenden

A ballast train from Meldon Quarry 'fresh off the bank', arrives on the 'up' through line at Exeter Central with M7 No. 30323 and N class No. 31838 at the head and with further assistance at the rear on 12 August 1958.

Rodney Lissenden

Having uncoupled from an 'up' train – Bulleid Pacific No. 21C105 trundles along the platform line heading for Exmouth Junction shed on 28 August 1945. The locomotive is not carrying nameplates but will eventually be named *Barnstaple*.

H. C. Casserley

The Southern Counties Touring Society ran a special train from Waterloo to Sidmouth Junction hauled by 'Lord Nelson' class 4-6-0 No. 30861 *Lord Anson* on 2 September 1962. At Sidmouth Junction – the special was headed by M7s Nos 30024 and 30025 for the leg to Exmouth and Exeter. No. 30861, after turning and engine requirements at Exmouth Junction, is seen here reversing into the bay platform at Exeter Central for the return journey.

S. C. Nash

Rebuilt 'Merchant Navy' class No. 35026 *Lamport & Holt Line* shunts stock at Exeter Central for a special to Waterloo on 15 October 1966.

S. C. Nash

Exeter Central looking west on 2 September 1959. No. 34104 *Bere Alston* using the scissors crossover, has just come off an 'up' service whilst a coach is being added to the rear of the train.

Derek Phillips Collection

No. 34013 *Okehampton* standing on the 'down' through road at Exeter Central, awaits clearance to run tender first to Exmouth Junction shed on 30 August 1964.

Barry Eagles

The former 'B' signal box at Exeter Central (opened 1925 – closed 23 February 1970) is pictured here standing out of use and disused on 10 July 1990.

John Scrace

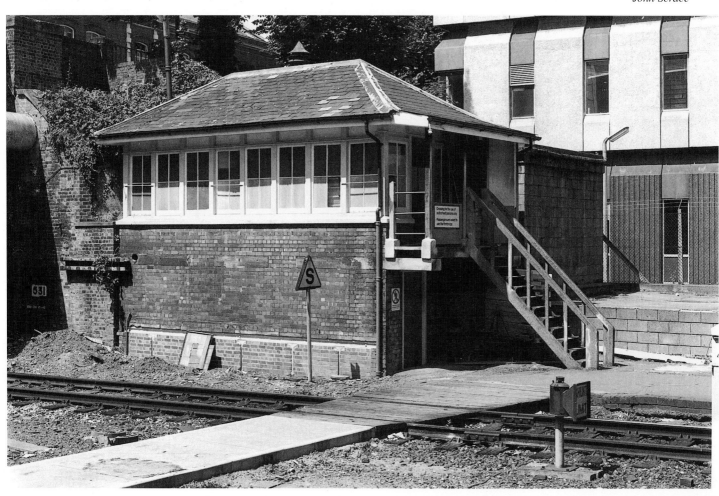

The top of the incline at Exeter Central and No. 34002 *Salisbury* tackles the last few yards of the climb up from St Davids station with the 4.2 pm Plymouth–Waterloo on 10 August 1960. The carriage sidings to the left were always busy with stock continually being shunted in or out. Note the wagon turntables leading off the No. 2 siding to the right.

Terry Gough

Mill–Yeovil Junction until closure of the terminal. The goods yard sidings have now been lifted except for one lying adjacent to the 'up' bay platform. The 'up' through road was taken out of use on 9 November 1969 and closure of the 'B' signal box came on 23 February of the following year. The large 'A' box was then renamed 'Exeter Central' and operated with a shortened frame of 50 levers. Carriage sidings to the east of the station on the 'down' side, and the carriage sidings west of the station at the top of the incline were removed in February 1970 leaving two sidings to the east of the station which lasted until 20 December 1982. The 'down' through road was taken out of use on 13 October 1984. The remaining signal box (former 'A) closed on 6 May 1985, with its sphere of operations taken over by a new panel at Exeter St Davids. Today, the station is but a shadow of its once bustling glory. Long echoing platforms needed for a former age seem incongruous in the modern era of two-car 'Sprinters', and three-car 'Super Sprinters'! The two signal boxes stand empty and unused, and no more will busy signalmen pull and slam back levers in the frames as the summer Saturday trains pour in. The 'down' line between Exeter Central and St Davids is signalled for bidirectional working allowing the Exmouth and 'Tarka Line' trains to run direct into the 'down' platform from St Davids station when no conflicting westbound services are around. The Exmouth branch, I am pleased to state, is still alive and thriving as it has been from its beginning in 1861, being

served today by a mixture of two-car and single-car 'Sprinters' on 30-minute intervals with additional trains in the summer season. Some trains run direct between Exmouth and Paignton, or Exmouth–Crediton–Barnstaple. The main line services to and from Salisbury and Waterloo are now worked by the Class 159 'Super Sprinters' of South West Trains. Exeter Central station, being only a few minutes' walk away from the City centre with its bustling shops and offices is *the* station for commuters and shoppers in the area – and long may it be so.

Footplate comments

I have so many memories of this station, working there so very often in steam days, it is difficult to know where to begin. However, the beginning is the best place to start – one day, when I was a young engine cleaner, I was informed by the shed foreman at Yeovil Town that for the next two weeks I was to attend the 'firing' school at Exeter Central to prepare me for my firing examination as a 'passed' cleaner. A travel pass was duly issued with instructions to travel down to Exeter each day on the 6.25 am Yeovil Town–Ilfracombe. I duly arrived at Exeter station on the following Monday, and in my country naivety I started to look around for a 'school' (as I had been led to believe by 'certain' old hand firemen at Yeovil!) consisting of buildings with classrooms etc. However, not being successful in my search I asked a nearby porter in my rustic Somerset accent, for assistance in finding the 'firing school'. He looked at me with a mixture of pity and surprise, evidently thinking that I had escaped from somewhere! Eventually the penny dropped and he guided me to the London end of the 'down' platform from whence I walked along the carriage sidings until I found the school which was formed of an ancient grounded L&SWR coach body! I must point out that what the building lacked in construction, it more than made up in professionalism and expert knowledge under the eagle eyes of Edgar Snow the Instructor, and occasioned by the trilby-hatted figure of the redoubtable Sam Smith, the Senior Locomotive Inspector for Exmouth Junction. They were halycon days spent in the old coach – with engine cleaners from other depots west of Exeter learning the rules and regulations applying to footplatemen, wrong line working, Rule 55, derailments on single and double lines etc., etc. Other duties of a footplateman's job were drummed into us over the week, and from the carriage windows we had a grand vista of the comings and goings of the station, and as we were near the carriage cleaning shed, long rakes of carriages were being propelled into and out of the shed all day long. We were warned 'not to upset' the female carriage cleaners, as they had a way of teaching cheeky cleaner boys a lesson which involved lots of axle grease and the like being placed on unmentionable parts! One week was spent in the old carriage learning the rules etc., for which a written test was taken, and the following week was spent at Exmouth Junction on practical work, to be followed about two weeks later with a firing test on the main line from Exeter to Yeovil with Inspector Sam Smith.

The Wilderness Years – Mismanagement and Ineptitude

The twin scourges of the line west of Salisbury – being taken over by the Western Region in 1963 and the proposals contained in the Beeching Report – did not auger well for the future. The news that we were to be taken over by the 'old enemy' under the guise of the Western Region was greeted with a stunned disbelief by the footplate crews and all staff on the line. Anger was tempered by a sense of betrayal, hardened steam men who had been known to be quick with their fists, were almost in tears. I well remember the sense of foreboding and gloom that settled on our shed at Yeovil – a situation to be found at the other locomotive sheds. We were Southern men – carrying on the tradition of the old Company (L&SWR) and the Southern Railway – and wanted nothing to do with the 'Western'. In fact, the absorption by the WR was regarded as a bigger disaster than the ending of steam traction. Even today, over 30 years since the WR takeover, the bad feeling, leading almost to hatred towards that *particular* Region, has not diminished amongst many surviving footplate crews, myself I hasten to add, included. The 'ACE' was reduced to portions for Exeter, Ilfracombe and Padstow in the 1963 Winter timetable with the Western Region in their usual policy of closure by stealth switching freight traffic to their tracks, of which, they (the WR) had considerable experience.

The 'Atlantic Coast Express', which had been hauled by a succession of superb locomotive classes over the years including T9s, 'King Arthurs', and the Bulleid Pacifics finally came to an end on 5 September 1964. The last steam-worked 'up' 'ACE' departed from Exeter Central on 14 August hauled by No. 35013 *Blue Funnel*, with No. 35022 *Holland America Line* powering the last 'down' 'ACE' in blistering style on 4 September. The Class 42 'Warship' diesel hydraulics appeared for the training of SR crews in May 1964 turning up on the odd train or two. One of our duties from Yeovil shed in 1964 involved working a Sunday night passenger train from Yeovil Junction to Salisbury and return with a 'down' goods. Instead of a Bulleid Pacific, one of the 'paraffin burners' appeared – not the best of swaps! The first booked appearance of one of the 'monoliths' on a passenger train between Exeter and Salisbury took place on 1 August of the same year. However, from 17 August one of the 'Warships' was rostered to work the 7.30 am Exeter-Waterloo and 1 pm return, followed by the 5.54 from Exeter and the return 1.10 am 'down' newspaper train.

For George Pryer and myself – including all staff who worked on the line in its prime – or for people who have studied the route in its heyday, what has happened since the Winter timetable of 1964 has seemed like a never-ending nightmare with things going from bad to worse, and worse still. From Monday, 7 September 1964 all trains from Waterloo ceased to run beyond Exeter St Davids, except for the 1.10 am 'down' newspaper train conveying through coaches for Plymouth, and the Brighton–Plymouth trains. The weekday service (1964) now consisting of five semi-

Class 50 No. 50009 *Conqueror* bursts out of St Davids Tunnel en route to Exeter Central with the 12.29 Exeter St Davids–Waterloo on 18 August 1989.

Hugh Ballantyne

Class 33 No. 33064 powers up the incline into Exeter Central on the bidirectional 'down' line with the 09.25 (Sundays) Exeter St Davids–Waterloo on 13 March 1988. The once-busy carriage sidings to the left, and freight sidings to the right now have other uses.

Hugh Ballantyne

Exeter Central is now but a shadow of its former self, as No. 50017 *Royal Oak* arrives with the 12.28 Exeter St Davids–Waterloo on 10 July 1990.

John Scrace

Above: Showing the major track rationalisation that has taken place since the ending of steam – Class 47 No. 47107 hauls a train of rails past the disused former 'A' signal box at Exeter Central on 17 August 1989.

Hugh Ballantyne

With locomotive and stock in Network SouthEast livery, No. 50029 *Renown* runs into the environs of Exeter Central with the 09.15 Waterloo–Exeter St Davids on 17 August 1989.

Hugh Ballantyne

St James Park looking west as No. 50043 *Eagle* runs past heading the 16.22 Exeter St Davids–Waterloo on 10 July 1990.

John Scrace

Pinhoe looking eastwards towards Honiton on 10 July 1990. The former station master's house stands at the end of the 'up' platform on the left. The CCTV cameras 'watching' the crossing are monitored from Exmouth Junction signal box. This is the end of the double-track section from Exeter – being single-track onwards to Honiton. Since re-opening on 16 May 1983, the station has had four 'down' and three 'up' weekday services for commuter traffic to and from Exeter in the peak times.

John Scrace

fast trains and no express timings of the previous years. DMUs operated west of Salisbury on the half a dozen or so local trains with two to three hours between each train. A lone Salisbury–Exeter Sunday steam-hauled stopping train lasted until well into 1965. The 1965/66 Summer timetables scheduled three through trains from Waterloo to Sidmouth and Exmouth in the peak weeks – with Bulleid Pacifics and Standard 4-6-0s (from Nine Elms) making a brief appearance on these last scheduled steam service trains west of Salisbury.

1967 was a disaster. The unreliable 'Warships' suffering breakdown problems, plus the difficulties with the singling of the main line and problems with the signalling, brought a whole barrage of complaints – unknown in their magnitude during L&SWR and Southern Railway days. Poor old Dugald Drummond must have been spinning around in his grave! The once superb main line had been brought to its knees by ineptitude. 'Warship' traction came to an end on 3 October 1971 when they were replaced by Class 33s hauling MkI stock. However, in 1980 came the Class 50s with MkII stock which had been 'cascaded' (another word for thrown

out!) from the Western Region. Yet again, another time-worn class of traction had appeared, although maintained to the best of ability, the failure of a locomotive on the singled main line could be catastrophic. The Class 50s often did fail, and passengers would wait a considerable time for an assisting locomotive – sometimes from Newton Abbot – as happened to a train at Chard Junction one day! At one time the failure rate and time-keeping was so bad that the line and the Class 50s were receiving the kind of media attention that may have been accorded to 'Attila the Hun' when he had a bad day! Between 1983 and 1985 only 65-70% of Waterloo–Exeter services were recorded as right time or five minutes late; compare this with Dugald Drummond reporting in 1912 that 97% of all L&SWR main line passenger trains had arrived to time, or not more than two minutes late. Remember, conditions on a T9 in 1912 with the engine steaming good or bad, eyes straining in fog to catch a glimpse of an oil-lit signal – without the benefit of a warm diesel cab and the AWS of a Class 50.

Network SouthEast took over the route in 1986 and things started to improve slightly. Eventually the Class 47/7s

A three-car DMU rolls over the level crossing at Sidmouth Junction with an 'up' service on 12 September 1964.

C. L. Caddy

No. 33026 *Seafire* powers up the bank towards Honiton Tunnel with the 07.45 Basingstoke–Exeter St Davids on 25 July 1992.

Hugh Ballantyne

Axminster looking east on 25 July 1990 showing the single line serving the former 'down' platform. The abandoned 'up' platform is still in situ; the footbridge and water tank have long gone.

John Scrace

Class 47/7 No. 47703 *The Queen Mother* sweeps westwards through Chard Junction with the 08.55 (Sun) Waterloo–Exeter St Davids on 6 October 1991. No. 47705 waits in the loop to the right ready to proceed light engine towards Yeovil Junction.

Hugh Ballantyne

No. 50017 *Royal Oak* in Network SouthEast livery matching the passenger stock, arrives at Crewkerne on 25 July 1990 hauling the 13.15 Waterloo–Exeter St Davids.

John Scrace

Class 47/7 No. 47709 scurries westwards between Yeovil Junction and Sutton Bingham with the 07.45 Basingstoke–Exeter St Davids on 7 September 1991.

John Scrace

'Warship' No. D831 *Monarch* stands on the run-round line behind the 'down' platform at Yeovil Junction on 31 August 1964.

John Scrace

allocated at Old Oak Common depot appeared on the line in 1990 to supplement and eventually replace the worn out 50s. The 47s had arrived from Scotland having being used on the 100 mph Edinburgh–Glasgow push-pull services and therefore were not exactly in 'showroom' condition, but they were an advance on the Class 50s which were withdrawn.

Network SouthEast introduced a revised timetable in 1991 for the Waterloo–Salisbury–Exeter route. Major rebuilding of station platforms to coincide with the new South Western Class 159 diesel multiple units was largely completed (as part of a £46½ million package) by the spring of 1993 with the new trains being gradually phased in and replacing the Class 47s and MkII stock, until 12 July 1993 witnessed the completion of the take-over by the new traction. A new maintenance and fuelling depot for all of the

Class 159s was constructed at Salisbury on the site of the former GWR terminus, the new depot consisting of a three-road single-ended building with each road capable of holding a three-car set. Five sidings, each capable of holding nine-car formations, are also in use at the depot.

The future of the line with the new 'Super Sprinters' is hopefully secure – although with privatisation – the tide could change either way. The disastrous mistakes of the 1960s including the singling of most of the track still haunt the route. An hourly service between Waterloo & Exeter is on the cards but much double-tracking and improved signalling are desperately needed if this is to be achieved, although this will of course involve a major capital expenditure – which may (or may not) be financed from the private sector. The line witnessed a resurgence of steam

Appearances can be deceiving – looking for all the world as if it is standing on the old 'down' through main line, when in reality standing on a siding – Class 33 No. 33013 propels a raft of ballast hoppers whilst shunting at Yeovil Junction on 25 April 1987.

C. L. Caddy

Yeovil Town Football Club (the 'Giant Killers'), were well known for their F.A. Cup games when many adversaries from the larger league clubs were lured to their doom during the early rounds of the tournament at their old sloping pitch at Huish. On 13 November 1965 the erstwhile Yeovil Team were drawn away to Brentford in the 1st round of the F.A. Cup; frost covers the sleepers as No. D803 *Albion* powers away from Yeovil Junction with the supporters special to Waterloo.

John Day

No. 33051 *Shakespeare Cliff* in Civil Engineers livery, and No. 33116 in Departmental livery, breast the top of the Sherborne bank at Milborne Wick and head east on 20 March 1993 with the 06.45 Exeter St Davids–Waterloo.

John Scrace

No. 47714 heads the 09.23 Plymouth–Waterloo past Tisbury Gates on 20 March 1993.

John Scrace

power in 1986 with special trains running to and from Salisbury to Yeovil Junction – locomotives using the turntable at Yeovil Junction – a sight to gladden many an old footplateman. Since then the route has become a firm favourite for steam running with *Clan Line, Taw Valley, Sir Lamiel*, and S15 No. 828 (all locomotives, that I have fired in my former years), plus other types of steam locomotives have traversed the route, some running from Exeter to Waterloo, bringing back working memories of bygone days on this once superb main line, pioneered and built by the finest railway company of them all – the London & South Western Railway.

Despite the appearance of double track, thanks to the disastrous Western Region 'rationalisation', this once magnificent main line was singled for much of its length. No. 820 *Grenville* is approaching Bridge 267 near the disused Chilmark Siding Box on 29 August 1970 with the 10.15 Exeter–Waterloo on what was once the 'down' line. The old 'up' line to the right is now a siding (from Dinton) at this point leading into RAF Chilmark depot. The Ministry siding can be seen curving away to the right behind the gate.

Hugh Ballantyne

Track rationalisation, plus the removal of signal boxes and semaphore signals, have taken their toll at the west end of Salisbury. Class 50 No. 50041 *Bulwark* arrives with the 09.40 Plymouth–Portsmouth Harbour on 28 April 1989.

John Scrace

Class 159 No. 159004 stands at Gillingham with the 12.17 Exeter St Davids–Waterloo (unit worked only to Salisbury) on 15 March 1993. A major rebuilding of the platforms on the route to cope with the new traction was mainly completed by the spring of 1993 and the Class 159s were gradually phased in until all of the units were in service by 12 July 1993 enabling the Class 47s to be replaced.

John Scrace

No. 33019 accelerates away from Gillingham with a train for Exeter on 28 April 1984.

C. L. Caddy

No. 47714 sweeps into the loop at Honiton with the 07.44 Waterloo–Exeter on 25 July 1992.

Hugh Ballantyne

No. 50009 *Conqueror*, in large logo livery, leaves Exeter Central with the 10.20 Exeter St Davids–Waterloo on 17 August 1989. The now-rationalised trackwork is apparent in this view.

Hugh Ballantyne

Index

'Merchant Navy' class 4-6-2 No. 35003 *Royal Mail* heads the 'up' 'ACE' (Padstow First Portion), between Gillingham and Semley on 21 August 1958.

Hugh Ballantyne

Rebuilt 'West Country' class 4-6-2 No. 34013 *Okehampton* simmers away in the 'down' bay at Salisbury on 18 April 1964 with the 3.5 pm local to Exeter Central. The Station pilot – M7 0-4-4T No. 30025 – stands in the background.

Hugh Ballantyne

After many years, steam traction returns to the now-singled main line on Honiton Bank as No. 777 *Sir Lamiel* heads west on 28 June 1992.

S. C. Nash